D0164350

WITHDRAWAL

SECOND EDITION

EARLY CHILDHOOD
EDUCATION

Education at SAGE

SAGE is a leading international publisher of journals, books, and electronic media for academic, educational, and professional markets.

Our education publishing includes:

- accessible and comprehensive texts for aspiring education professionals and practitioners looking to further their careers through continuing professional development

- inspirational advice and guidance for the classroom

- authoritative state of the art reference from the leading authors in the field

Find out more at: **www.sagepub.co.uk/education**

SECOND EDITION

EARLY CHILDHOOD EDUCATION

History, Philosophy and Experience

CATHY NUTBROWN
and **PETER CLOUGH**

Los Angeles | London | New Delhi
Singapore | Washington DC

LB
1139.23
.N878
2014

HARVARD UNIVERSITY
GRADUATE SCHOOL OF EDUCATION
MONROE C. GUTMAN LIBRARY

Los Angeles | London | New Delhi
Singapore | Washington DC

SAGE Publications Ltd
1 Oliver's Yard
55 City Road
London EC1Y 1SP

SAGE Publications Inc.
2455 Teller Road
Thousand Oaks, California 91320

SAGE Publications India Pvt Ltd
B 1/I 1 Mohan Cooperative Industrial Area
Mathura Road
New Delhi 110 044

SAGE Publications Asia-Pacific Pte Ltd
3 Church Street
#10-04 Samsung Hub
Singapore 049483

Editor: Marianne Lagrange
Assistant Editor: Rachael Plant
Project Manager: Jeanette Graham
Production Editor: Thea Watson
Copyeditor: Rosemary Campbell
Proofreader: Isabel Kirkwood
Marketing Manager: Catherine Slinn
Cover design: Naomi Robinson
Typeset by: C&M Digitals (P) Ltd, Chennai, India
Printed in Great Britain by Henry Ling Limited at
The Dorset Press, Dorchester, DT1 1HD

© Cathy Nutbrown and Peter Clough, 2014

First published in 2008
Reprinted in 2009, 2010 (twice) and 2012
This edition © Cathy Nutbrown and Peter Clough,
2014

Apart from any fair dealing for the purposes of
research or private study, or criticism or review, as
permitted under the Copyright, Designs and Patents
Act, 1988, this publication may be reproduced, stored
or transmitted in any form, or by any means, only with
the prior permission in writing of the publishers, or in
the case of reprographic reproduction, in accordance
with the terms of licences issued by the Copyright
Licensing Agency. Enquiries concerning reproduction
outside those terms should be sent to the publishers.

Library of Congress Control Number: 2013943691

British Library Cataloguing in Publication data

A catalogue record for this book is available from the
British Library

MIX
Paper from
responsible sources
FSC
www.fsc.org   FSC™ C013985

ISBN 978-1-4462-6786-8
ISBN 978-1-4462-6787-5 (pbk)

For the new pioneers ...

Contents

Go to www.sagepub.co.uk/nutbrownclough for a downloadable recording of Conversations 1, 2, 3 and 6.

About the Authors

Professor Cathy Nutbrown is Head of the School of Education at the University of Sheffield, where she teaches and researches in the field of early childhood education.

Cathy began her career as a teacher of young children and has since worked in a range of settings and roles with children, parents, teachers and other early childhood educators. Cathy is committed to finding ways of working 'with respect' with young children, and sees the concept of quality in the context of what it means to develop curriculum and pedagogy in the early years with the ambition of working in a climate of 'respectful education'.

She established the University of Sheffield MA in Early Childhood Education in 1998 and a Doctoral Programme in Early Childhood Education in 2008. In 2010 she contributed to the Tickell Review of the Early Years Foundation. In June 2012 she reported on her year-long independent review for government on early years and childcare qualifications (The Nutbrown Review). In May 2013 Cathy won the ESRC prize for Research with Outstanding Impact in Society and in September 2013 she was presented with the NW Lifetime Achievement Award. She is Editor-in-Chief of the *Journal of Early Childhood Research* (Sage) and author of over fifty publications on aspects of early childhood education.

Peter Clough is Honorary Professor of Education at the University of Sheffield. Peter taught English and Drama, in the 1970s, in London and later in a number of special schools. His research interests include the use of narrative and fictional writing in research and research report. Peter has taught Inclusive Education and Early Childhood Education at the University of Sheffield, has been Professor of Inclusive Education at Queen's Belfast and Liverpool Hope, and Research Fellow at the University of Chester. Peter is an Honorary Professor at the School of Education, University of Sheffield, where he teaches Masters and Doctoral students. Amongst over 50 publications focusing on equality, inclusion, difference, early childhood education, and teachers' lives are several books, including *Narratives and Fictions in Educational Research* (OUP) and *A Student's Guide to Methodology* (Sage).

Acknowledgements

We should like to thank the many people who wrote to us about the first edition of this book and we thank them for suggestions which have influenced the development of this second edition.

The numerous students and academic colleagues who have shared their ideas with us and allowed us to try out some of the new conversations in this book have been most helpful and we thank them warmly.

Special thanks go to our Undergraduate, Masters and Doctoral students who told us how important it was to bring alive the ideas of past pioneers and commented on our attempts to do this.

The keepers of the archives we consulted have been particularly helpful, as have librarians at The University of Sheffield. We thank Sheffield Local Authority for allowing us to quote from their 1987 Nursery Education Guidelines. We wish to acknowledge the important contributions played by Sage Publications, in particular Marianne Lagrange for inviting us to make this second edition, Rachael Plant for her help with recording four of the conversations, and Jeanette Graham for her care in the production of this book.

Cathy Nutbrown and Peter Clough

Sheffield

September 2013

Introduction

Though history per se does not change, the way we view the events of history, and the political contexts of those events, can lead to re-interpretation and reviewing, resulting in new meanings and insights. Since this book was first published in 2008, we have continued to think about the impacts of many key figures in the history of early childhood education, and have been conscious of living through events that will themselves form a part of the history of early childhood education and care.

This book, whilst maintaining the central feature of imagined dialogues, is considerably different from the first edition. In this edition we have taken the opportunity to update our view of the legacy of early childhood education and, in particular, the last 20 years. As well as adding new detail to the section on pioneers, we have included three more figures whose contribution to early childhood education deserves celebration: Alec Clegg, Loris Malaguzzi and Chris Athey. The imagined dialogues themselves have also changed. Our opening and closing conversations have been revised, reflecting the changing times and our current perspectives on the issues we discuss. Conversations featuring Robert Owen, Susan Isaacs, Johann Pestalozzi, Jean Piaget, Friedrich Froebel and Rudolf Steiner have been revised and updated. Three new conversations have been added: Alec Clegg's work on policy for creativity is highlighted in Conversation 5 with Peter Clough; Susan Isaacs, Maria Montessori and Margaret McMillan are imagined in Conversation 6 discussing aspects of childcare policy which dominated debate in 2012–2013; Conversation 8 sees Charlotte Mason talking with Cathy Nutbrown about children's rights and early education. We chose to add these new conversations because they provide an opportunity to consider the impacts of policy on creativity, children's rights and provision and because we feel that these issues have come more urgently to the fore in the last five years.

The final section of the book examines eight themes, first by reflecting back on history and then by considering current related policy. We have added an additional theme in this edition and so conclude the book with a final discussion on professional development and training for nursery teachers and other professionals working with young children.

'What is early education for?'

This question of what education is 'for' must have been in the minds of many of the figures who feature in this book. At the same time they were probably driven by a profound belief in the capacity of education to bring about change.

So what, then, is early education for? For us, in the spirit of Vygotsky's theory of learning, learning is about relationships, and in the early years relationships are key. This is why the central role of the parent in a child's development and learning is vital, much as Mason described. Young children are full of drive to discover the potential within themselves and the world around them, and relationships support discovery.

In this book we look back at the work of the past and examine present policies, practice and research in order better to understand what is happening now and to be equipped with a better understanding of ideas which may come in the future. It was in 1953 that L.P. Hartley wrote in *The Go-Between* 'The past is a foreign country; they do things differently there'. The past may well be a foreign country but, as we know, travellers to other countries often learn something new, collect an interesting artefact, a different recipe, a new idea, bring something back which changes their lives, even just a little. Look at the past and we see our present, and perhaps our future, through new lenses .... and, as Comenius wrote in the 1600s:

> We are all citizens of one world, we are all of one blood. To hate a man because he was born in another country, because he speaks a different language, or because he takes a different view on this subject or that, is a great folly. Desist, I implore you, for we are all equally human. ... Let us have but one end in view, the welfare of humanity; and let us put aside all selfishness in considerations of language, nationality, or religion. (Comenius, *The Great Didactic*, 1649)

Different views and practices may be foreign to us, but understanding how they came to be puts us in a position to understand, or to challenge.

As we were writing this book we have constantly asked each other 'What would Susan Isaacs say about that?' or 'How would Pestalozzi have responded to this?' But we suggest that Christian Schiller was right to urge a focus on the future when he said:

> ... there have been great men and women whose vision and action have inspired a generation: Robert Owen, Friedrich Froebel, in our own time Margaret McMillan and others. But they pass away, and their ideas pass away with them unless these ideas are fashioned into new forms which reflect new circumstances and stand the test of new practices in the contemporary scene.

The pioneers take such ideas and refashion and temper them in their daily work in school. Patiently, day after day, week after week and year after year they make the pathway from the past through the present towards the future.

(Schiller, 1951: xvii)

The important thing in early childhood education is not what Susan Isaacs, or Charlotte Mason, or Katherine Bathurst might have said... Rather, the important thing is what those who live with, or work with and for young children in our present times and settings, actually say and do. The important thing is that the new pioneers, those working in early childhood settings and elsewhere in the pursuit of the best provision for young children's learning and care, take these ideas into the future and make them their own. The task, then, becomes less a question of counting up quotations or learning dates than of each practitioner discovering the meaning and value of historical ideas as they are realised in their own practices. There is no better tribute to those who have gone before than to remould, revisit and revise their ideas for a new today.

'So who needs history?'

We suggest that we need to understand the history of early childhood education because it provides a 'rootedness' to our work. It means we are building our work on solid ground and travelling along well-trodden paths. We can be inspired by some whose ideas came – as it were – before their time but yet were not reticent in articulating or realising their ideas. History can remind us that it is worth working for the things we believe in, and the study of history shows how important it is to record ideas and practices for those who follow to ponder.

With burgeoning development in the field of early childhood education and care, and new interest in alternative approaches to early years provision internationally, there is a danger that an understanding of the histories and legacies on which present-day provision for care and education is built might be allowed to slip away. There is the potential, amidst constant and persistent policy changes, that those whose work involves a concern with early childhood education will have fewer and fewer opportunities to ask where ideas began, how ideas and practices have developed and what roots lie beneath present-day practices and philosophical ideas.

This book traces the work of some pioneers of early childhood education. It provides brief biographies and critical insights into their work and compares their principles and practices to those of others past and present. The book takes an innovative and accessible approach to the histories, philosophies and experiences of early childhood education over the years, and gives necessary, meaningful detail about individual educators and contributors to the field in order to help readers understand how contributions and developments in the past have created routes to present thinking and practice. We then work with these pioneers' ideas and hold them up to interrogation in the light of twenty-first-century life, testing them to see what such thinkers and practitioners might still have to offer the field of early childhood education and care today.

In this way, the book offers four things:

- An historical overview of the development of some key ideas and practices in early childhood education
- A series of biographical accounts of 27 key contributors to the field, with brief summaries of their major achievements and key texts
- An exploration of the ways in which their individual ideas compare with others through imagined conversations based on their writings and our own interpretations of their work
- An analysis of ways in which certain common themes can be seen in both early writings and current practices, and an exploration of how the ideas of key pioneers of the past might be interpreted and incorporated in modern-day early childhood provision.

Part 1

A Short History of Early Childhood Education

The legacy of history

We begin this book with a short chronology of the developments in thinking and practice which have taken place in the history of early childhood education in the UK. We have identified key moments and key international figures in history who have, in different ways, influenced thinking, research, policy and practice in the development of education and care for the youngest children. In beginning with an overview of early years developments from the 1600s to present day we have created a foundation for the rest of the book with our view of the contributions of individual women and men who, in one way or another, made their distinctive mark on the development of early childhood education in the UK.

History is what humanity creates, and policy itself is *real*ised by people; as Hesse (1939) reminds us, history helps to generate a concept of humanity. In the sense that people *are* the history-makers, early childhood educators make both history and policy, though in another sense the inheritance of history is something from which they stand apart and the impact of policy is something over which they may feel they have no control. But, as Merleau-Ponty (1962: ix) has it, 'although we are born into a [pre-existing] world, we [yet] have the task of creating it…'

One of the aims of this book is to help readers to consider current policies and practices in early childhood education through the lens of history; it seeks to use history as a means of understanding present states and challenges of early childhood education, and as a tool for informing the shape of early childhood education in the future – that is, in our *own* lives and careers.

Of course, we could say that nothing is new, and ideas simply recur; perhaps most topical at the end of the twentieth century was the example of the planned re-introduction of 'Payment by Results', signalled in a DfEE Green Paper (DfEE, 1999), and, again, a trial of a new policy of Payment by Results was introduced in 2012[1] whereby Children's Centres were to be rewarded for the results they achieved in effective early intervention programmes and family support. This policy echoed the 'Payment by Results' in the Revised Code of 1862, where the notion of raising standards through the use of testing was introduced and teachers' pay was linked to the achievements of their pupils. This is not so much a case of history repeating itself but perhaps more of an example of how events, developments and ideas can rhyme, or chime, or echo over time.

This book is structured to encourage critical engagement with historical ideas and developments, reflecting on influences on early childhood education, issues of policy development and implementation, and the impact of research on policy. The development of early childhood education provision, and the key figures in that development, form the starting points for considering where early childhood education has come from and where present policies 'fit', or do not fit, with the lessons of history. The ways in which childhood has been constructed throughout recent history is also a topic which helps to inform the critique of policy which has moved from the central aim of 'nurturing childhood' to a situation where 'raising educational achievement' is the main goal. Central to this argument about the shift in priorities of policy in early childhood education and care is the change in language and the new terminologies imposed year after year upon early years provision.

Finally, we are aware that there is no single history; it needs always to be seen from multiple perspectives, viewed through different lenses. In understanding what has happened in the UK, it is important, too, to look at international developments in early childhood education and the many influences from figures throughout history working around the world.

Early childhood education in the UK: a brief history

During the mid-1700s there were moves in political and social spheres to provide some form of education for young children. 'Monitorial' schools were set up from the end of the 1700s by the Quaker, Joseph Lancaster, and the New Lanark worksite elementary school was set up by Robert Owen in the early 1800s. The National Society was founded on 16 October 1811, its aim

[1] http://www.education.gov.uk/childrenandyoungpeople/earlylearningandchildcare/delivery/surestart/a0076712/sure-start-children's-centres

that the National Religion should be made the foundation of National Education, and should be the first and chief thing taught to the poor, according to the excellent Liturgy and Catechism provided by our Church.[2]

The National Society established a national system of education, supplemented by the State from 1870. In 2007 there were some 5,000 Church of England and Church in Wales schools (originally known as National Schools), most of which are primary schools, educating almost a million children. However, it was the protestant 'Evangelicals' who, through the Home and Colonial School Society (founded in 1836), had the insight to consider the development of schools for the youngest children and open 'infant schools'.

Thus, throughout the eighteenth and nineteenth centuries schools were being developed and systems devised and expanded, not only by religious organisations and benefactors, but also, of course, by the socially and politically motivated, who were driven, not by religious conviction but by a belief that the education of young children could contribute to the development of a better society. By 1862, the Revised Code was introduced whereby grants were awarded to elementary schools, depending upon the achievement of their pupils. Forster's Education Act of 1870 established school boards in areas where there was a lack of elementary school provision.

Simultaneously, there was pioneering work on the nature of curriculum for young children, with the Mundella Code of 1882 advocating 'enlightened' teaching of young children. Particular figures can be seen as distinctly influential in such 'curricular development' (though of course it would not have been known as such!); these include: Johann Pestalozzi, Friedrich Froebel, Rachel and Margaret McMillan, Maria Montessori, Charlotte Mason, Susan Isaacs and, more lately, Loris Malaguzzi and Chris Athey. All advocated ways of working with children which centred around the children themselves and where play was a central component of what was offered.

It was the development of industry which first prompted schooling for young children, and discussion about the age at which compulsory schooling should begin. The view was put forward in parliament during the enactment of Forster's Education Act (1870) that sending children to school a year earlier than other countries in Europe would give them some sort of advantage in educational achievement (Szretzer, 1964). Indeed, it was Mundella who, in an address to the 'National Education League' said: 'I ask you Englishmen and Englishwomen, are Austrian children to be educated before English children?' (Birmingham, 1869: 133). A further reason, put forward in the Hadow Report (1911) for supporting an early start to schooling was the desire to prevent

---

[2] http://www.churchofengland.org/education/national-society

childhood ill-health by the introduction of medical inspections of young children whilst at school. Legislation for the introduction of nursery schools for 2–5-year-olds was passed by Lloyd George's coalition government in 1918. However, the early start to compulsory schooling was paralleled by early leaving too, a view supported by the industrialists who needed young workers, as well as many families who needed their children to work to earn enough to put food on the table.

Later, during the First World War, with the need for mothers of younger children to work, the development of nursery education flourished. The following account of the setting up of nursery education in Sheffield is typical of many cities in the north of England.

The Development of Nursery Education in Sheffield has paralleled National trends. Nursery Education began in this country at the beginning of this [the twentieth] century at the instigation of people who were concerned about the plight of children in industrial cities: Sheffield children were typical of these. The social climate was such that by the late 1920s Sheffield was beginning to suffer in the Depression: unemployment was rife and poverty was very real. The then centre of the city buildings consisted of many terraced houses and factories, with little opportunity for the children to grow and develop in a healthy environment. In Scotland, Robert Owen had seen the necessity for young children to have good food, fresh air and rest in uncrowded conditions and started a nursery for his workers' children at the turn of the nineteenth century. Rachel and Margaret McMillan began their Nursery School in Deptford with the intention of providing an 'open-air' school for young children in 1913. This was the beginning of thinking that young children needed special provision.

Children from poorer areas were often under-nourished with poor skin and pale complexions: rickets were common. Colds, coughs and catarrh seemed to perpetuate. Clothing was inadequate and unattractive: there was very little colour in their lives. The children were often stitched into their clothes for winter. Flea bites, sore eyes and lack of sleep were common and infection was easily passed on. The local Women Councillors (in Sheffield) decided to fight for a nursery school and, although it was an uphill battle Denby Street Nursery School was opened in 1928 based on the McMillan open-shelter type. It was open from 8.30 am to 5.00 pm and holidays. There was practically no money, very little equipment and a skeleton staff.

The emphasis was on physical care. The children were fed, washed, rested and loved. The food was simple and plentiful – buttered rusks, dripping toast, hash stew, shepherd's pie, lentil roast, milk puddings, custard and fruit and steamed puddings. The nurse and doctor visited regularly. Cod liver oil was administered and children monitored for impetigo, rickets, poor eyesight, etc. School became a haven especially if children were from families living in only one room, although the schools were very careful not to usurp the home.

Outdoor play was robust and skilful as many of the children had played in the streets from a very young age. The imaginative play – particularly domestic play – was very real. The children were independent, practical, capable and resilient, many having to be so from a very young age, especially if they came from a large family.

Sheffield Nursery Education grew slowly from its beginnings: there were only 4 nursery schools by 1939 when most children were evacuated or spent quite a lot of time in the air raid shelters after the outbreak of war. Nurseries did close at the beginning of the war but opened again in 1940 on a short-time basis because of the bombing campaign. Gradually the day became extended again as it was felt that children could catch up on sleep at the nursery and there was a need for the regular routine and stability it provided.

The war years did give an impetus to nursery education: there was some expansion because of the demand for married women in the labour force. The expansion of nursery education became a high priority and resources were found. For example in 1941 a new joint circular was sent out to set up special war nurseries financed by the Ministry of Health and the Maternity and Child Welfare Department. The full-time nurseries were open in some cases for 12–15 hours and only for children of working mothers. Part-time nurseries also gave priority to evacuated children and those of working mothers. The emphasis moved to include children's social and emotional needs.

Although the extension in provision of nursery education because of the pressures of war was considerable, compared with earlier years, it could not be regarded as 'spectacular' as only a very small proportion of the total child population in the age group were receiving some kind of nursery education. However, the war nurseries did much to popularise the idea of a nursery stage in education. In the emergency situation of the war, where married women were needed to work, the care of the children had been met by the nursery school. The idea that only mothers can look after children, lost its force during the war.

The 1944 Education Act implied that nursery education would become universal but the 50s and 60s marked a decline in state provision for a variety of reasons – economic pressures, demand for space and teachers for the over fives during the 'bulge' years. (Government) Circular 8/60 effectively stopped expansion until Addendum No. 2 in 1965 when a controlled expansion was allowed where this would increase the return to service of married women teachers.

In 1960, however, the Pre-school Playgroup Movement was formed, the lack of nursery places having given mothers the impetus to make their own provision. The continuous expansion of the movement and the commitment and dedication of those working in it has contributed significantly to greater awareness of the needs of the under fives.

Interest in the state provision of nursery education came to the fore once again when stimulated by the Plowden Report in 1967. It was recommended that nursery classes should be extended, and that an immediate start on building of new nursery schools should be made in 'educational priority areas': the idea being that good nursery schools could begin to offset the consequences of social deprivation. (Sheffield LEA, 1986: 2–3)

Denby Street Nursery School officially closed on 31 August 2003; the last roll had 84 boys and 83 girls on register. It is now a temporary car park, mostly used by fans of Sheffield United Football Club who play at Bramall Lane. The school was one of many to go by the wayside in times of reduced expenditure and 'rationalisation' of provision, and closures of other early years settings have continued in 2013.

Whilst nursery education was under development in England, there were parallels in Scotland. Following Robert Owen's initiatives, Nursery education began with voluntary contributions in the early 1900s through the commitment of those who saw the need to provide something particular for younger children:

> At the beginning of the 20th century as people became more aware of social and physical conditions, public interest was directed to the welfare of children under five years old. The first nursery school in Scotland was opened in Edinburgh in 1903.

> Edinburgh's Free Kindergarten was established in 1903. Miss Howden, infant headmistress at Milton House School in 1881, who was concerned at 'babies' accompanying siblings to school, left her savings to found the free kindergarten which started in Galloway's Entry, Canongate in 1903.

> St Saviour's Child Garden was established in 1906 by Miss Lileen Hardy in co-operation with Canon Laurie, Rector of Old St Paul's Episcopal Church in the church's hall in Browns Close. (Hardy, 1999)

Thus, His Majesty's Inspector of Schools reported in 1913:

> This school is a bright spot in a rather dark neighbourhood ... with two groups of about 20 children under 5 years of age. To these school lessons are not given. They engage in a variety of interesting kindergarten occupations and they learn to draw and sing. The rest of the time they spend taking care of pets, in attempts at gardening and in playing at housework. They mostly live in the open air and are obviously happy. Regular lessons in elementary subjects are given to those children whose ages are from 5–7 years. (City of Edinburgh/Early Education, 1999)

All such developments in early education had social and welfare issues at their heart, as fundamental concerns. These, combined with the effects of war years and a recognition of the needs of young children, fuelled the development of early education provision, where establishments set up to care for the physical needs of young children also began to develop ways of providing opportunities for young children to learn. The summary of the HMI report on St Saviour's School describes what many would recognise as elements of an appropriate curriculum for young children. Extended opening hours for working mothers was often normal practice and balancing children's needs was a central feature of many nursery establishments.

Foundation stones: some key figures whose work has influenced thinking and development of provision for young children

The following section outlines some of the politicians, social pioneers and educationalists who in different ways contributed to the development of early education in the UK. Table 1.1 provides a brief summary (in chronological order by date of birth) of some of the women and men who influenced these developments in the UK, up to recent times. This summary helps to identify 'key moments' in particular periods of history, and the links between the work of a number of individuals and the development of policies. It is not a comprehensive summary, but serves to provide an indicative 'archaeology' behind current UK practices.

Table 1.1 Some influential figures and key events in the development of Early Education in the UK, up to the present day

Name	Summary of achievements
Jan Amos Comenius 1592–1670	In 1631 published *The School of Infancy* focusing on the early years of a child's education and in particular on education by mothers within the home. In 1658 his *Orbis Sensualium Pictus*, the first picture book for children, was published.
Jean-Jacques Rousseau 1712–1778	In 1762 published *Emile* which expounded his view for a universal system of education through the experience of the child Emile.
J.H. Pestalozzi 1746–1827	In 1780 published *Leonard and Gertrude: A Book for the People* in which he set out a view of education as central to the regeneration of a community. He wrote: 'The school ought really to stand in closest connection with the life of the home'. He believed that mothers should be educated sufficiently to teach their children at home.
Robert Owen 1771–1858	Mill owner in New Lanark, Scotland. In 1816 established schools for children of his workers. Schools were for children under 12 years with particular emphasis on the infant school. James Buchanan was the first teacher in the New Lanark school, exemplifying Owen's ideals of kindness, activity and co-operation.
Joshua Watson 1771–1855	A retired wine merchant and government contractor during the Napoleonic Wars, he was once referred to by Bishop Lloyd of Oxford as 'the best layman in England'. He was an influential Church of England figure in the nineteenth century, and one of the founders of The National Society for the Education of the Poor in the Principles of the Established Church in 1811.

(Continued)

Table 1.1   *(Continued)*

Name	Summary of achievements
Joseph Lancaster 1778–1838	One of the founders of mass education for the poor in the industrial age and pioneer of the Monitorial school system. In 1798 set up the Borough Road School using the system of monitors to teach them. Supported by other Quakers, the system spread and 826 British schools were established by 1851. Borough Road also became the earliest teacher training institution.
Friedrich Froebel 1782–1852	In 1826 published *The Education of Man* in which he argues for the importance of play in education. Froebel's ideas became influential in Britain around the mid-nineteenth century.
James Buchanan 1784–1857	In 1814 worked with Robert Owen in New Lanark to run the infant school. Though reported not to have been a good manager, he enjoyed working with children using methods that reflected 'progressive' infant school work.
Samuel Wilderspin 1791–1866	In 1820, after meeting James Buchanan, took charge of the new Quaker Street Infant School in Spitalfields.
Elizabeth Mayo 1793–1865	In 1829, wrote *Lessons with Objects* which claimed that by arranging and classifying objects and discovering their qualities the child would be stimulated to learn. This influenced elementary education throughout the rest of nineteenth century, including some rote learning.
William Ewart 1798–1869	In 1850 successfully introduced a Bill to establish free public libraries supported from local rates.
Sir James Phillips Kay-Shuttleworth 1804–1877	1839–40 established a training college at Battersea which became the model for nineteenth-century training of elementary school teachers.
Robert Lowe 1811–1892	Introduced the Revised Code in 1862 which included the introduction of 'Payment by Results' whereby grants to elementary schools were based principally upon pupils' performance in annual examinations in reading, writing and arithmetic. Payment by Results continued for 35 years until 1899.
Charles Dickens 1812–1870	Through his novels he drew attention to the poor social conditions which affected children and the importance of education.
Emily Anne Eliza Shirreff 1814–1897	Campaigned for the education of girls and women. In 1875 became president of the Froebel Society (founded in 1874). She emphasised the importance of the proper training of kindergarten teachers.
William Edward Forster 1818–1886	The 1870 Elementary Education Act established school boards in areas where there was a lack of elementary school provision.

Name	Summary of achievements
Anthony John Mundella 1825–1897	Member of the Hadow Committee and responsible with Lord Spencer for the Mundella Act which became known as the Education Act of 1880 and which introduced universal compulsory education in England.
	The 'Mundella' Code of 1882 encouraged 'enlightened' teaching methods in schools and allowed for a variety of subjects in the curriculum.
Sir William Hart Dyke 1837–1931	Played a leading part in promoting and distributing the 1890 Education Code which paved the way for the ending of the system of 'Payment by Results'.
	In 1891 introduced the Free Education Bill which opened up the way to providing free elementary education to children.
Sir James Crichton-Brown 1840–1938	In 1884 as Vice President of the Committee of Council on Education investigated cases of alleged 'overpressure' in London schools caused by the demands of the Mundella Code.
Charlotte Mason 1842–1923	Headmistress of one of England's first infant schools at 22 years of age. Pestalozzi-trained, she started the first infant school in the country and championed home education and play as being as important as lessons, with the key phrase 'Education is an atmosphere'.
Edmond Gore Alexander Holmes 1850–1936	In 1911 published *'What Is and What Might Be: A Study of Education in General and Elementary Education in Particular'*. This book condemned the formal, systematised, examination-ridden education system and advocated co-operation, self-expression and activity methods.
	Holmes also, importantly, criticised the system of 'Payment by Results'.
Mary Augusta Ward (Mrs Humphry) 1851-1920	In 1890 founded a centre for social work, Bible teaching and 'children's play hours' at Gordon Square, London. The 'Children's Play Hours' scheme led to the establishment of recreational centres for London children. The Centre transferred to Tavistock Square in 1897 and became the Passmore Edwards Settlement. In 1898 Mary Ward began a scheme for 'crippled' children which contributed to the general recognition of the need for special resources and provision for some children.
Edward Parnell Culverwell 1855–1931	In 1913 published: *The Montessorian Principles and Practice* advocating modern, Montessorian teaching methods and thus introducing the method to the UK.
Sigmund Freud 1856–1939	Developed an approach to psychoanalysis which provided a way of interpreting the behavoiur of young children.

(Continued)

Table 1.1   *(Continued)*

Name	Summary of achievements
John Dewey 1859–1952	Promoted progressive and child-centred education through teaching based on integrated learning through projects rather than discrete subjects.
Rachel McMillan 1859–1917	In 1913 established the Rachel McMillan Open Air Nursery School in London, based on her ideas about pre-school education, with a large garden incorporating shelters and other outdoor facilities. She focused particularly on work with children from slum areas.
Margaret McMillan 1860–1931	In 1899 Margaret McMillan participated in one of the first medical inspections of children under government auspices. In 1902 she campaigned successfully for school medical inspections. In 1913, with her sister Rachel she established Camp schools and a nursery school. She established the Rachel McMillan Training College in memory of her sister in 1930.
Catherine Isabella Dodd 1860–1932	In 1902 opened an experimental elementary school and kindergarten based on new teaching methods.
Dame Maude Agnes Lawrence 1864–1933	School inspector and administrator. Became Chief Woman Inspector in 1905 when the Woman Inspectorate was set up. The six women, at first, inspected the education of very young children and girls in elementary schools, mainly in domestic subjects.
Maria Montessori 1870–1952	In 1907 opened, in Rome, the first House of Childhood, for children living in tenement housing aged between 3 and 7 years. Montessori's work emphasised the importance of children's environments. She developed successful methods of working with children described as 'mentally defective'.
Edith Mary Deverell 1872–1937	In 1900 appointed to the Inspectorate. Joined five other women inspectors who were inspecting girls' and infants' departments in elementary schools. Campaigned to secure the interest and co-operation of parents in the work of the school.
Melanie Klein 1882–1960	Psychoanalyst who employed 'free [therapeutic] play' techniques with children. In 1932 published *The Psycho-Analysis of Children*. A pioneer of knowledge of the 'mental life' of infant children and an important influence on general attitudes to young children.
Alexander Sutherland Neill 1883–1973	In 1924 A.S. Neill founded his own school in Lyme Regis, which on moving to Suffolk became known as the famous 'Summerhill School', based on radically liberal, humanist and child-centred principles.

Name	Summary of achievements
Susan Sutherland Isaacs 1885–1948	In 1924–1927 established the Malting House School, Cambridge, with a curriculum and pedagogy designed to further the *individual* development of children. Author of several books which included observations and reflections of children at the Malting House School. (Thus an early *systematic* researcher.)
Henry Caldwell Cook 1886–1939	In 1917 published *The Play Way, an Essay in Educational Method*. He believed that the existing school system hampered 'true' education, arguing (as Dewey was to) that: 'Proficiency and learning come not from reading and listening but from action, from doing and from experience'.
Marion Richardson 1892–1946	Mostly influential as Inspector for Art during the 1930s in London. Influenced the teaching of handwriting during the late 1930s, with the publication *Writing and Writing Patterns* (1935) which influenced the teaching of handwriting in primary schools.
Louis Christian Schiller 1895–1976	Her Majesty's Inspector of Schools, promoted child-centred learning and education through the arts. Worked closely with Robin Tanner running courses for serving teachers.
Lev Vygotsky 1896–1934	Psychologist and educational theorist best known for his emphasis on learning as an act of social interaction and his theory of the 'Zone of Proximal Development'.
Donald Woods Winnicott 1896–1971	A paediatrician and psychoanalyst who developed a framework of human emotional development which supports the development of environments and practices to enable children to develop as secure and emotionally 'whole' human beings.
Jean Piaget 1896–1980	Psychologist who put forward stages of cognitive development which informed practice in early years teaching. Corresponded with Susan Isaacs.
Sir Fred Joyce Schonell 1900–1969	Most renowned for influence on primary school methods of teaching, in particular, approaches to teaching children with learning difficulties. In 1944 wrote the *Happy Venture* reading scheme and developed the reading test named after him.
Erik Erikson 1902–1994	Psychologist and psychoanalyst, his theory of human development prompted the development of early childhood programmes which supported healthy social and emotional development.
Sir James Pitman 1901–1985	Inventor of the Initial Teaching Alphabet (ita) a simplified format to aid learning of reading which was in vogue in some schools during the 1960s but which did not become universally established infant teaching practice.

(Continued)

Table 1.1 *(Continued)*

Name	Summary of achievements
Carl Rogers 1902–1987	Psychologist and psychotherapist who put forward an approach to education which was based on reciprocal relationships between children and between children and their teachers.
Burrhus Frederick Skinner 1904–1990	Psychologist who developed theory of behaviourism which promoted a system of learning which involved a 'stimulus-response' approach in order to modify undesirable behaviour.
Robin Tanner 1904–1988	Promoted the arts in education and ran courses for teachers, with Christian Schiller, at the Institute of Education in London.
John Bowlby 1907–1990	Psychoanalyst renowned for his 'attachment' theory.
Sir Alec Clegg 1909–1986	Chief Education Officer of the West Riding 1945–1974. Clegg emphasised the importance of creativity in all educational processes, made key contributions to teachers' in-service education (INSET) and to the organisation and curricula of schools. He made an extensive collection of children's artwork from West Riding schools from the 1930s to 1974 and expounded the importance of creativity.
Sir John Hubert Newsom 1910–1971	Like Clegg, a pioneer of the systematic development of school needs and processes. In 1963 Chair of the Central Advisory Council on education which produced the Newsom Report – *Half Our Future* – reporting on the education of 'average and below average' children. Deputy Chair of the Central Advisory Council, Children and their Primary Schools which produced *The Plowden Report* (1968) and wrote several books, including *Willingly to School* (1944), *The Education of Girls* (1948) and *The Child at School* (1950).
Loris Malaguzzi 1920–1994	Founder of the Reggio Emilia Approach to preschool education. Famously championed children's rights in education and the 'hundred languages of childhood'.
Chris Athey 1924–2011	Director of the Froebel Early Childhood Project which identified 'Schematic Theory' as a way of understanding children's learning. Advocate of parents and professional educators sharing pedagogic knowledge.

Into the twenty-first century: twenty-five years of policy change

Understanding recent history: 1988–2013

When we look back over these last few years, it seems that the slow and fitful development of early childhood education in the UK is now central to educational and social change. There has been something of an explosion of activity, a burgeoning of initiatives, interest and resources. Thus in the last 25 years alone, from 1988 to 2013, there have been at least 25 major new policies (an average of one per year) which, apart from their individual effects, have, as a whole, changed the shape and status of Early Childhood Education and Care almost beyond recognition. A few years ago a teacher told us:

> It's odd, I started teaching in 1988 and I've been looking back at old files and things and clearing out planning sheets, class lists, those kinds of things. Looking back I found myself plotting these 20 years almost exactly in terms of a policy a year!

A brief survey of this period reveals how policy changes have involved early childhood educators in the following:

- implementing the National Curriculum and subsequent revisions
- rigorous and (sometimes) stressful inspection processes
- implementation of the Children Act 1989
- interpretation of expected 'desirable outcomes' of nursery education
- implementing new codes of practice for the identification of children with Special Educational Needs
- implementing changes in relation to national assessment of children on entry to school, known as 'Baseline Assessment'
- the National Childcare Strategy in 1998
- working, during the 1990s, with diminishing resources followed by high-profile, funded activity and increasing expectations during the early 2000s and savage cuts to public spending and progressive closure of provision since 2011, whilst policy continued to claim progress on quality
- working with diminishing support and limited opportunities for professional development followed by expectations of further qualifications and funded professional development
- grappling with issues affecting the teaching of 4-year-olds in school
- Early Years Development and Childcare Partnerships (EYDCPs)
- working within a developing network of diversity of provision and Early Years Child Care Partnerships
- implementing aspects of the National Literacy Strategy

(Continued)

(Continued)

- implementing aspects of the National Numeracy Strategy
- implementing the new Foundation Stage curriculum developed from government guidance
- transforming the Foundation Stage from policy to practice
- implementing the Foundation Stage Profile
- *The Ten Year Childcare Strategy* 2004
- implementing the Birth to Three Matters Framework
- establishment of the Children's Workforce Development Council (2006)
- implementing the revised Early Years Foundation Stage (2007)
- acquiring Early Years Professional Status
- review of The Early Years Foundation Stage (Tickell, 2011) and implementation of the revised EYFS (2012)
- review of Early Years and Childcare Qualifications (Nutbrown Review, 2012)
- launch of the Childcare Commission[3] (DfE and DWP, 2012)
- provision for 40% of the most vulnerable 2-year-olds in England[4]
- new policies announced in 'More Great Childcare' (DfE, 2012)
- new assessment policy announced (2013)

It is important to remember that this list is by no means exhaustive and, of course, is supplemented by other social and educational policies which have – equally if less directly – impacted on the culture, structure and status of early childhood education and care. As well as these demanding policy shifts, recent years have seen the establishment of what might be called a new recognition for the early childhood workforce with:

- unprecedented government investment followed by unprecedented spending cuts
- professional development opportunities (and expectations)
- networks of support
- expectation of further qualifications of some staff working with children from birth to five.

Into the future, learning from the past

Learning from the past is one way of trying to ensure that new policies and investment do not repeat the mistakes of previous generations but,

---

[3] https://www.education.gov.uk/childrenandyoungpeople/earlylearningand childcare/a00211918/childcare-commission

[4] http://www.education.gov.uk/childrenandyoungpeople/earlylearningand childcare/delivery/free%20entitlement%20to%20early%20education/ a0070230/eigel

of course, history shows that it is not that simple! We shall come to this later in the book where we examine the ways in which influential people and their actions contributed to the history and development of early childhood education the UK and how this has helped to shape present-day policy and practice and serves to locate current experience within a history of ideas, beliefs and values. However, throughout the book it will become apparent that policy-makers do not always learn from the past and, as we shall see, ideas sometimes seem to return, are sometimes re-invented and appear in 'new clothes' but nevertheless bear a distinctly familiar shape (even if bringing new intentions).

The point of this examination of the work and thinking of people who have contributed to the development of early childhood education, is to try to understand how the most useful ideas can be drawn upon and developed. There is no 'history for the sake of history' here, rather a reflection on some of the lessons which might be learned in order to try to understand the present state of early childhood education and how it has come to be what it is.

Suggestions for further reading

Giardiello, P. (2013) *Pioneers in Early Childhood Education: the roots and legacies of Rachel and Margaret McMillan, Maria Montessori and Susan Isaacs.* London: Routledge.

Selbie, P. and Clough, P. (2005) 'Talking early childhood education fictional enquiry with historical figures', *Journal of Early Childhood Research*, 3(2) 115–26.

Part 2

The Pioneers: Their Lives and Works

In this part of the book we have presented a chronologically arranged series of biographies of 27 key figures who contributed as pioneers to the development of early childhood education and care through their work in: child development; philosophy; psychology; curriculum; pedagogy; social policy; and different forms of provision of early childhood education and care. We should emphasise that this is neither a systematic nor exhaustive collection; rather, we have chosen people in whose work we can see distinctive contributions to the development of early childhood education. Some of the names will be familiar (if not famous) and certainly widely acknowledged as 'pioneers' worthy of the name. But we believe that those less well known can no less be seen as pioneers, even if their spheres of influence were smaller, local and less celebrated.

These brief biographies are intended as short introductions to the people, their most important contributions to the early childhood field and their key writings. Those featured here have been chosen because some of them have influenced our own beliefs, research and practices and some were suggested by our students and other contemporary contributors to the field of early childhood education. It will be clear that some of the people we have included here have an obvious place, while for others their contribution and inclusion may be less immediately apparent. We do not claim a comprehensive 'who's who' – or 'who *was* who'! – in the history of early childhood, but those included here, we feel, provide a starting point for explorations of 'old' ideas.

How this section is used is a matter of reader preference. Some may wish to read it through chronologically, others may wish to refer to selected biographies. However, we suggest that before the conversations in Part 3 are read, the biographies of the people featured in them are consulted because they include important background material which further illuminates the conversations.

The Biographies

Name	**Socrates**
Born	Athens, 469 BC
Died	Athens, 399 BC
Personal details	Son of Sophroniscus (thought to be a stonemason) and Phaenarete (a midwife). He studied geometry, music, literature and gymnastics in his youth, whilst also immersing himself in the ideas of philosophers. Married with children, he spent most of his life in Athens, where his student, Plato, recorded all of his ideas: Socrates himself never wrote anything down. He was executed for his lack of belief in Athens' gods and for corrupting the young: in public areas of Athens, he engaged citizens in philosophical discussions, where he also encouraged them to practise more self-analysis.
Profession/s	Socrates fought in the Greek army, fighting as a foot soldier in the Peloponnesian War with Sparta, and served on an executive council of the Greek Assembly.
Key contributions to early childhood education	According to Plato's writings it is perhaps his idea of teaching through the learners' questions which is most useful to early childhood education. He emphasised the importance of philosophy and of talking with others about life's questions.
Key texts	He wrote nothing himself, the main evidence of his thinking was recorded by his contemporaries: Plato and Xenophon.
Quotations	'Wisdom begins in wonder'.
Biographies	Kraut, R. (1984) *Socrates and the State.* Princeton, NJ: Princeton University Press.
	Penner, T. (1992) 'Socrates and the early dialogues', in R. Kraut. (ed.), *The Cambridge Companion to Plato.* Cambridge: Cambridge University Press.
	Santas, G.X. (1979) *Socrates: Phiolosophy in Plato's Early Dialogues.* London: Routledge and Kegan Paul.

Name	**Jan Amos Komenský (more widely known as Comenius)**
Born	28 March 1592 in the southern part of Moravia (now the Czech Republic)
Died	15 November 1670 in Amsterdam, Netherlands. His grave has been declared Czech soil by the Dutch government thus his desire to be buried in Czech soil was fulfilled.
Personal details	Orphaned at the age of 12, Comenius was eventually exiled by the outbreak of religious wars. He married twice, and both wives died, as did his two sons. In 1628, Comenius settled in Lezno, Poland, where he wrote his first books advocating the reform of the education system. His whole library was lost in a fire. He is variously referred to as the 'Teacher of Nations' and the 'Father of Modern Education'.
Profession/s	Comenius was educated at Heidelburg University, Germany, and ordained a clergyman. He was asked to be the first President of Harvard College, but declined. He returned to Moravia to become a schoolmaster and church pastor at Fulnek. He was a Bishop of the Unitas Fratum (Moravian Church) and became its President in the Thirty Years' War.
Key contributions to early childhood education	His books, *The Great Didactic* and *The School of Infancy*, proposed that education should not be limited to the action of the school and family but is part of general social life. He believed in what is sometimes called a 'holistic' view of education, teaching that education begins in the early days of childhood and continues throughout life. He believed that teachers should understand how a child's mind develops and believed that all children should receive the same education, whatever their gender and social class. He promoted education that was 'thorough, natural and enjoyable' and opposed rote learning, and was also the first to encourage continuing education, as well as equal education for all.
	He visited England in 1641 and worked in Sweden and Hungary to reform school systems.
	Orbis Sensualium Pictus (The Visible World in Pictures), published in 1658, is believed to be the first illustrated textbook for children.
	He was greatly respected by many in seventeenth-century Europe but less popular with some figures who are thought to have been responsible for his name being absent from any history of philosophy for two centuries.

(Continued)

(Continued)

Key texts	In his life, he published 154 books, the majority of which concerned educational philosophy and theology.
	The School of Infancy (1631)
	The Great Didactic (1657)
	Orbis Sensualium Pictus (1658)
Quotations	'Teach gently so that neither the teacher nor the pupils feel any difficulties or dislike; on the contrary, both find it very pleasant. And teach thoroughly, not superficially, but bring everyone to a real education, noble manners and devout piety'. (*The Great Didactic,* 1657)
	'The ideas of Comenius do not have to be updated, merely translated.' (Jean Piaget on Comenius, *Prospects,*1999)
Biographies	Laurie, S.S. (1904) *John Amos Comenius, Bishop of Moravians: His Life and Educational Works* (6th edn). Cambridge: Cambridge University Press.
	Spinka, M. (1967) *John Amos Comenius: That Incomparable Moravian* (2nd edn). New York: Russell and Russell.
	Murphy, D.J. (1995) *Comenius: A Critical Reassessment of his Life and Work.* Dublin: Irish Academic Press.

Name	**Jean-Jacques Rousseau**
Born	1712, Geneva
Died	2 July 1778, Ermenonville, near Paris
Personal details	Son of a watchmaker whose mother died days after his birth, Rousseau had little formal education. He lived with Thérèse Levasseur and had five children whom he left to an orphanage, later this was used by those who opposed his theories on education and child care to attack him. Rousseau's writings were controversial and he eventually fled to and settled in Paris where his ideas continued to attract attention and criticism.
Profession/s	He became an apprentice and then an engraver. Between 1740 and 1741 he was private tutor to two sons of a French nobleman, then moved to Paris in 1742. From 1743 to 1744, he was secretary to the French ambassador in Venice. Rousseau pursued his interest in music and in 1752 his opera *Le Devin du Village* was performed for King Louis XV.
Key contributions to early childhood education	Rouseau is best known for *Emile*, his work on developmental psychology and its implications for education. In *Emile*, Rousseau details the growth of a young boy under his care. In this largely fictional work *Emile* grows up in what Rousseau saw as the natural setting for a child, the countryside, where his education is designed to help him learn how to live. Rousseau discusses Emile's development in three stages: up to 12 (a period which Rousseau characterised as more animal like); 12 to 16 (the beginning of reasoned thought), and 16 onwards (the beginning of adulthood).
	Emile sets out Rousseau's ideals for living. The boy is protected from bad influences whilst he learns how to follow his instincts and to think for himself. It is education designed by Rousseau for a boy, and this is not what he would have proposed for a girl, who would be taught to obey.
	Emile has been criticised for being impractical, and Rousseau was aware of much of the criticism that his ideas attracted and made it clear that *Emile* was an ideal, not a reality, a philosophical position rather than a 'true treatise on education'.
Key texts	*Discourse on the Arts and Sciences* (1750)
	Emile: or, on Education (1762)
	The Social Contract (1762)

(Continued)

Quotations

'The strongest is never strong enough to be always the master, unless he transforms strength into right, and obedience into duty.' (Rousseau, 1762)

'Childhood is the sleep of reason.' (Rousseau, 1762)

'I long remained a child, and I am still one in many respects.' (Rousseau, 1782)

'Man is born free, but everywhere he is in chains.' (Rousseau, 1762)

'The training of children is a profession, where we must know how to waste time in order to save it.' (Rousseau, 1762)

'The person who has lived the most is not the one with the most years but the one with the richest experiences.' (Rousseau, 1750)

Biographies and commentaries

Bertram, C. (2003) *Rousseau and the Social Contract*. London: Routledge.

Cooper, L. (1999) *Rousseau, Nature and the Problem of the Good Life*. Pennsylvania: Pennsylvania State University Press.

Cranston, M. (1982) *Jean-Jacques: The Early Life and Work*. New York: Norton.

Damrosch, L. (2005) *Jean-Jacques Rousseau: Restless Genius*. New York: Houghton Mifflin.

Dent, N.J.H. (1988) *Rousseau: An Introduction to his Psychological, Social and Political Theory*. Oxford: Blackwell.

Dent, N.J.H. (2005) *Rousseau*. London: Routledge.

Lange, L. (2002) *Feminist Interpretations of Jean-Jacques Rousseau*. University Park: Penn State University Press.

Wokler, R. (1995) *Rousseau*. Oxford: Oxford University Press.

See also The Rousseau Association: http://www.rousseauassociation.org/

Name	**Johann Heinrich Pestalozzi**
Born	12 January 1746, Zürich, Switzerland
Died	17 February 1827, Brugg, Switzerland
Personal details	Pestalozzi had Italian Protestant roots and was from a middle-class family. His father was a surgeon and oculist who died when Pestalozzi was young and the family then lived under less affluent circumstances. He is said to have had a happy childhood, his mother influencing his thinking about how young children should spend their early years, playing and enjoying family activities.
	He married at 23 and tried farming as a livelihood, but failed.
	At the University of Zürich he became part of the political reform party working to improve conditions for ordinary people. He later focused his work on education.
	In 1798 the French invaded Switzerland and Pestalozzi rescued several children who had been abandoned on the shores of Lake Lucerne and cared for them personally in a disused convent until the French claimed the building in 1799.
Profession/s	Pedagogue and educational reformer, dedicating his life to children's education.
Key contributions to early childhood education	In terms of his educational philosophy, he did not limit education to mean academic achievements, but also defined it as developing social awareness and practical skills. This philosophy was summarised as 'Head, Heart and Hands'.
	His early educational experiments were unsuccessful but he opened a school in his farmhouse and in 1801 published *How Gertrude Teaches Her Children,* a book that influenced the pedagogical thinking of the period. In it he explained his ideas for a form of instruction that was in line with the laws of nature; children should learn through activity, through things rather than words and be free to pursue their own interests and draw their own conclusions. Putting some of Rousseau's ideas into practice, his major contribution to education came from 1804, when he spent 20 years at Yverdon. He and his wife established an educational institute for poor and underprivileged children. Some 150 boys (aged between 7 and 15 years) were cared for and educated according to their individual needs. In 1806 a similar school for girls was established, and in 1813 the first school in Switzerland for children with hearing and/or speech difficulties was set up. Social scientists of the time were greatly interested in the Pestalozzi philosophy and practices. His work was not easy, not all the teachers agreed on how things should be done, and around 1815 there were difficulties with the teachers and he struggled to maintain the schools as he believed they should be until his retirement in 1825.

(Continued)

(Continued)

Whilst his schools were important achievements, the most important contribution was in the principles of education which he established and demonstrated: observation, the 'whole' person, and the sympathetic approach of teachers. Key themes in his work are a refusal to allow 'method' to dominate what teachers did and a reluctance to make young children conform to views of what was 'correct'.

Pestalozzi saw education as central to the improvement of social conditions and believed that schools could play an important role. Victorian reformers took up his vision for education as the cornerstone of welfare policy through the nineteenth and twentieth centuries.

Key texts	*How Gertrude Teaches her Children: An Attempt to give Directions to Mothers how to Instruct their own Children* (1801) *Help for Teaching, Spelling, and Reading* (1801) 'Pestalozzi's Elementary Books' (1803). Six short books: three on *Intuitive-instruction in the Relations of Number,* two on *Intuitive-instruction in the Relations of Dimensions,* and *The Mother's Manual or Guide to Mothers in Teaching their Children how to Observe and Think.*
Quotations	'The wish to be acquainted with some branches of knowledge that took hold of my heart and my imagination even though I neglected the means of acquiring them, was, nevertheless, enthusiastically alive within me, and, unfortunately, the tone of public instruction in my native town at this period was in a high degree calculated to foster this visionary fancy of taking an active interest in, and believing oneself capable of, the practice of things in which one had by no means had sufficient exercise'. (Pestalozzi, 1801) 'life for the young child should be happy and free, and education in self-control should be gradual and careful. Punishment and restraint should rarely be necessary. Pressure to learn beyond the child's natural pace is harmful, and the denying of opportunities to learn by trial and error retards the development of character as well as of learning.' (Pestalozzi, 1801)
Biographies	Biber, G.E. (1831) *Henry Pestalozzi and his Plan of Education.* London: John Souter School Library. Silber, K. (1960) *Pestalozzi: The Man and his Work.* London: Routledge and Kegan Paul.

Name	**Robert Owen**
Born	14 May 1771, Newtown, Montgomeryshire
Died	1858
Personal details	Owen's father (also Robert Owen) was a saddler, ironmonger and postmaster. His mother, Anne Williams, had seven children, of which Owen was the sixth. He developed an early love of reading. At the age of 9 Robert Owen worked as a grocery boy and when he was 10 he worked with his brother in London as a saddler and became an apprentice to a clothier, where his employer had an impressive library, leading to Robert Owen spending much time reading. By the age of 19 Owen was the superintendent of a cotton mill in Manchester. He married Ann Dale, daughter of David Dale who owned the mills at New Lanark, in 1799.
Profession/s	In 1790 Owen went into business manufacturing yarn. Later he managed a large Manchester fabric mill before moving to manage the New Lanark Mills in 1800. Owen refused to employ pauper children in the mills and promoted a standard for community living in New Lanark mill homes which included sanitation, education and what were considered to be less exploitative working conditions. He also insisted that good behaviour of employees was rewarded. Out of the 2,000 workers at New Lanark, 500 were children from poorhouses and charities in Edinburgh and Glasgow.
Key contributions to early childhood education	He opened Britain's first infant school at New Lanark Mills in 1816. In these schools corporal punishment was avoided and the focus was placed upon 'character development', with dancing and music also being included in the curriculum. His clear enjoyment of, and liking for, children showed in his views of how they should be treated in school. As well as being strongly opposed to corporal punishment, he believed in rewarding cleanliness and good conduct. He insisted that his teachers treated pupils well and did not instil fear in them but promoted a love of reading and learning.
	Owen limited the working hours of children in the mills by his contribution to the Factory Act of 1819. Children under 10 were not employed in the mills, and instead went to school.
Key texts	*A New View of Society and Other Writings* (1812)

(Continued)

(Continued)

Quotations	'[there is] something fundamentally wrong with all religions' (*Glasgow Herald*, 20 April 1812)
	'The object is no less than to remove gross ignorance and extreme poverty, with their attendant misery, from your population, and to make it rational, well disposed, and well behaved.' (*Glasgow Herald*, 20 April 1812)
	'...human nature is radically good, and is capable of being trained, educated, and placed from birth in such manner, that all ultimately ... must become united, good, wise, wealthy, and happy.' (Owen, 1920: 181)
Biographies	Owen, R. (1920) *The Life of Robert Owen: Written by Himself*. London: G.Bell and Sons.

Name	**Friedrich Froebel**
Born	21 April 1782, Oberweissbach, Saxony (now Germany)
Died	21 June, 1852, Marienthal, Saxony
Personal details	Froebel was born into a clergyman's family. His mother died when he was only nine months old, and he was neglected as a child until an uncle took him in and sent him to school where he began to study maths and languages. Upon leaving school he served an apprenticeship to a forester, furthering his knowledge of natural phenomena and his love of plants.
Profession/s	Froebel taught at a progressive school in Frankfurt that was run on the lines advocated by Johann Heinrich Pestalozzi where he became convinced of his vocation as a teacher and after two years went to teach at Yverdon in Switzerland under Pestalozzi.
	He opened his own school with a colleague and settled at Keilhau in 1818. It was here that Froebel began to put many of his educational theories into practice in the school that took the form of an educational community. Whilst there, he wrote various articles, however his most important work was *Menschenerziehung, The Education of Man.*
Key contributions to early childhood education	In 1826 Froebel published his most important work, *The Education of Man*. This was a presentation of the principles and methods that had been pursued at Keilhau.
	In 1831 he accepted the Swiss government's invitation to train elementary school teachers, at which time he became convinced of the importance of the early stages of education.
	He returned to Keilhau in 1837 and opened an infant school, which he eventually named the Kindergarten or 'Garden of Children'.
	Froebel started a publishing business for play and other educational materials to stimulate learning through well-directed play activities accompanied by songs and music. His experiments at the Kindergarten attracted widespread interest – especially the use of 'gifts' (play materials) and 'occupations' (activities) – and other Kindergarten schools soon became established. His publishing firm published a collection of *Mother-play and Nursery Songs*, which included explanations of the songs' meanings and details for their use.

(Continued)

(Continued)

Froebel's ideas were soon brought to the attention of educators in England, France and the Netherlands and eventually the United States, where they became a cornerstone of standard educational provision for children from 4 to 6 years of age.

Key texts   *The Education of Man [Die Menschenerziehung]* (1826)

Mother Songs [Mutter und Koselieder] (1843)

Quotations   'The purpose of education is to encourage and guide man as a conscious, thinking and perceiving being in such a way that he becomes a pure and perfect representation of that divine inner law through his own personal choice; education must show him the ways and meanings of attaining that goal.' (Friedrich Froebel, 1826, *Die Menschenerziehung*, p. 2)

'Play is the highest expression of human development in childhood, for it alone is the free expression of what is in a child's soul.' (Friedrich Froebel, 1887, *The Education of Man*)

Biographies   Kilpatrick, W. H. (1916) *Froebel's Kindergarden Principles Critically Examined.* New York: Macmillan.

Lawrence, E. (ed.) (1952) *Friedrich Froebel and English Education.* London: University of London Press. (A series of essays on key elements of Froebel's thought and practice.)

Name	**Charles Dickens**
Born	7 February 1812, Portsmouth
Died	9 June 1870, Gad's Hill
Personal details	When Dickens was 12 years old, his father was imprisoned for debt, leading to Charles being sent to work in a boot-blacking factory in order to help support his family financially. Dickens worked from 1827 to 1832 in a solicitors', office and as law-court reporter. He was a Parliamentary reporter from 1832 to 1836. He began writing stories in 1833. He had 10 children.
Profession/s	He is best known as a novelist.
Key contributions to early childhood education	Dickens' concerns around education arise in his writing about society and crime. His ideas about education of the poor appear to stem from a view of crime prevention. He became involved in Ragged Schools from 1843, and drew attention to social issues and the effects of poverty on children through his novels and in his letters. The kindergarten movement was first mentioned by Dickens in a letter written on 1 February 1855. Dickens also helped Angela Coutts create Urania House, a place where former prostitutes were offered the opportunity to learn to read and write.
Key texts	Numerous novels but perhaps most relevant to early childhood are:
	Nicholas Nickelby (1839)
	David Copperfield (1850)
	Bleak House (1852)
	Hard Times (1854)
	Great Expectations (1861)
Quotations	To teachers of the Ragged Schools: 'Good intentions alone will never be sufficient qualification for such a labour, while this world lasts' (Dickens in Collins, 1963: 138)
	'I think it is right that the State should educate the people; and I think it is wrong that it should punish ignorance, without enlightening or preventing it. ... But I would limit its power and watch it very carefully. ... I apprehend that there are certain sound rudiments of a good education, and certain moral and religious truths, on which we might agree. I would have those taught in State Schools, to the children of parents of all Christian denominations; favouring no one Church more than another.' (Letter to Edward Baines 7 June 1850 in Collins, 1965: 252)

(Continued)

'Little Red Riding Hood was my first love. I felt that if I could have married Little Red Riding Hood, I should have known perfect bliss.' (Dickens in Bettleheim, 1988: 23)

Biographies   Hughes, James L. (1900) *Dickens as an Educator.* New York: D. Appleton.

Manning, J. (1956) *Dickens on Education.* Toronto: University of Toronto Press.

Collins, P. (1963) *Dickens and Education.* London: Macmillan.

Name	**Charlotte Mason**
Born	1 January 1842, Bangor
Died	16 January 1923, Ambleside
Personal details	Charlotte Mason was an only child, from a reasonably affluent family. Her father was a Liverpool merchant and she was educated by her parents at home. Her mother died when she was 16 years old and her father when she was 17. She lived with friends until she was 18 when, in 1860, she moved to London to train at the first teacher training college, 'The Home and Colonial School Society' established by Elizabeth and Charles Mayo, who used the ideas of Pestalozzi. Mason endured ill-health and suffered a breakdown which forced her to take breaks from her work. She travelled widely and wrote travel books as well as education books.
Profession/s	Mason became headmistress of the Davison School for infants in 1861, before she was fully trained. She was later to be Mistress of Method at Bishop Otter College, Chichester. She opened the House of Education, a women's teacher training college, in 1892. The House of Education was renamed Charlotte Mason College and later became part of St Martin's College, Lancaster – now the University of Cumbria.
Key contributions to early childhood education	Drawing on the work of Rousseau and Pestalozzi, Charlotte Mason promoted education for girls and women. She promoted the use of the senses in learning and learning through experiences and the outdoors.
	She developed a clear and distinctive philosophy and wrote 20 articles on education which became known by some as a Child's Bill of Rights. She established a teacher Training College in Ambleside in 1892 which also had a Parents' Union School, where young children could attend without charge if their parents subscribed to the monthly *Parents' Review* journal, which Charlotte Mason published to promote, her work on home education through her home education network, the Parents' National Education Union.
	Her promotion of parents as educators and home education makes her a key figure in the home education movement in the twenty-first century.
	The Charlotte Mason method revolves around the idea that 'Education is an Atmosphere, a Discipline, a Life'.
Key texts	*The Home Schooling Series.* Oxford: The Scrivener Press, 1955.

(Continued)

(Continued)

(1886) *Volume 1: Home Education. The Training and Education of Children Under Nine.*

(1896) *Volume 2: Parents and Children. A Practical Study of Educational Principles.*

(1904) *Volume 3: School Education. The Training and Education of Children Over Nine.*

(1904) *Volume 4: Ourselves, Our Souls and Bodies. Book 1: Self Knowledge. Book 2: Self Direction.*

(1905) *Volume 5: Some Studies in the Formation of Character.*

(1923) *An Essay Towards a Philosophy of Education.* Oxford: The Scrivener Press, 1955.

This may be a useful website for more information about her methods: http://simplycharlottemason.com/basics/what-is-the-charlotte-mason-method/

Quotations	'It stultifies the child to bring down his world to the "child's level"'. (Mason, 1923)

'...my object is to show that the chief function of the child – his business is the world during the first six or seven years of life – is to find out all he can, about whatever comes under his notice, by means of his five senses; that he has an insatiable appetite for knowledge got in this way; and that the endeavour of his parents should be to put him in the way of making acquaintance freely with nature and natural objects'. (Mason, 1886: 96–7)

'Children have a right to the best we possess; therefore their lesson books should be, as far as possible, our best books.' (Mason, 1923)

'There is no part of a child's education more important than that he should lay – by his own observation – a wide basis of facts towards scientific knowledge in the future.' (*on Nature Study Volume 1, Home Education,* 1886)

Name	**Rudolf Steiner**
Born	1861 in a small village called Kraljevec in the Austro-Hungarian Empire (now in Croatia)
Died	1925, Dornach, Switzerland
Personal details –	Rudolf Steiner was Austrian. He founded *Anthroposophy* meaning – in Greek – 'Wisdom of Man'. Anthroposophy is a way of looking at one's whole life in connection with the spirit. For many Steiner-educated pupils and Steiner teachers and parents of children in Steiner schools, Anthroposophy is a way of life, not just a basis for a system of education.
	Whilst at University, he focused on maths, chemistry and physics, and earned his doctorate having written his thesis on philosophy.
Profession/s	Steiner was a scientist and a philosopher. In the 1890s, he worked at the Goethe Archive in Weimar for seven years. In later life Steiner was greatly concerned with social issues, and this promoted the foundation of the Steiner-Waldorf school movement which, some 80 years after his death, is still active internationally and offers a comprehensive, socially inclusive co-educational alternative to State education systems in many countries.
Key contributions to early childhood education	Rudolf Steiner conceived of education as an art – creative, progressive, social and individual. Teaching is essentially vocation, a challenging yet fulfilling task and teachers, in common with their pupils, remain learners. Not limited to schooling, teaching and learning mean taking one's place in the world, working with enthusiasm, acting with consideration, involving oneself responsibly. Now an international movement, Steiner-Waldorf kindergartens are found in many countries, with over 40 in the UK.
	Steiner-Waldorf kindergartens are early childhood settings which follow pedagogical practices based on the anthroposophical work of Rudolf Steiner. Steiner-Waldorf kindergartens are immediately recognisable for their homely characteristics. Furniture is often wooden, and the equipment available for the children is made of natural materials. Plastic toys are not a feature in Steiner kindergartens.
	The first Waldorf school was opened in 1919 with funding from the Waldorf Astoria company. Emil Molt wrote:

> I felt the tragedy of the working class: to be held back by lack of money from sharing the education of the rich middle class. I also had a sense of what it would mean for social progress if we could support a new educational endeavour within our factory...
>
> (Molt, 1991: 3)

(Continued)

(Continued)

The first Waldorf kindergarten was opened in 1926, the year after Steiner died. It was developed and run under the direction of Elizabeth von Grunelius, a teacher who had worked closely with Steiner in defining what kindergarten education in a Steiner school should look like. The Waldorf plan for early childhood education was published in *Educating the Young Child* (Grunelius, 1974) in England in 1955 and set out the underpinning structures of Steiner-Waldorf kindergarten provision which were built upon *imitation* and *example*.

Key texts	Steiner, R. (1947) *The Study of Man*. London: Anthroposophic Press.
	Steiner, R. (1980) *Rudolf Steiner: An Autobiography*. Blauvelt, NY: Steinerbooks.
	Steiner, R. (1995) *The Kingdom of Childhood: Introductory Talks on Waldorf Education*. Seven lectures and answers to questions, given in Torquay 12–20 August 1924. Hudson, NY: Anthroposophic Press.
	Steiner, R. (1996) *The Foundations of Human Experience*. Hudson, NY: Anthroposophic Press. (Originally published as *The Study of Man* 1947.)
	Oldfield, L. (2001) *Free to Learn: Introducing Steiner Waldorf Early Childhood Education*. Stroud: Hawthorn Press. (Provides a clear discussion of Steiner-Waldorf pedagogy and several examples illustrate aspects of this work.)
Quotations	'The child has fantasy, and this fantasy is what we must engage. It is really a question of developing the concept of a kind of "milk for the soul"' (Steiner, 1995: 14)
	'You must teach and educate out of the very nature of the human being, and for this reason education for moral life must run parallel to the actual teaching ...' (Steiner, 1995: 52)
	'Reverence, enthusiasm, and a sense of guardianship, these three are actually the panacea, the magical remedy, in the soul of the educator and teacher.' (Rudolf Steiner, *The Kingdom of Childhood*, 1924)
	'Accept the children with reverence, educate them with love, send them forth in freedom.' (Rudolf Steiner, *The Kingdom of Childhood*, 1924)
Biographies	Aeppli, W. (1986) *Rudolf Steiner Education and the Developing Child*. Hudson, NY: Anthroposophic Press.
	Lissau, R. (1987) *Rudolf Steiner: Life, Work, Inner Path and Social Initiatives*. Stroud: Hawthorn Press.
	Molt, E. (1991) *Emil Molt and the Beginnings of the Waldorf School Movement*. Edinburgh: Floris Books.

Name	**Sigmund Freud**
Born	6 May 1856, Freiberg, Moravia (Czech Republic)
Died	1939
Personal details	His father Jacob was 41 and his mother 21 when Freud was born to a family which eventually totalled eight children. In 1859 the family moved to Vienna and in 1873 Freud graduated from secondary school able to read in several languages. He then studied medicine at Vienna University, and after graduating went on to work at the Vienna General Hospital. His early career involved him in research in psychiatry and neurology, and he collaborated with Josef Breuer in the treatment of hysteria through the use of hypnosis. After military service in 1880 he rejected medical practice in favour of research and teaching, but nevertheless graduated with a degree in medicine in 1881. He began psychiatric work in 1883 and treated 'nervous' disorders by 'electrotherapy' before developing his work on hypnosis from 1885. He married in 1886 and had six children, and in that year also set up a private practice that specialised in nervous and brain disorders. He spent much of his life in Vienna until the Nazis annexed Austria in 1938 and Freud, being Jewish, left for England where he died of cancer in 1939.
Profession/s	Freud was a medical doctor specialising in physiology and psychology. He is known as the 'father' of psychoanalysis, and was a highly influential thinker of his time who put forward the concepts of the unconscious, infantile sexuality and repression of experiences. He developed a radically new approach to the analysis and understanding of the human mind. His work on the interpretation of dreams and the role of subconscious symbolism is still influential in many aspects of life and work today.
Key contributions to early childhood education	Freud's theory on infantile sexuality and the 'Oedipus complex' has been used to interpret the behaviour of young children. His identification of three structural elements in the mind, *id*, *ego* and *super-ego* has been used to understand and interpret children's behaviour.
Key texts	*The Standard Edition of the Complete Psychological Works of Sigmund Freud* (ed. J. Strachey with Anna Freud), 24 vols. London, 1953–1964.
Quotations	'My life is interesting only if it is related to psychoanalysis.' (*The Psychopathology of Everyday Life*, 1904) 'Children are completely egoistic; they feel their needs intensely and strive ruthlessly to satisfy them.' (*The Ego and the Id*, 1923)

(Continued)

(Continued)

'When you were incontestably the favourite child of your mother, you keep during your lifetime this victor feeling, you keep feeling sure of success, which in reality seldom doesn't fulfill'. (*The Interpretation of Dreams*, 1900)

Biographies

Bettelheim, B. (1982) *Freud and Man's Soul*. New York: Knopf.

Frosh, S. (1987) *The Politics of Psychoanalysis: An Introduction to Freudian and Post-Freudian Theory*. New Haven, CT: Yale University Press.

Jones, E. (1953–1957) *Sigmund Freud: Life and Work* (3 vols). New York: Basic Books.

Wallace, E.R. (1983) *Freud and Anthropology: A History and Reappraisal*. New York: International Universities Press.

Wollheim, R. (1971) *Freud*. London: Fontana.

Name	**Rachel McMillan**
Born	25 March 1859, New York
Died	25 March 1917, London
Personal details	Following the death of her father and sister Elizabeth, Rachel she returned to Scotland with her mother and sister Margaret in 1865. On the death of her mother Jean McMillan, in 1877, Rachel took over the care of her very sick grandmother. She became a Christian Socialist in 1887 and on the death of her grandmother joined her sister Margaret in London in 1888, where she became a house mother in a home for girls in Bloomsbury. Rachel lived with Margaret for the rest of their lives. Rachel attended socialist meetings with her sister, and wrote for the magazine *Christian Socialist*. She gave free lessons to working class girls in the evening. Both Rachel and Margaret became aware of the relationship between workers' physical environment and their intellectual development and after the sisters helped workers during the London Dock Strike in October 1889, they moved to Bradford in 1892 where they promoted Christian Socialism and visited the poor. Politically aware and active, both sisters joined the Labour Party in 1902 and went on to support the campaign for universal suffrage but not the extreme actions of the Women's Social and Political Union.
Profession/s	Rachel McMillan was a political campaigner and health worker. She developed nursery provision for children of poor families as a means of promoting healthier lives.
Key contributions to early childhood education	In 1902 in London, Rachel worked closely with leaders of the Labour movement including James Keir Hardie and George Lansbury to campaign for school meals, because they believed that hungry children could not learn, and her work was instrumental in the passing of the School Meals Act in 1906. In 1908 Rachel and Margaret McMillan opened the first school clinic and a 'Night Camp' where children living in the slums of London could wash and put on clean nightclothes. In 1914 their Open-Air Nursery School and Training Centre was opened in Peckham, for 30 children aged from 18 months to 7 years. Rachel was responsible, in the most part, for the kindergarten and her sister worked on health issues. The classrooms in the Open-Air Nursery were called 'shelters' as the two sisters believed that children should be in the open air as much as is possible.

(Continued)

(Continued)

Key texts   Rachel was not the writer in the family – her sister Margaret was
                   responsible for writing and publishing their ideas and work.

Quotations   'I think that, very soon, when these teachings and ideas are
                   better known, people generally will declare themselves
                   Socialists.' (McMillan,1927)

Biographies   McMillan, M. (1927) *The Life of Rachel McMillan.* London:
                   J.M.Dent.

Name	**John Dewey**
Born	1859, Vermont
Died	1952, New York
Personal details	Dewey came from a family of Vermont farmers, and was the third of four sons of Archibald Dewey and Lucina Artmesia. He graduated in philosophy from the University of Vermont and gained a PhD in 1884 before teaching and later becoming Professor of Philosophy at the University of Michigan, where he taught for 10 years. Whilst there, he wrote *Psychology* (1887) and *Leibniz's New Essays Concerning the Human Understanding* (1888), his first two books, which both expressed his commitment to Hegelian idealism. He married Alice Chipman in 1886 and moved to the University of Chicago in 1894 and then to Columbia University, New York, in 1904.
Profession/s	Philosopher, educationalist and university professor.
Key contributions to early childhood education	His ideas on the contribution education might make to alleviate social problems have pervaded many early education programmes.
	The Dewey Laboratory School became a well-established centre for 'progressive education' which employed a pedagogy based on ideas of democracy and child centredness. What became known as the 'project method' involved teachers and children working on ideas and finding solutions to questions. Dewey was critical of misinterpretations of these ideas: 'Many so-called projects are of such a short time-span and are entered upon for such casual reasons, that extension of acquaintance with facts and principles is at a minimum. In short, they are too trivial to be educative' (Dewey, 1931: 31). The project method did not falsely divide knowledge into subjects but encouraged a more holistic approach to learning. The role of the teacher was to ensure that children's project ideas were realisable and to offer help and teaching at all stages where needed and where opportunities for teaching arose.
	Dewey promoted (in line with Vygotsky and Montessori) ideas of child-centred education, of activity and interaction, of education as a part of the social world of children and their communities.

(Continued)

(Continued)

His ideas and the methods he coached have been considered as his most valuable and lasting contributions to culture today. His ideas about education mainly focused on education that was below university level, and were built upon ideas that were first raised by Rousseau, Pestalozzi and Froebel. Dewey fused ideas of viewing children as individuals with their own rights with the notion that class-based educational organisation did not meet the requirements of a new era, calling for the educational system to be overhauled because of the changes occurring in American civilisation. Dewey wanted to integrate school with society, believing that learning the actual problems of life and learning the application of the principles and practices of democracy should serve a broader social purpose of helping people become more effective members of a democratic society.

The Progressive Education Association, inspired by Dewey's ideas, codified his doctrines as follows:

1. The conduct of the pupils shall be governed by themselves, according to the social needs of the community.
2. Interest shall be the motive for all work.
3. Teachers will inspire a desire for knowledge, and will serve as guides in the investigations undertaken, rather than as task-masters.
4. Scientific study of each pupil's development, physical, mental, social and spiritual, is absolutely essential to the intelligent direction of his development.
5. Greater attention is paid to the child's physical needs, with greater use of the out-of-doors.
6. Cooperation between school and home will fill all needs of the child's development such as music, dancing, play and other extra-curricular activities.
7. All progressive schools will look upon their work as of the laboratory type, giving freely to the sum of educational knowledge the results of their experiments in child culture.

These rules for education sum up the theoretical conclusions of the reform movement begun by Colonel Francis Parker and carried forward by Dewey at the Laboratory School he set up in 1896 with his first wife in connection with the University of Chicago. With his instrumentalist theory of knowledge as a guide, Dewey tried out and confirmed his new educational procedures there with children between the ages of 4 and 14.

Key texts	*Experience and Education* (1897). New York: Macmillan Publishing Co.
	How We Think (1897). New York: Dover Publications.
	My Pedagogic Creed (1897). Washington, DC: Progressive Education Association.
	The School and Society (1899). Chicago: University of Chicago Press.
	Experience and Education (1938). New York, NY: Kappa Delta Pi.
Quotations	'...the fundamental issue is not of new versus old education nor of progressive against traditional education but a question of what, if anything whatever, must be worthy of the name Education.' (Dewey, 1897)
	'I believe that education ... is a process of living, not a preparation for future living.' (Dewey, 1897)
	'While the child of bygone days was getting an intellectual discipline whose significance he appreciated in the school, in his home life he was securing acquaintance in a direct fashion with the chief lines of social and industrial activity. Life was in the main rural. The child came into contact with the scenes of nature, and was familiarized with the care of domestic animals, the cultivation of the soil, and the raising of crops. The factory system being undeveloped, the house was the center of industry. Spinning, weaving, the making of clothes, etc., were all carried on there.' (*My Pedagogic Creed*, 1897)
	'The actual interests of the child must be discovered if the significance and worth of his life is to be taken into account and full development achieved. Each subject must fulfill present needs of growing children . . . The business of education is not, for the presumable usefulness of his future, to rob the child of the intrinsic joy of childhood involved in living each single day.' (*Experience and Education,*1938)
Biographies	Tanner, L.N. (1997) *Dewey's Laboratory School: Lessons for Today.* New York: Teachers College Press.

Name	**Margaret McMillan**
Born	20 July 1860, New York
Died	29 March 1931, London
Personal details	Margaret McMillan returned to Scotland with her mother and sister Rachel in 1865, following the death of her father and sister Elizabeth from scarlet fever, from which she had suffered herself, resulting in deafness until the age of 14.
	In 1877 after the death of her mother, Margaret went to London to train as a governess. From 1888 Margaret and Rachel lived and worked together for the rest of their lives. She was converted by her sister Rachel to socialism and attended political meetings. Margaret gave free evening lessons to working-class girls in London and became aware of the connection between working and living conditions and capacity to learn.
	Rachel and Margaret moved to Bradford in 1892 where they promoted Christian Socialism and visited the poor. In 1894 Margaret McMillan was elected Independent Labour Party member for the Bradford School Board, thus influencing work in Bradford Schools.
Profession/s	She was a suffragist and campaigner for nursery education and health care for young children.
Key contributions to early childhood education	In 1911, she published *The Child and the State*, in which she criticised the way schools situated in working-class areas often concentrated on preparing children for jobs that were monotonous and unskilled, insisting that schools should be offering a broader education.
	She established medical inspections in elementary schools and pioneered, with her sister Rachel, the first open-air nursery for under fives, where disadvantaged children could enjoy 'light, air and all that is good' (1917).
	When Rachel McMillan died on 25 March 1917, Margaret continued to run the Peckham Nursery which they had opened together. She also served on the London County Council and wrote several books, including *The Nursery School (1919)* and *Nursery Schools: A Practical Handbook (1920)*. Margaret McMillan became interested in nursing and in 1930 she established a college in Deptford to train teachers and nurses which was named the *'Rachel McMillan College.'*

Key texts

Child Labour and the Half Time System (1896). London: George Allen and Unwin.

Early Childhood (1900). London: George Allen and Unwin.

The Camp School (1917). London: George Allen and Unwin.

The Nursery School (1919). London: George Allen and Unwin.

Nursery Schools: A Practical Handbook (1920). London: George Allen and Unwin.

Childhood, Culture, and Class in Britain (1925). London: George Allen and Unwin.

Quotations

'Our mother was possessed by one aim – to give us children a proper education. She spared nothing in the pursuit of this end. The first experience of school was a little disconcerting and in some ways even alarming. The children sat in a large room with a desk that looked like a pulpit. This desk contained, as we afterwards learned with horror, a tawse, or leathern strap, with four tongues, which the masters used with energy, not indeed for the punishment of girls, but only of boys. In spite of our immunity, we were filled with anxiety and distress, and had a deep sympathy with the unruly boys.' (McMillan, 1927)

'The condition of the poorer children was worse than anything that was described or painted. It was a thing that this generation is glad to forget. The neglect of infants, the utter neglect almost of toddlers and older children, the blight of early labour, all combined to make of a once vigorous people a race of undergrown and spoiled adolescents; and just as people looked on at the torture two hundred years ago and less, without any great indignation, so in the 1890s people saw the misery of poor children without perturbation.' (McMillan, 1927)

Name	**Maria Montessori**
Born	31 August 1870, Chiaravalle, Italy
Died	6 May 1952, The Netherlands
Personal details	Maria Montessori graduated from technical school in 1886. She was a very bright student and studied modern languages and natural sciences. From 1886 to 1890 she attended Regio Instituto Tecnico Leonardo da Vinci. She is said to be the first woman in Italy to qualify as a physician. She had one son, Mario Montessori, in 1898. Montessori had a love affair with her colleague, Dr Montesano, but they never married. Montessori was exiled by Mussolini mostly because she refused to compromise her principles and make the children into soldiers.
Profession/s	Maria Montessori was an Italian medical doctor who worked with children with learning difficulties in socially deprived areas of Rome after developing an interest in the diseases of children and in the needs of those that were said to be 'ineducable'. In 1907 she began work with 50 children living in the slum areas of Rome who, within two years, were considered to be achieving educationally alongside other children of their age. Her success brought her worldwide acclaim. Her first *Casa dei Bambini* (Children's house or household) was opened in Rome in 1907.
	Whilst well known for her distinctive work on early childhood curriculum and pedagogy, Maria Montessori was well respected in the world of science, and was invited to the US in 1915 by Alexander Graham Bell and Thomas Edison to address an audience at the Carnegie Hall. She was politically active and her expression of anti-fascist views forced her into exile during World War Two. She was twice nominated for the Nobel Peace Prize and – until the adoption by Italy of the Euro – her face appeared on the 1,000 lire note, in recognition and honour of her achievements.
Key contributions to early childhood education	From her early work, Montessori developed a set of principles, based on her observation of these children, which she argued were applicable to the learning of all children. The Montessori Method is based on a philosophy which encompasses a range of issues, namely: multi-age grouping of children according to periods of development; human tendencies; the process of children's learning; the prepared environment; observation; work centres; teaching method; class size; basic lessons; areas of study; daily schedule; assessment; learning styles; and character education. Within

these many elements the notion of 'human tendencies' is perhaps key. Montessori developed her methods by building on her observations that learning is brought about by human tendencies to do – to act, to explore, to create. She observed that learning happened through repetition, concentration, and imagination, and that learners needed to be independent in their actions whilst making their own decisions about what 'work' they should do and learning how to control their own actions.

Between 1907 to the mid-1930s, Maria Montessori dedicated herself to the development of schools throughout Europe and North America. From around 1935–1947 she worked in India and Sri Lanka, training teachers in the Montessori curriculum and method.

Montessori was, undoubtedly, a pioneer in the field of child care and education, and, though famous for her influence on early childhood education, her work included ways of working with children of all ages. Montessorian approaches are used, internationally, in education settings and in home-based provision for children. In the case for those said to be 'ineducable', she argued that training for teachers should be developed along Froebelian lines. She also developed a teaching programme to help enable 'defective' children to learn to read and write. Her methods not only included teaching speech skills through repetitions, but also through developing exercises that prepare children for learning skills: *looking becomes reading; touching becomes writing* (Montessori Method).

Key texts

Montessori, M. (1914) *Dr Montessori's Own Handbook.* New York: Schocken Books.

Montessori, M. (1962) *Education for a New World.* Wheaton, IL: Theosophical Press.

Montessori, M. (1963) *The Secret of Childhood.* Calcutta: Orient Longmans.

Montessori, M. (1964) *The Absorbent Mind.* Wheaton, IL: Theosophical Press.

Montessori, M. (1964) *The Montessori Method.* New York: Schocken Books.

(Continued)

(Continued)

Quotations	'Like others I had believed that it was necessary to encourage a child by means of some exterior reward that would flatter his baser sentiments, such as gluttony, vanity, or self-love, in order to foster in him a spirit of work and peace. And I was astonished when I learned that a child who is permitted to educate himself really gives up these lower instincts. I then urged the teachers to cease handing out the ordinary prizes and punishments, which were no longer suited to our children, and to confine themselves to directing them gently in their work.' (*Education for a New World*, 1962)
	'We should really find the way to teach the child how, before, before making him execute a task.' (The Montessori Method)
	'First the education of the senses, then the education of the intellect.' (*The Absorbent Mind,* 1964)
Biographies	Kramer, Rita (1976) *Maria Montessori*. Toronto: Longman Canada Limited.

Name	**Alexander Sutherland Neill (A.S.Neill)**
Born	17 October 1883, Forfar, Scotland
Died	23 September 1973
Personal details	Neill's father was a teacher, and Neill became a pupil-teacher in his father's school. He later spent three years working as a teacher in a school in Fife, where he received a teaching certification. When he was 25 he enrolled at Edinburgh University to study agriculture and graduated with an MA in 1912. By 1914 he was headmaster of the Gretna Green School in Scotland. Neill married twice; his second wife, Ena Wood Neill, administered Summerhill School until 1985 when their daughter, Zoe Neill Readhead, took over the school as headteacher.
Profession/s	Neill was a progressive educator, author and founder of Summerhill School, which remains open and continues to follow his educational philosophy to this day. He is best known as an advocate of personal freedom for children.
Key contributions to early childhood education	Neill's ideas of freedom in education were highly controversial in their time. However, his work influenced many progressive educators who came after him. Perhaps the main influence on the early years was an ethos of respect for children and a fluid approach to learning and curriculum. The central tenet of Neill's philosophy was the freedom of the child and the resistance to oppressive routines and regimes.
	In 1921, Neill, along with several others, founded Summerhill, an international school in Suffolk, where class attendance and extracurricular activites were optional and there was no prescribed teaching method, which left children to learn by their own initiative.
Key texts	*A Dominie's Log* (1916). London: Herbert Jenkins.
	The Last Man Alive (1939). London: Gollancz.
	Summerhill: A Radical Approach to Child Rearing (1960). New York: Hart Publishing.
	Neill, Neill, Orange Peel! (1973). New York: Hart Publishing.
Quotations	'[I am] ... just enough of a Nietzschian to protest against teaching children to be meek and lowly.' (Neill, 1960)

(Continued)

(Continued)

'[I am] trying to form minds that will question and destroy and rebuild.' (Neill,1960)

'The function of the child is to live his own life – not the life that his anxious parents think he should live, nor a life according to the purpose of the educator who thinks he knows best.' (Neill,1960)

'No one is wise enough or good enough to mould the character of any child. What is wrong with our sick, neurotic world is that we have been moulded, and an adult generation that has seen two great wars and seems about to launch a third should not be trusted to mould the character of a rat.' (Neill,1960)

Biographies

Croall, Jonathan (1983) *Neill of Summerhill – The Permanent Rebel.* London: Routledge & Kegan Paul.

Walmsley, John (1969) *Neill and Summerhill: A Pictorial Study.* Baltimore: Penguin.

Name	**Susan Sutherland Isaacs**
Born	24 May 1885, near Bolton, Lancashire, England
Died	12 October 1948, London, England
Personal details	Susan Sutherland Isaacs was the last of nine children, whose mother died when she was six. Her own schooling was difficult and she was removed from school at the age of 14 although she continued to self-educate vigorously.
Profession/s	Isaacs trained and practised as a psychoanalyst and such training and experience clearly influenced her work, particularly with regard to observing young children's behaviour. Isaacs trained as a teacher and in 1912 obtained an Honours degree in Philosophy and a scholarship to Cambridge. After two lecturing posts she founded the experimental Malting House School, Cambridge, in 1924.
Key contributions to early childhood education	The Malting House School had an experimental philosophy with no fixed curriculum and placed an emphasis on individual development and joy in discovery.
	For Isaacs, children quite naturally experience intense feelings of fear, hate, jealousy and guilt, and she argued that they should have the freedom to express them in a free yet carefully contained environment.
	In 1930 she published *Intellectual Growth in Young Children* and three years later *Social Development in Young Children*. Also in 1933 she became the first Head of the Child Development Department of the Institute of Education, University of London, from where she was a great advocate of nursery schooling. She corresponded with Piaget but the two never met.
	Susan Isaacs was a powerful mix of 'educationalist' and 'psychologist' and at the core of her child-centred philosophy was the need to understand the child from within. She argued that young children need a subtle balance between explorative freedom and emotional expression, and mild yet firm supporting control in order to protect them from their inner anxieties and aggressive impulses.
	Between 1929 and 1936, Isaacs replied to parents' questions concerning their children in *Nursery World*, under the pseudonym Ursula Wise.

(Continued)

(Continued)

Key texts	*The Nursery Years* (1929). London, Routledge & Kegan Paul.
	Intellectual Growth in Young Children (1930). London: Routledge & Kegan Paul.
	Social Development of Young Children (1933). London: Routledge & Kegan Paul.
Quotations	'The nursery school teacher no less than the mother must have love and sympathy, natural insight and the patience to learn; but children need more than this in their struggles with the many problems we have glimpsed. They need true scientific understanding as well as mother-wit and mother-love.' (Isaacs, 1954: 30).
	'The nursery school is an extension of the function of the home, not a substitute for it; but experience has shown that it brings to the child such a great variety of the benefits that it can be looked upon as a normal institution in the social life of any civilised community.' (Isaacs, 1954: 31).
Biographies	Gardner, D.E.M. (1969) *Susan Isaacs.* London: Routledge and Kegan Paul.
	Graham, P. (2008) *Susan Isaacs: A Life Freeing the Minds of Children.* London: Karnac Books.

Name	**Louis Christian Schiller**
Born	20 September 1895, New Barnet, London
Died	11 February 1976, Kenton, London
Personal details	Christian Schiller fought and was wounded in World War I. In 1917 he was awarded the Military Cross. He studied maths at Cambridge (1919–1920). He married Lyndall Handover in 1925 and had four children: three daughters and one son, Russell.
Profession/s	Schiller taught maths until 1923. He was a student at London Day Training College from 1923 to 1924. He took an interest in elementary and primary education and gained a teaching diploma in 1924. He became an Assistant Inspector in 1924 and District Inspector in Liverpool in 1925. Schiller ran HMI residential courses for serving teachers, often in collaboration with Robin Tanner, who also promoted progressive education and the arts in primary education.
	In 1946 he was appointed first Staff Inspector for Primary Education, following the 1944 Education Act.
	Schiller became Senior Lecturer at the University of London Institute of Education and ran courses for teachers there between 1955 and 1963. He was a member of the Plowden Committee.
Key contributions to early childhood education	An HMI who promoted child-centred teaching, Schiller was a strong advocate for education and the arts in the early years. He influenced many teachers who went on to develop careers in teaching and promoting progressive methods.
Key texts	Griffin-Beale, (ed). (1979) *Christian Schiller in His Own Words*. London: A. & C. Black.
	Many lecture scripts are in the Institute of Education archives: http://www.ioe.ac.uk/services/606/.html
Quotations	'Curriculum is not an attractive word... it leaves an impression of something sharp ...' (Schiller, 1950 in Griffin-Beale, 1979)
	'Assessment must take place "in the round". To see her assessment in the round we must observe *how* she reads. With what quality of understanding.' (Ibid.)

Name	**Lev Semyonovich Vygotsky**
Born	1896, Russia
Died	1934
Personal details	Born into a middle-class family, Vygotsky studied literature at the University of Moscow. As a secondary teacher he became interested in the processes of learning and the role of language in learning. He then pursued his interest in psychology, despite having no formal training in the subject, studying Freud, Piaget and Montessori in particular.
	Vygotsky died at the age of 38 of tuberculosis, curtailing the contribution he might have made to the field.
Profession/s	Psychologist and educational theorist.
Key contributions to early childhood education	Vygotsky put forward the idea of learning as a social exchange, that young children learn through interaction with other children and with adults – Vygotsky's sociocultural theory. This theory suggests that social interaction results in changes to children's thought and behaviour, that will vary between cultures. Vygotsky proposed that the development of a child depends on the interactions they experience, the people they experience them with, and what the culture they are in provides to enable them to form their own view of the world.
	The 'Zone of Proximal Development' was a key contribution to present understanding of the role of the adult (or another child) in children's learning and is a cornerstone of present-day pedagogy where children work together in groups and of teachers' use of observation to inform their practice in the early years.
Key texts	Vygotsky, L. and Vygotsky, S. (1980) *Mind in Society: The Development of Higher Psychological Processes*. Cambridge: Harvard University Press.
	Vygotsky, L. (1986) *Thought and Language*. Boston: MIT Press.
Quotations	'Learning and development are interrelated from the child's very first day of life.'(Vygotsky, 1980)
	'... development is subject to the influence of the same two main factors which take part in the organic development of the child, namely the biological and the social.' (Ibid.)
	' ... human learning presupposes a specific social nature and a process by which children grow into the intellectual life of those around them.' (Ibid: 88)
Biographies	Newman, F. and Holzman, L. (1993) *Lev Vygotsky: Revolutionary Scientist*. London: Routledge.

Name	**Donald Woods Winnicott**
Born	28 January 1896, Plymouth, Devon
Died	1971, London
Personal details	Winnicott's family were wealthy Methodists. His father, Sir Frederick, was a merchant and his mother was Elizabeth Martha Woods. He grew up in Plymouth, completed a medical degree at Cambridge in 1920 and served, during his student years, as a probationary surgeon in World War I. Winnicott married Alice Taylor in 1923. His second wife was psychoanalyst Elsie Clare Nimmo Britton, whom he married in 1958.
Profession/s	A paediatrician and psychoanalyst for children at Paddington Green Hospital for Children, 1923–1963.
Key contributions to Early Childhood Education	Winnicott took an interest in Object Relations Theory, and developed concepts such as the 'holding environment', and the 'transitional object' (often referred to as the comfort blanket). His work has helped many teachers and early childhood educators to understand the needs of stressed and distressed children and to support children at times of transition in their lives. Winnicott put forward the idea of the *good-enough mother*, a mother whose physical and emotional attunement to her baby helps her baby to adapt without trauma to changes, including the eventual realisation on the part of the baby that she or he is separate from his/her mother.
	He was author of some fifty publications on parent–child relationships, child psychoanalysis, transitional objects, play, disorders and behaviour.
	The principal concepts he developed in his work are:
	<ul><li>The transition object: For comfort and not-me identification</li><li>The good-enough mother: Providing the 'holding environment' and facilitating transition</li><li>True self, false self: Integrity and growth</li><li>Winnicott's development stages: Unity, transition, independence.</li><li>Play: Development and learning.</li></ul>
Key texts	Winnicott, D. (1953) 'Transitional objects and transitional phenomena', *International Journal of Psychoanalysis*, 34: 89–97.
	Winnicott, D.W. (1957) *Mother and Child: A Primer of First Relationships*. New York: Basic Books.
	Winnicott, D.W. (1964) *The Child, the Family and the Outside World*. Harmondsorth: Penguin.
	Winnicott, D.W. (1965) *The Family and Individual Development*. London: Tavistock Publications.

(Continued)

(Continued)

Winnicott, D.W. (1971) *Playing and Reality*. London: Tavistock Publications.

Winnicott, D.W. (1984) *Deprivation and Delinquency*. London: Tavistock Publications.

Winnicott, D.W. (1988) *Human Nature*. London: Free Association Books.

Winnicott, D.W. (1993) *Talking to Parents*. Wokingham and Cambridge, MA: Addison-Wesley.

Winnicott, D.W. (1996) *Thinking about Children*. London: Karnac Books.

Quotations	'The good-enough mother ... starts off with an almost complete adaptation to her infant's needs, and as time proceeds she adapts less and less completely, gradually, according to the infant's growing ability to deal with her failure.' (Winnicott, 1953) 'I suggest that the mother hates the baby before the baby hates the mother, and before the baby can know his mother hates him.' (Winnicott, 1947) 'The potential space between baby and mother, between child and family, between individual and society or the world, depends on experience which leads to trust. It can be looked upon as sacred to the individual in that it is here that the individual experiences creative living.' ('The location of cultural experience,' 1967)
Biographies	Rodman, F.R. (2003) *Winnicott: Life and Work*. Cambridge, MA: Perseus Publishing.

Name	**Jean Piaget**
Born	9 August 1896, Neuchatel, Switzerland
Died	16 September 1980, Geneva, Switzerland
Personal details	Jean Piaget was the oldest child of a professor of medieval literature. At the age of 11, while studying at the local Latin high school, Piaget wrote a short paper on an albino sparrow – the first paper which perhaps sparked a career which resulted in over sixty books.
	After he graduated from high school, Piaget went on to study natural sciences at the University of Neuchâttel and obtain a PhD.
	Piaget was married to Valentine Châtenay in 1923, had three children, Jacqueline, Lucienne and Laurent. Much of Piaget's theory of intellectual development in childhood was informed by his observations of his own children.
Profession/s	Piaget trained as a zoologist and began studying psychology as the result of his interest in the connection between biology and logic. As Professor of Psychology at Geneva University his work became mainly concerned with the cognitive stages of development in children. Such studies have had an influence on practices for teaching in schools, as Piaget believed that learners assimilate and accommodate new knowledge at times of 'conflict' with their existing understanding of the world.
Key contributions to early childhood education	Piaget's many experiments were concerned with observing and analysing egocentric behaviour in young children in the belief that overcoming such behaviour was the goal of development. He saw learning as a process, which evolves as the result of children interacting with the environment and moving through certain stages of cognitive development. He corresponded with Susan Isaacs though the two never met. Bärbel Inhelder (1913–1997) was Piaget's research companion for 50 years.
	Piaget described four developmental stages: the Sensori-Motor stage lasts from birth to 2 years, followed by the Preoperational stage (2 to 7 years), the Concrete Operational Stage (7 to 12 years) and the Formal Operational Stage (12 to adult).
	In more recent times some researchers have questioned the basis of some of Piaget's theories. Most notably, Margaret Donaldson in her book *Children's Minds* (1978) considered that Piaget's experiments were too abstract for children to really perform appropriately well in. The belief is that some of Piaget's conclusions about young children's cognitive abilities do not have enough credibility and therefore do not accurately reflect the intellectual accomplishments of which many very young children are capable.

(Continued)

(Continued)

Key texts	Piaget, J. and Inhelder, B. (1969). *The Psychology of the Child.* New York: Basic Books. (Original work published 1966.)
	Piaget, J. (1990) *The Child's Conception of the World.* New York: Littlefield Adams.
	Piaget, J. (1952) 'Jean Piaget (Autobiography)', in E.G. Boring (ed.), *A History of Psychology in Autobiography, Vol. 4.* Worcester, MA: Clark University Press, pp.237–56.
Quotations	'The teacher-organiser should know not only his own science but also be well versed in the details of the development of the child's or adolescent's mind'. (Piaget and Inhelder, 1969)
	'Intelligence organizes the world by organizing itself'. (Ibid.)
	'During the earliest stages the child perceives things like a solipsist who is unaware of himself as subject and is familiar only with his own actions'. (Ibid.)
	'It is with children that we have the best chance of studying the development of logical knowledge, mathematical knowledge, physical knowledge, and so forth'. (Piaget,1990)
	'The principal goal of education in the schools should be creating men and women who are capable of doing new things, not simply repeating what other generations have done'. (Piaget,1952, Autobiography)
Biographies	Gattico, E. (2001) *Jean Piaget.* Milan: Bruno Mondadori.
	Kitchener, R. (1986) *Piaget's Theory of Knowledge.* New Haven, CT: Yale University Press.
	Smith, L. (1996) *Critical Readings on Piaget.* London: Routledge.

Name	**Erik Erikson**
Born	15 June 1902, Frankfurt, Germany
Died	1994
Personal details	Erikson's Danish father left Erikson's mother before his birth. His Jewish mother, Karla Abrahamsen, was a lone parent for the first three years of his life until she married Dr Theodor Homberger and the family moved to southern Germany. The young Erik Homberger first learned of his Jewish roots as a young man and was taunted in the synagogue school for being Danish and at grammar school for being Jewish. Perhaps this is the root of Erikson's professional interest in identity.
	He taught art and studied for a certificate in Montessori education and another from the Vienna Psychoanalytic Society. He was married with three children, and some of his life was spent on the move to avoid Nazi occupation. He left Vienna,moving to Copenhagen, and then to Boston when the Nazis entered Austria. He worked at the Harvard Medical School and practised child psychoanalysis. He was attracted to the work of anthropologists of the time as well as to that of psychoanalysts. He taught at Yale and the University of California at Berkeley and carried out studies of the relationship between society and culture. He became Erik Erikson on taking American citizenship.
	From 1950, he spent 10 years working and teaching in Massachusetts, returning to Harvard in 1960 where he worked until his retirement in 1970.
Profession/s	Psychologist and psychotherapist.
Key contributions to early childhood education	Erikson embellished Freud's suggestion of five stages of development, adding three more stages and extending the theory into adulthood. He promoted the notion of interaction between generations – mutuality – and highlighted the impact that children had on their parents and vice versa. Erikson believed that development took place in stages, and that identity and convictions become stronger with time and experience. He believed that the stages of development are determined by nature and the limits within which nurture operates. According to Erikson, everyone moves through every stage, and healthy development and learning in each stage are crucial to progression. In Erikson's view, physical, emotional and psychological stages of development are linked to specific experiences. For example, if an infant's physical and emotional needs are met, the infant completes his/her task of developing the ability

(Continued)

(Continued)

to trust others. Unmet needs make it harder, if not impossible, to complete the various 'tasks' associated with each stage. And even though they may progress developmentally to the next 'stage', children lack something in their development. For example, if an 18-month-old is not given opportunities to explore and learn through his or her actions, the result can be a toddler who harbours self doubt, thus hindering the later development of independence.

His work supports the development of programmes in early childhood education which foster positive self-esteem and exploratory learning through play.

Key texts

Childhood and Society (1950). New York: W.W. Norton.

Young Man Luther (1958). New York: W.W. Norton.

Youth: Change and Challenge (1963). New York: Basic Books.

Insight and Responsibility (1964). New York: W.W. Norton.

Identity: Youth and Crisis (1968). New York: W.W. Norton.

Quotations

'Hope is both the earliest and the most indispensable virtue inherent in the state of being alive. If life is to be sustained hope must remain, even where confidence is wounded, trust impaired.' (Erikson,1950)

'Babies control and bring up their families as much as they are controlled by them; in fact the family brings up baby by being brought up by him.' (Ibid.)

'Healthy children will not fear life if their elders have integrity enough not to fear death.' (Ibid.)

'Children love and want to be loved and they very much prefer the joy of accomplishment to the triumph of hateful failure. Do not mistake a child for his symptom.' (Erikson,1963)

'Doubt is the brother of shame'. (Ibid)

Biographies

Coles, R. (1970) *Erik H. Erikson: The Growth of His Work.* Boston, MA and Toronto: Little, Brown.

Friedman, L.J. (1999) *Identity's Architect: A Biography of Erik H. Erikson.* New York: Charles Scribner.

Miller, P. (1983) *Theories of Developmental Psychology.* San Francisco: W.H. Freeman and Company.

Roazen, P. (1976) *Erik H. Erikson: The Power and Limits of a Vision*. New York: The Free Press.

Santrock, J. (1996) *Child Development*. Dubuque, IA: Brown and Benchmark Publishers.

Welchman, K. (2000) *Erik Erikson, His Life, Work, and Significance*. Philadelphia, PA: Open University Press.

Name	**Carl Rogers**
Born	8 January 1902, in Oak Park, Illinois
Died	1987
Personal details	Rogers' father was a civil engineer and his mother a devout Christian who brought her children up strictly; he was the fourth of six children. Aged 12, his family moved to a farm outside Chicago. He initially studied agriculture at the University of Wisconsin but changed to study religion and then later doubted some of his basic religious views.
	He married Helen Elliot and moved to New York and studied at the Union Theological Seminary, but eventually rejected religion in favour of psychology. He gained a PhD in clinical psychology from Columbia University in 1931, after which he worked as a child psychologist and began to develop his own approach to therapy.
	In 1942, he wrote *Counselling and Psychotherapy* and set up a counselling centre at the University of Chicago in 1945. In 1957 he returned to the University of Wisconsin, moving to La Jolla, California in 1964 to continue his research. He worked as a therapist and lectured and wrote until he died.
Profession/s	Psychologist and psychotherapist.
Key contributions to early childhood education	Rogers saw people as basically good or healthy, and for him mental illness, criminality, and other such problems, were not natural tendencies but arose because the person was not in a healthy state of mind. This theory was simple. He believed that human beings had it in their nature to do the very best they can. The self-actualisation of the human being was the goal, and all that a person did contributed (or detracted) to the ability of that person to reach that goal. He is best known for his non-directive therapy.
	His view of freedom and non-directive approaches has underpinned some thinking about how young children learn and how their needs in the early years might be best met in order to ensure positive mental health and growth. He advocated 'facilitating learning' through a genuine relationship between teacher and pupil. His work held notions of prizing, trusting and accepting the learner and of working through and with 'empathic understanding'. These concepts are central to many early childhood programmes which seek to adopt an holistic approach to learning and development. Key to Rogerian approaches was the relationships on which learning was based and through which learning took place, and how person-centred learning can be used in education settings.

As a humanistic psychologist, Rogers agreed with much of Maslow's work, however he added to this that in order for a person to 'grow', they need an atmosphere that provides 'genuineness ... acceptance ... and empathy', as without these, relationships and personalities will not develop in the way that they should.

Key texts

Rogers, C.R. (1961) *On Becoming a Person: A Therapist's View of Psychotherapy*. Boston: Houghton Mifflin.

Rogers, C.R. (1980) *A Way of Being*. Boston: Houghton Mifflin.

Rogers, C. and Freiberg, H.J. (1993) *Freedom to Learn* (3rd edn). New York: Merrill.

Quotations

'When I look at the world I'm pessimistic, but when I look at people I am optimistic.' (Rogers, 1961)

'The only person who is educated is the one who has learned how to learn and change.' (Ibid).

'In my early professional years I was asking the question: How can I treat, or cure, or change this person? Now I would phrase the question in this way: How can I provide a relationship which this person may use for his own personal growth?' (Rogers, 1969)

'The good life is a process, not a state of being. It is a direction not a destination.' (Rogers, 1980)

'I believe that the testing of the student's achievements in order to see if he meets some criterion held by the teacher, is directly contrary to the implications of therapy for significant learning.' (Rogers)

Biographies

Cohen, D. (1997) *Carl Rogers: A Critical Biography*. London: Constable.

Kirschenbaum, H. (1979) *On Becoming Carl Rogers*. New York: Delacorte Press.

Thorne, B. (1992) *Carl Rogers*. London: Sage.

Name	**Robin Tanner**
Born	1904, Wiltshire
Died	1988
Personal details	Married Heather Sprackman in 1931.
Profession/s	Artist, etcher and printmaker.
	From 1924, after attending Goldsmith's College, Tanner taught in Greenwich, Corsham and Chippenham.
	He was an HMI of primary schools from 1935 to 1964 and promoted the teaching of fine art to young children. As an HMI he ran courses for primary teachers, often with Christian Schiller.
Key contributions to early childhood education	Tanner believed that it was essential for teachers and children to study natural things and that the arts and crafts, music and poetry should be central to primary education.
	He worked with Schiller on professional development courses for teachers.
Key texts	Tanner wrote a number of books on printmaking aimed at children, including *Wiltshire Village,* which was reprinted 1978.
	His papers are held at the Institute of Education of the University of London archives: http://www.ioe.ac.uk/services/715.html
Quotations	'We know we are right and we are unassailable! But because we want all children to grow their roots deep into the finest strata of the civilisation of which they are a part we need to be constantly vigilant and alert to possible inroads. And if we need any reward for our devotion it is surely to see children finding themselves and learning and growing to their full structure.' (Tanner, 1977)
Biographies	Roscoe, Barley (1990) 'Robin Tanner and the Crafts Study Centre', in Barley Roscoe (ed.), *Tributes to Robin Tanner 1904–1988.* Bath: Holburne Museum and Crafts Study Centre.

Name	**Burrhus Frederick Skinner**
Born	20 March 1904, Susquehanna, Pennsylvania, USA
Died	18 August 1990, Cambridge, Massachusetts, USA
Personal details	Skinner's father was a successful lawyer, his mother a housewife. He had one younger brother.
	He studied at Hamilton college, then worked in a bookshop where he read the work of psychologists Pavlov and Watson. He gained a PhD in psychology from Harvard in 1931. By 1936, aged 32, Skinner was married with two daughters. He then became a teacher. During World War II he was funded to work on a secret project to train pigeons to keep pecking a target that would keep a missile locked on to a target. Later in his life he focused on the moral and philosophical implications of behaviourism, completing his last paper the day he died.
Profession/s	In 1945 he became Chair of the Psychology Department at the University of Indiana. He returned to Harvard in 1948 and became Edgar Pierce Professor of Psychology there in 1958.
Key contributions to early childhood education	Skinner developed and promoted a controversial philosophy of 'radical' behaviourism which involved (re)training people using a stimulus response technique, known as 'operant conditioning'. His ideas have been applied to programmes for bringing up children, training animals and classroom control. Skinner developed teaching machines based on the idea of programmed instruction, where, through careful sequencing, students responded to material broken into small steps. Some of these ideas, particularly the breaking of behaviour into small learning steps, have been used in work with children with autism.
Key texts	B.F. Skinner (1938) *The Behavior of Organisms: An Experimental Analysis*. New York: Knopf.
	B.F. Skinner (1953) *Science and Human Behavior*. New York: Macmillan.
	B.F. Skinner (1972) *Beyond Freedom and Dignity*. New York: Knopf.
	B.F. Skinner (1974) *About Behaviorism*. New York: Knopf.
	B.F Skinner (1976) *Walden Two*. New York: Macmillan.

(Continued)

(Continued)

Quotations	'Behaviourism removes us from the pedestal of god-like, and it places us with our ancestors, the animals'. (Skinner, 1938)
	'Man is a complex chicken'. (Ibid.)
	'The hypothesis that man is not free is essential to the application of scientific method to the study of human behaviour'. (Skinner, 1953)
	'The consequences of behaviour determine the probability that the behaviour will occur again'. (Skinner, 1974)
	'Society attacks early, when the individual is helpless.' (Skinner, 1972)
	'Education is what survives when what has been learned has been forgotten.' (Skinner, 1974)
	'We shouldn't teach great books; we should teach a love of reading.' (Skinner, 1972)
Biographies	B.F. Skinner (1976) *Particulars of My Life.* New York: Alfred A. Knopf.
	See also the B.F. Skinner Foundation: http://www.bfskinner.org

Name	**Sir Alexander Bradshaw Clegg (Alec Clegg)**
Born	13 June 1909, Long Eaton, Derbyshire
Died	1986, Yorkshire
Personal details	Alec Clegg was the son of a Derbyshire teacher and headteacher. He attended Long Eaton Grammar School and Bootham School in York before reading modern languages at Clare College, Cambridge, then training as a teacher at the London Day Training College. Between 1932 and 1937 he taught French and PE at the St Clement Danes' Holborn Estate Grammar School.
	Between 1939 and 1945 Clegg worked in Birmingham, Cheshire and Worcestershire education authorities. He then joined the West Riding, first as Deputy and quickly becoming Chief Education Officer. He founded Bretton Hall College for the training of teachers, in 1949.
Profession/s	Teacher, Chief Education Officer.
Key contributions to early childhood education	Alec Clegg was a pioneer of the arts in education. He was also an advocate of continuing professional development for teachers, establishing and supporting residential summer vacation courses for teachers to support their teaching of *all* children and enhance their love and understanding of the arts in education.
	He advocated the education of the mind and spirit.
Key texts	*The Excitement of Writing* (1964). London: Chatto and Windus.
	Children in Distress (1969).
	'Recipe for Failure' (National Children's Home convocation lecture, 1972)
	Changing Primary School: Its Problems and Priorities (1972). London: Vintage.
	Enjoying Writing: Further Collection of Children's Poetry and Prose (1973). London: Chatto and Windus.
Quotations	'I began my professional life as a teacher, I am the son, son-in-law, grandson, husband, brother, brother-in-law, nephew, father and father-in-law of teachers.' (After dinner speech, Making the whole world wonder, Sir Alec Clegg, Bingley College of Education, 3 August 1972)

(Continued)

(Continued)

'... an education service is not a factory which produces glass bottles or motor cars or radio sets or other inanimate devices. It produces people.' (*Children in Distress*, 1969)

'But there are two kinds of education: the education of the mind by imparting facts and teaching skills, and the education of the spirit, and the material to be worked on here is the child's loves and hates, his hopes and fears, or in other terms, his courage, his integrity, his compassion and other great human qualities.' (After dinner speech, Making the whole world wonder, Sir Alec Clegg, Bingley College of Education, 3 August 1972)

Biographies   Darvill, P. (2000) *Sir Alec Clegg: The Man, His Ideas and His Schools*. Knebworth: Able Publishing.

Name	**Loris Malaguzzi**
Born	23 February 1920, Correggio, Italy
Died	30 January 1994, Reggio Emilia, Italy
Personal details	Malaguzzi was born in Correggio, Italy, in the midst of Fascist Italy. His father encouraged him to enrol in a teacher training course in 1939, which he completed during the war. In 1936 he enrolled in the first post-war psychology course in Rome. He married Nilde Bonaccini and they had one son.
Profession	A teacher and, most famously, founder of the Reggio Emilia Approach to early childhood education.
Key contributions to early childhood education	The Reggio Emilia approach to early education centres around a conviction that children are powerful people, and that they have within them the will and potential to create their own knowledge, and the right and need to generate knowledge in community with other children and adults.
	Malaguzzi's ideas about education were far reaching, with the Reggio Emilia approach centring around the observation of children at work and play and the documentation of their projects. Teachers continually make notes, take photographs and record children's discussions; they review and discuss the work and use these discussions to plan next steps.
Key texts	Baldini, R., Cavallini, I., Moss, P. and Vecchi, V. (2012) *One City, Many Children: Reggio Emilia, a History of the Present.* Reggio Emilia: Reggio Children.
	Malaguzzi, L. (1995) *Valpino: Last of the Chicken Thieves.* Reggio: Edizioni Junior. (A children's story about Volpino the fox, a very clever, very hungry and very frustrated chicken thief.)
	Rinaldi, C. (2005) *In Dialogue with Reggio Emilia: Listening, Researching and Learning: Contextualising, Interpreting and Evaluating.* London: Routledge.
Quotations	'Learning and teaching should not stand on opposite banks and just watch the river flow by; instead, they should embark together on a journey down the water. Through an active, reciprocal exchange, teaching can strengthen learning how to learn.' (Edwards, C., Gandini, L. and Forman, G. (eds) (1993) *The Hundred Languages of Children*, Ch 3)

(Continued)

(Continued)

'Our task, regarding creativity, is to help children climb their own mountains, as high as possible. No one can do more.' (Ibid.)

'They [children] are autonomously capable of making meaning from their daily life experiences through mental acts involving planning, coordination of ideas, and abstraction. ... The central act of adults, therefore, is to activate, especially indirectly, the meaning-making competencies of children as a basis of all learning. They must try to capture the right moments, and then find the right approaches, for bringing together, into a fruitful dialogue, their meanings and interpretations with those children.' (Ibid.)

Biographies

Hall, K., Cunneen, M., Murphy, R. and Ridgway, A. (2010) *Loris Malaguzzi and the Reggio Emilia Experience*. London: Continuum.

Smidt, S. (2013) *Introducing Malaguzzi: Exploring the Life and Work of Reggio Emilia's Founding Father.* London: Routledge.

Name	**Chris Athey**
Born	1924, North East of England
Died	2011, London
Personal details	Chris Athey left school in 1938, two weeks before she was 14 years old. She worked on her Aunt Kate's farm in Devon and looked after her baby cousin. Returning to Croydon she took a job 'toasting teacakes in a sweet factory'. Leaving home at 16, Chris worked at the Creed and Company factory near East Croydon Station. She became involved in trade union and labour movements and attended Workers' Educational Association classes. She was an avid reader from childhood. After a year of studying philosophy, psychology and economics at Hillcroft College, Surbiton, Chris was accepted, in 1947, for the emergency teacher training course at Wall Hall, Hertfordshire.
Profession/s	Teacher and researcher.
	Studying with Molly Brearly and Honour Southam at the Education Department at Goldsmiths College, Chris encountered Piaget, commenting 'I was immediately engrossed because he was maintaining that intelligence was not fixed and unchanging and that intelligence could be created'.
Key contributions to early childhood education	She was director of the Froebel Early Education Project from 1973 to 1978. She identified schemas (repeatable patterns of behaviour) and shared ideas about children's schematic learning with parents – bringing together 'parents, professionals and pedagogy'. This work has stimulated interest in many countries and inspired other researchers and writers (Tina Bruce, Cath Arnold, Cathy Nutbrown and Frances Atherton).
	Chris Athey inspired many nursery teachers through continuing professional development courses to look differently at young children's learning and take a constructivist approach.
Key texts	Athey, C. (1990) *Extending Thought in Young Children: A Parent–Teacher Partnership*. London: Paul Chapman.
	Athey, C. (2006) *Extending Thought in Young Children: A Parent–Teacher Partnership* (2nd ed). London: Sage.

(Continued)

(Continued)

Quotations	'Nothing gets under a parent's skin more quickly and more permanently than the illumination of his or her own child's behaviour.' (Athey,1990: 66)
	'Parents, Professionals and Pedagogy' (Ibid.)
	'Constructivists are child-centred teachers who are trying to become more conscious and more theoretically aware of what is involved in the process of "coming to know".' (Ibid.)
	'fitting not flitting'. Athey described the way in which viewing children's activity from a schematic viewpoint could demonstrate that they were connecting ideas together rather than moving randomly from one thing to another. (Ibid.)
	'…you can learn to do anything if it becomes inconvenient not to be able to do that thing.' (Ibid.)
Biographies	*A Learning Story* by Chris Athey. Available at: http://www.pengreen.org/uploads/article1816/A%20Learning%20Story%20by%20Chris%20Athey.pdf
	Arnold, Cath (2005), 'Our understanding of how children's thinking develops owes much to the work of Chris Athey, Who is Chris Athey?, *Nursery World*, 20 October.

Suggestions for further reading

Throughout this section we have listed the writings of those whose biographies have featured. In addition, the following books trace histories of early childhood education from Canadian and US perspectives.

Wolfe, J. (2002) *Learning from the Past: Historical Voices in Early Childhood Education* (2nd ed.) Canada: Piney Branch Pr.

Lascarides, V.C. and Hinitz, B.F. (2011) *History of Early Childhood Education* (2nd ed.) New York: Routledge.

Part 3

Talking of Early Childhood Education: Nine Conversations

This third part of the book brings together the ideas and practices of some whose biographies were presented in Part 2. They are, as it were, 'brought to life' in a series of imagined exchanges between some of those characters in conversation. In this way a range of issues which lie at the very heart of the development and practice of early childhood education and care in the present day is explored by reaching back into history and relating past happenings and perspectives to present concerns and contexts. Throughout these conversations we highlight familiar themes: curriculum and pedagogy; ideologies of childhood; play; literacy; the role of the adult; the roles of parents; and social and economic deprivation. Whilst the conversations focus more specifically on a small number of historical figures, many contributors to early childhood education in the past are referred to in the conversations as their ideas play into the topic under discussion.

But before we begin to imagine how figures from history might have talked with us and with each other, we have included a recent conversation which took place between us. We asked, 'Do we need history?' (in early childhood education) and this led us to talk about the part history has played in each of our careers and how it has informed our interests in early childhood and in education more generally. This conversation is then followed by seven imaginary conversations which address different themes through the perspectives and work of different historical figures. The final conversation, again between us, explores underpinning beliefs and values.

List of Conversations

Conversation 1

So, Who Needs History?

In conversation: Peter Clough (PC) and Cathy Nutbrown (CN)

Go to www.sagepub.co.uk/nutbrownclough for a downloadable recording of the conversation.

> It is a 6.47 am on a cold day in April 2013. Peter and Cathy are on a train, travelling from Sheffield to London, talking about something they have explored on several occasions over their years of working together: what is important in early childhood education and why history matters …

PC   Let's go back one more time – my old question! Why was it that you … how did you get involved in early childhood education? What was the attraction?

CN   I've been asked that many times before, and I'm not entirely sure! I think I always wanted to be a teacher, though I'm not sure quite what it was that attracted me to young children. I did a course to teach children from 3 to 11 years and did my three practices in a nursery school, a reception class with 5-year-olds, and an older infant class. Thinking back, I saw so many examples of how quickly young children learn and how fascinated they are by so many things. Maria Montessori's book *The Absorbent Mind* is so well titled (not that I agree 100% with Montessori), it is as if young children just 'soak up' experiences and learn from them … and so teaching an age phase where part of the work was to watch children learn and support them in that learning, felt like the right place for me …

PC   What would you have been if you hadn't been a nursery teacher?

CN   No idea! I think it would have had to have something to do with learning in some way … learning is fascinating. … In the early years … because learning is so rapid and tangible you really can almost see young children thinking. And given the right circumstances very young children really thrive – they develop language, pose interesting questions (those 'why' questions Piaget wrote about), apply themselves to solve problems that they themselves have decided to tackle. It is fascinating to be part of that …. and now, at the University, I get some of that joy being part of the learning and the excitement with students at all levels of study...

PC   There's been a lot of talk recently about 'early intervention', various reports[1], and extra funding to support the most 'vulnerable' 2-year-olds to attend nurseries ... do you think that early years provision in the form of early childhood education really can bring about change – can it really make the difference to young children's later life chances ...?

CN   ...I wouldn't say *the* difference, not always, but providing what young children need early on can make a big difference. It goes along with other things that affect their lives too of course, that goes without saying, so early childhood education – or other forms of early intervention – can't stand alone ... it needs to accompany wider support for families, including issues relating to housing, poverty, health, well-being – all those things. And these are all big issues at the moment – lots of families are struggling in the recession with many different issues, largely because of financial difficulties and unemployment. Early childhood education can't solve all of those things – it's not a panacea for all ills – but it can help. And learning, learning in the early years is so elastic! And yes, I do believe that good early education is crucial, 'the gap' – the achievement gap – that people talk about can be narrowed early on with good teaching – but if children enter school behind their peers, they remain behind throughout their school career.

PC   And I met a lot of those children, of course, in my own teaching ... Left behind somehow because of one reason or another, then termed 'maladjusted' or 'remedial', and it was only later in my teaching that the idea of curricular approaches to learning difficulties came to the fore; up until the early 80s it was the child who was the problem ... I think in terms of Special Educational Needs it was always about 'repairing' damage – such as sending the 'slow readers' to the 'remedial' group – and partly about 'containing' children who would always be different and have difficulties of many different kinds, in a school system that was not really up to meeting their specific and different needs.

---

[1] Field, F. (2010) *The Foundation years: Preventing Poor Children Becoming Poor Adults: The Report of the Independent Review on Poverty and Life Chances*. London: HMSO. Available at: http://webarchive.nationalarchives.gov.uk/20110120090128/http:/povertyreview.independent.gov.uk/media/20254.poverty-report.pdf

Allen, G. (2011) *Early Intervention: The Next Steps An Independent Report to Her Majesty's Government*, Graham Allen MP, http://www.dwp.gov.uk/docs/early-intervention-next-steps.pdf

CN And meeting specific and different needs early is important, and good pedagogy can do this. When I was a young nursery teacher there were three women who really inspired me: Ann Sharp was the Adviser for Early Childhood Education in Sheffield ... she had such vision about multi-agency provision and she really made things happen. Her work led to the setting up of excellent services which combined education and care in innovative ways with staff from education and social services departments working in the same settings. She gave me many opportunities to think, and of course she introduced me to Chris Athey[2] whose work on schemas and young children's learning was truly ground breaking. Chris talked about parents, practitioners and pedagogy as the three key components to quality in young children's learning. And the third inspiration was Ann Hedley ... she was the headteacher in a school where I taught in the nursery, and I learned so much from her about working with parents, providing beautiful environments for learning, watching children and planning for their learning around what I saw, and she had a genuine human concern for everyone she worked with. So my understanding, my 'take' on pedagogy is born out of my continued professional development in which these three women played a strong part, so that they form some of my own history as a teacher.

PC ... interesting, that personal history ... I have often thought about how my own education, and the opportunities it gave me, was very much down to the policies of the day. ... you know, if it wasn't for the 1944 Education Act I wouldn't have gone to a Grammar School – and I know for sure I'd not be doing what I'm doing today... I don't mean that Grammar Schools were all good, or anything, but that ... well, that was one piece of policy that located me – fairly directly – in expanded opportunities – that my elder brother didn't get, for example ...

CN Yes, and I can say the same: I benefited from specific education policies during my school career, undoubtedly, and I suppose it isn't going too far to say that my career as a nursery teacher wouldn't have happened if legislation in 1918 hadn't been passed to allow Local Education Authorities to spend money on nursery schools, and Sheffield – where I did my initial training and where I worked as a nursery teacher – was quick to build nursery schools.

PC Yes, I can trace issues of Special, and later Inclusive Education policies in the same way ... in my working in certain kinds of schooling ... but you know, it wasn't until much later – I mean after I'd spent

---

[2] Athey, C. (1990) *Extending Thought in Young Children: A Parent-Teacher Partnership*. London: Paul Chapman Publishing.

years working with difficult adolescent boys – 'Bad Lads', as I used to say – that the penny dropped about not trying to repair in later years, but … putting resources in from the start, from the early years so that difficulties don't arise – or at least can be lessened … Now that will just seem like blindingly obvious to you, but …

CN Yes, beginning early, for me, is vital … whether we are talking about children who have some identified learning difficulties or not. I have long since said that early education at its best is inclusive education – it's all there – differentiated learning, learner-centred, individual assessment, partnership with families, flexibility …

PC … and with that goes a sense of the investing in the future?

CN Well that's an interesting one – yes – it is about investing in the future but it is also about giving children what they need now. And by that I mean the immediate moments and years of childhood are important in their own right, and they need high quality early education and care – when they need it – because they need it – not simply because it will help build important foundations for the future.

PC But aren't those two the same thing – investing in now for the future?

CN Yes – but philosophically I think there is a difference. It's about acknowledging the importance of childhood itself, it's about the *nowness* of childhood. And that is something fundamental for me; valuing the moments of young children's learning for what they are in and of themselves, as well as for the contribution that learning makes to children's later schooling and lives.

PC So that notion of the *nowness* of childhood as you put it – you think that informs what happens in ECE, how people create and construct policy?

CN Yes … it should … It's a subtlety, but yes – it's about the importance of every moment in young lives – it's about not wasting time – it's about what children need now. And so it informs my thinking about 'school readiness'. We can spend too much time rushing children to make them 'ready' for the next stage and we should just be a bit more patient – allow children to be three when they are three and four when they are four rather than treating them as 'nearly five' or nearly at school, do you see what I mean? We presently rush children on too much – but solid foundations take time to build and you can't erect a lasting building without digging and setting the foundations.

PC Foundations! And Foundation Stages and … it brings us back, really, to why we started this project about the historical foundations of

ECE and why it's important … So let me put another question – for the second time – to you: it's the 'And so what has history got to offer the field of Early Childhood Education these days?', do you think? I know that your views are … but do you think that others' views … about pedagogy and childhood … are informed by the work of those who pioneered work in early years?

CN Whilst I was working on the qualifications review[3], I was thinking about the future, and in so doing considered what had happened in the past, and how we had reached the point that we were at in England. During the consultation meetings someone said 'this is a young workforce' meaning that it was only in recent years that people worked with young children. And I remember being surprised, somewhat taken aback, because, of course, it's not a young workforce, it's hundreds of years old, and for the last hundred years in particular, much work has been done. Some think that the idea of teachers working with the youngest children is a new idea – but nursery teachers were being trained to work with children from 2 to 5 years in the late 1800s at the House for Education at Ambleside![4] This is one reason why history is important, because it reminds us of work that has been done, of things that were successful, of policies that were badly designed, and of how crucial it is always to be vigilant about new policies, new developments and new legislation. Knowing the history of one's profession is part of the root of professional identity, and can help answer some questions about why we do what we do.

PC True, knowing that it happened before and was bad doesn't stop repetition, but it's interesting though, that few government documents recognise their histories. So many documents have been published that seem to come out of nowhere, no references to the work they draw on, no acknowledgement of what went before, often little recent evidence that it's a good idea! Indeed, now that everything is published on the internet, no hard copies … the archaeology of policy may well become more and more difficult to trace. We don't – politicians don't – always learn from the past, bad ideas get repeated, good ones (like the NHS) get dismantled, but at least some knowledge of history would tell us when we have 'been there before', even if the same mistake is made again …

---

[3] Nutbrown, C. (2012) *Foundations for Quality the Independent Review of Early Education and Childcare Qualifications, Final Report.* London: DfE.

[4] Charlotte Mason, http://www.cumbria.ac.uk/AboutUs/History/CharlotteMason.aspx

From the diary of Lady Margaret Smith[5]

A New Lanark imagining…

It is 1817, late spring. I had arrived from London yesterday, having visited the opening of the exhibition of the Elgin Marbles at the British Museum, a fine display, and something which lifted the depression in this terrible post-war period. I stayed in Mr Owen's house last evening and, over dinner with him and other guests we talked of his vision for society and consequently of his plans for education which would contribute to the development of such a society. He greeted me warmly as his guest and made it very clear that he did not hold the views of other eminent figures of the time that women should not be involved in social reform of educational progress. 'Women', he said 'Women will be no longer made the slaves of, or dependent upon men. … They will be equal in education, rights, privileges and personal liberty'[6]. When I read these very words some 20 or more years later, I was transported in my mind back to the dinner table and that spring evening in 1817. There was talk of the typhus epidemic breaking out in Edinburgh and Glasgow and I recall my host discussing the opening of his Institute for the Formation of Character when he said that a better society was one 'formed so as to exist without crime, without poverty, with health greatly improved, with little, if any misery, and with intelligence and happiness increased a hundredfold'. And I know he truly believed that only ignorance (at all levels) would prevent his vision from becoming a reality.

The first New Lanark school has been open for about a year and we visited the very next morning. Walking into the school yard I saw hordes of little children playing and a tall figure amongst them. He was Mr James Buchanan, the first teacher in the New Lanark school, chosen by Mr Owen from his own workforce in the mills. I could see from his interactions with the children that he too holds dear Mr Owen's ideals of kindness, activity and co-operation. And my first impression was that the importance of the outdoors, good wholesome food and space for rest were very apparent.

Some little children spotted Mr Owen and ran to him, enjoying his hand on their head, and smiling up as he spoke gently to them. Next I was taken to the dancing room, where there were some 70 or more pairs of children, really very young, dancing with amazing accuracy to the piano music of the maypole celebrations. They smiled, sang and danced with real joy.

There was good food available in a public kitchen, adult education classes, parent classes and support, community involvement and health care. Truly there was something special at New Lanark which we should try to emulate throughout the Kingdom.

Lady Margaret Smith, London

---

[5] Note: Lady Margaret Smith is a fictional character but the words of Owen and the events are taken from real happenings of the time.

[6] Robert Owen (1841) *Book of the New Moral World: Sixth Part.* London, 1836–44. Published as one volume, New York: G. Vale, 1845.

Conversation 2

Why Early Childhood Education?

In conversation: Robert Owen (RO) with Cathy Nutbrown (CN)

(Biography: RO p. 29)

Go to www.sagepub.co.uk/nutbrownclough for a downloadable recording of the conversation.

> It is June 2013, around the world there are many stories of poverty and neglect in childhood, and in England the UK Conservative-led coalition government is implementing measures to cut public spending, following a recession which took hold whilst the last (Labour) government was pursuing an intervention policy designed to address some of the difficulties associated with poor beginnings in life. Sure Start, launched in 1998, was designed as a multi-agency programme of provision to alleviate the difficulties associated with social disadvantage such as ill health, unemployment, under achievement. In this imaginary conversation Robert Owen talks with Cathy about why early education is important and how provision for young children is important to the development and well-being of wider society.

CN So why ... and how did you get into education? Surely a businessman's biggest concern is his profits ...

RO OK, so I'm a business man, yes: but I think that industry has a vital part to play in this business of education; people get jobs after school, yes? But I'd go further than that: for me, industry can only really succeed if it is truly part of a community and its education system. I've tried to develop this in New Lanark. I really do think that the environment in which people live makes a difference to them as people – it's obvious really – but I feel a responsibility to my mill workers to do something about this. I believe that it's possible to nurture rational, good and humane people, but harsh treatment, by teachers, employers, whoever, can really corrupt and damage people. Education is so important, that's why I built the school at New Lanark. Do you know that when I got there, children as young as five – as young as five! – were working in the mills – sometimes 12 or more hours a day – can you believe that? I said right away this must stop; we will not employ any children under 10; and I saw to it that the young children went to the nursery and infant schools. I also banned any form of physical punishment in my schools and in my factories.

CN   Do you see any necessity – I mean ever – for punishment? Would you, for example ...

RO   Cruelty by 'superiors' – teachers, employers, whoever – only ever ultimately results in badness – corruption in children's minds and people's hearts. On that basis I support a philosophy of education that reduces any need for punishment. You have to make people want to work – and yes, I know the work they do in my factories is hard and it's repetitive, but somehow you have got to make that work worthwhile so that their lives are enriched outside of work. ... Ensure workers are fit and well to work by providing housing, reward hard work with opportunities for recreation. Working seven days a week is bad and in the end would not be the best for my business – it's as simple as that. And in just the same way you've got to make children want to learn ... and you've got to reward children's efforts in school with times to play – indeed make then fit to learn by having them spend time outdoors, too.

CN   So that it's the complete child who is educated, not just ...

RO   Couldn't really have put it better myself! I would want to add other things – the economy, and people as individuals – but essentially I agree.

CN   In the UK recently there's been a lot of talk about work-based learning ... and lifelong learning and ... learning at the very centre of things ...

RO   Just so, absolutely; I am in total agreement about the importance of learning – that's why I have schools for the young children and also insist that when the children begin working in the factory from 10 years old they still go to school for a period each weekday. And it has never occurred to me to exclude the girls from schooling, after all they make equally good workers, as well as intelligent and caring mothers.

CN   Is this a sort of 'Education for All'?

RO   From my point of view it is about making education part of the community – I need the parents and the older children in the mills, working. But the young children need to learn while their parents are working, so I built a school where they would be safe, where they would learn the things I believe are important to them for later life, and where they would have an experience of well-being. In my time it meant that young children were safe, doing something useful and not playing on the streets without supervision.

CN   You could say, then, that you are investing in your workers, so that …

RO   I agree totally! In a way I have 'bought' the opportunity to control the education for these children in New Lanark and my other schools, and, yes, I can control what happens there – who teaches there, what they teach … because I have that power, those powers. That's the power that I have as an owner. And you know power isn't evil in itself – they say that God has the 'power and the glory' so power need not be bad. Power to educate is a responsibility so those who have the power must use it with humility, responsibility and conscience. And you yourself have written about how teachers and adults generally have power, but that they must use it – what is it you say: respectfully? … as 'respectful educators'[7] – am I not right?

CN   Thank you for the citation! Yes; what I was trying to say in that book, above everything, was that our philosophy of education must be visible … must be seen in what we actually do, how we respect our children.

RO   Yes, I like that: the philosophy must be evident and – yes – I think this is true in what I have established. There is a clarity about why my schools exist, why the young children attend and why the teachers teach what they teach. And it is important to know what underpins what is done.

CN   Can I push you a little on this question of respect… How does that fit in with your role as an industrialist … a capitalist who, after all, needs to show a profit …?

RO   As I have said, education must be a way of nurturing respect for individuals and for ensuring that communities have a cohesion whereby there is well-being and harshness is shunned. Education is about bringing out the maximum potential of people who will become contributors to the local economy and who will play a part in the smooth running of an industrial community.

CN   So any educational argument is … is also a financial one? Is it that simple?

RO   Correct! It is! Teachers have a great responsibility for young minds, to prepare children for the future and to be kind and fair

---

[7] Nutbrown, C. (ed) (1996) *Respectful Educators–Capable Learners*. London: Sage.

to them all. And they are powerful too, in a different way – a different sort of power from mine! – but they are the powerful adults in the classroom and they have a duty to use that power in the long run to create a just and a fair society …

CN   Fascinating, and you make a strong business case for getting early education right that's important – early education provision makes good economic sense.

Circa 1924 the *British Journal of Psychology*, carried the following, uncharacteristic, notice:

WANTED – an Educated Young Woman with honours degree – preferably first class – or the equivalent, to conduct education of a small group of children aged 2½–7, as a piece of scientific work and research.

Previous educational experience is not considered a bar, but the advertisers hope to get in touch with a university graduate – or someone of equivalent intellectual standing – who has hitherto considered themselves too good for teaching and who has probably already engaged in another occupation.

A LIBERAL SALARY – liberal as compared with research work or teaching – will be paid to a suitable applicant …

The advertisement was placed by Geoffrey Pyke, owner of the Malting House School, Cambridge, and answered by Susan Sutherland Isaacs, who founded the experimental school, between 1924 and 1927.

Source: *International Journal of Psycho-Analysis*, 31 (1950): 279–85.

Conversation 3

What Motivates Young Children to Learn?

In conversation: Susan Sutherland Isaacs (SI) with Peter Clough (PC)
(Biography: SI p. 53)

Go to www.sagepub.co.uk/nutbrownclough for a downloadable recording
of the conversation.

It is June 2013, new curriculum plans have been drawn up and implemented
in England for the teaching of children aged from birth to 5 years. A recent
review of qualifications to work with young children has recommended some
fundamental changes to improve quality. The education and care of the
youngest children remains at the forefront of policy developments and investment in provision for the education and care of young children continues to
be made. New targets have been set, for provision and for achievement of
young children following the Early Years Foundation Stage. Funding for 40%
of the most vulnerable 2-year-olds heralds consideration of how best to support their early learning and development in the coming years. There have
been continued concerns over the formalisation of the curriculum and of the
'top-down' pressure on young children to learn; the 'education' or 'care'
debate rumbles on. But, whatever the policy context, what really motivates
young children to learn? In this imaginary conversation Peter Clough talks
with Susan Sutherland Isaacs about her experimental work at the Malting
House School and her beliefs about learning and the role of teachers.

PC Thank you for agreeing to meet and talk, Mrs Isaacs.

SI Susan.

PC Susan ... I've been thinking about young children's learning and this
notion of 'motivation' – what makes them tick as learners. ... I was
reading some of Comenius' work – do you know it? – and he seems
to hold to a notion of the teacher as 'gardener' and the child as a sort
of 'seed' to be nurtured[8] and in that idea there is an implicit relationship between the 'gardener' and the 'seed' – the teacher and the
child. His thesis would be, I think, that given the right environment,

---

[8] 'Is there any who denies that sowing and planting need skill and experience? ... the
trained gardener goes to work carefully, since he is well instructed, where, when, and
how to act and what to leave alone, that he may meet with no failure.' (Komenský,
translated in Keatinge, 1896: 111).

motivation can be an intrinsic as well as extrinsic factor. But I don't think we have really got to the bottom of this idea of 'motivation' when it comes to young children's learning, do you?

SI   Well, Comenius would argue, I think, that the issue of motivation in young learners is a significant issue; he would say that too many young children are denied the intellectual and emotional growth they are capable of and therefore not only their own lives, but also those of society in general, are robbed of a great inheritance.

PC   Robert [Owen] was saying something similar recently when he was talking with Cathy about New Lanark and the School there…

SI: But I think we must consider motivation as something from the inside – something that's already there. … It's there in young children – all young children – a deep desire to do, to create, to learn, to explore. What happens then is that this motivation can be nourished and encouraged to promote learning or it can be crushed – as so many earlier teaching techniques have done. You only have to watch young children play and you can see their motivation for learning. And the right teacher, the skilled and intelligent teacher, knows when to add that something extra to fuel their learning.

PC   I'm glad we got straight to play; I've got here … it's what you wrote for the Nursery Schools Association. May I read this?

If we are to mention one supreme psychological need of the young child, the answer would have to be 'play' – the opportunity for free play in all its various forms. Play is the child's means of living, and of understanding life. … He needs opportunity for imaginative play, free and unhampered by adult limits or teachings, just as much as he needs the chance to run and jump and thread beads. It is in this regard that our understanding of the child's mind and the way in which he develops has deepened and broadened in recent years[9].

So is it play, then, that is the real motivator? Do you believe that play is intrinsic? The built-in motivator?

SI   Let me put it this way: children can generate some interesting scientific questions in their play and then they must find the answers. That's why the teacher must be an intelligent woman and why observation is so important in helping us to plan teaching. And I think it is a mistake to believe that young children should be treated so gently that they always have their own hearts' desire – play alone is not what

---

[9] Isaacs (1954) *The Education Value of the Nursery School*. London: The Nursery School Association of Great Britain and Northern Ireland, p. 23.

I advocate. I think there should be a toughness ... yes a tough edge to learning – children must think and teachers must be more than gentle-minded mothers. 'They need more than mother wit and mother love they need true scientific understanding'[10] Sometimes education must be unsympathetic – yes, unsympathetic – and make a situation where children struggle in their learning. If they are really keen to know then they will seek, and they'll find the answer to their own questions.

PC   There's a lot there – can you give me an example?

SI   My observations show that children can, in the right kind of challenging environment, pose for themselves the most complex of scientific questions, and the good teacher – and there are many of them – can then help them to find the answers to those questions. If we think, for example, of John Dewey's work[11] we see that it is demonstrating ... it's seeing ... and knowing ... but above all doing that lead to understanding – not pure, abstract instruction.

PC   Well that takes us straight to Malting House, and some of the ... the risks you took ... Some would say – particularly in these recent times of Health and Safety tyranny! – that the environment you created at the Malting House was one which contained too much risk – Bunsen burners, bonfires, all kinds of living creatures, laboratory samples preserved in jars ... You emphasise the scientific, the place of 'discovery', as it were, and the role of teachers in encouraging the scientific thinking of young children; today's early years settings would ban most of those things as too risky, and as putting children in danger...

SI   And perhaps I would say that the sanitised environment is not one where real learning can happen. At the Malting House we aimed to create an environment which included social realities as distinct from fantasies.[12]

PC   Real live encounters with real-life things ... discovering the wheel? Is that perhaps what really motivates children? Have we got to the bottom of what actually makes them tick?

SI   Much education of young children wastes opportunities. And from what I see today there is too much readiness to take on 'accepted' practices without thinking about the circumstances in

---

[10] Ibid., p.30.

[11] Dewey, J. (1897) *My Pedagogic Creed*. Washington DC: Progressive Education Association.

[12] Issacs, S. and Issacs, N. (1930) *Intellectual Growth in Young Children*. London: Routledge.

which learning takes places. Teachers should be well qualified thinkers – and graduates, I think – with a scientific mind and a capacity continually to adapt their methods to circumstances and to individual children's needs.

PC   Are you saying that early years practitioners today don't take into account the needs of the children they work with?

SI   I'm saying that young children need adults who understand about young minds but also have a good knowledge themselves, can impart information, encourage enquiry in lively inquisitive minds – yes – motivate their learning.

PC   OK, before we look at the question of what teachers might do at a practical level to motivate young children's learning, I'd like to put your experience into some sort of context. ... Susan, you trained to be a teacher in the early part of the twentieth century and entered the profession with a background in psychology as well as education – psychoanalysis too, I believe – in other words, you had a critical and scientific training. Thinking about your work and the Malting House experiment, would you agree that there might be too many practitioners now who do not critically examine their practice for one reason or another?

SI   Well yes, of course, yes! In my opinion it is the prime responsibility of a teacher, or anyone who works with young children, to observe the children closely and to learn from them in such a way that how they teach and what they teach is tailored to the individuality of each child. And part of that is intense reflection on what is happening in the children they observe and their own interactions with the children.

PC   In that case how does a teacher begin to balance the need to observe and reflect on a personal level and the need to teach more formally? And what of Monsieur Piaget's belief in the importance of particular age-related stages as a basis for planning in teaching young children?

SI   I am not sure that there is such a clear distinction to be made between the two. Both observation and teaching roles are tightly interwoven in a healthy and fruitful teaching and learning relationship. Although the teacher, or practitioner, is the 'guide' in one sense, it could be possible that a child could be a guide in learning too.[13]

---

[13] 'The grown-ups who are tending little children need to have a sense of fitness and proportion, to know when to give and when to withhold, when to see the baby in the child, and when to respond to the man that he is to be' (Isaacs, 1954: p.22).

PC Well you're very clear about the importance of a well educated teacher too, but can you say more about this idea of a child leading the learning?

SI Well, as Comenius would say, a teacher who uncritically follows precedent when teaching young children, or indeed any individual child, is very unlikely to teach them as well as someone who is willing to modify their approach in the light of their experiences. My own observations lead me to believe that young children have a natural desire to understand the world around them but they also have a desperate need to be understood by those who are significant in their lives. Obviously parents and friends and, yes, other children too, are examples of such people, but so too are teachers – guides in their learning.

PC To stay with Comenius for a moment and his idea that some teachers seemingly work a great deal and achieve proportionately very little … He suggests that there are times when children can benefit from teachers who consciously seek to 'do' less. Do you, like him, believe that a great deal of learning takes place when children can actually be left to discover their world uninterrupted by the teacher?[14] When I watch young children they seem, often, quite attuned to their surroundings, to the physical and emotional environment. And I think there are particular kinds of environment which promote children's ability to learn? Yes?

SI Say more, what kind of environment would you create? Physical and emotional, tell me …

PC First of all the adults are crucial, I think; their attitude to the children is key for me … friendliness, interestedness, warmth. … And then, I think boundaries and rules and expectations? They're important too aren't they – to avoid a sort of 'chaos'? And others emphasise too the layout of the room, what's available … Montessori [15], for example, and her planned experiences, and Nutbrown[16] with the idea of 'workshops' to foster schematic interests. Much is written about what a place of learning for young

---

[14] 'Let the main object of this, our Didactic, be as follows: To seek and to find a method of instruction, by which teachers may teach less, but by which learners may learn more; by which schools may be the scene of less noise, aversion, and useless labour, but of more leisure, enjoyment and solid progress' (Komenský, translated in Keatinge, 1896: 4).

[15] M. Montessori (1964) *The Absorbent Mind*. Wheaton, IL: Theosophical Press.

[16] C. Nutbrown (2011) *Threads of Thinking: Schemas and Young Children Learning* (4th edn.). London: Sage.

children would look like – so there must be a level of importance in the physical environment … But I think young children, first and foremost need emotional security in a nursery environment and that's about people and continuity, routine, knowing where you stand, who's going to pick you up if you fall, knowing that – Oh I don't know … Sarah doesn't eat cabbage – that sort of thing. In any early years environment these things have a huge impact on children's well-being, which in turn has to affect their interest, their motivation to do things, to … to learn. Some children can't wait to get to nursery or playgroup or whatever, but others are just not there yet – still very happy at home, thank you, with their own things, whatever they might be. And so it's relationships that are important in learning, that's true of adults too, even at university, even at PhD level – getting on with your supervisor, tuning in, that's really vital in the motivation stakes. I think it goes without saying that all of us, adults as well as children, are more motivated if we feel confident in, about ourselves.

SI   Yes, but I need to say something … Before a child even comes to school, it is important to consider that they have already learnt a great deal in the home environment. Perhaps the most important thing a child has realised is that they have a place and an identity, they have relationships within a family and, of course, they are beginning to understand a little of what they can and cannot yet accomplish on their own. And this connects with our comment about the relationship between self-confidence and motivation in children's learning. It is my opinion that the provision of an environment that meets the emotional needs of a young child as they make the transition from home to school is fundamental in enabling a young child's intrinsic motivation to learn to flourish, uninterrupted.

PC   OK, a fluid transition from home to school, and an emotionally supportive environment, but what should the place look like? What do you consider important for the adult to do in a practical sense to ensure that young children are as motivated to learn in the early years setting as they were at home?

SI   Well, I don't agree with this 'rationed' environment – that wouldn't happen at home – but I would add to that: I think it's necessary not to underestimate the importance of extending such qualities to the outside environment. The outdoors is often sadly neglected as a learning environment. And despite many projects and pioneers of such things as 'Forest Schools',[17] there is still a lack

---

[17] http://www.forestschools.com/

of real knowledge from the adults and a lack of will from some adults to really make maximum use of the outdoors. Young children's confidence in themselves is promoted a great deal by being given space to simply run and jump and express themselves freely and enjoy games with other children too.[18] But more than that – the outdoors is a natural science classroom. You'll see from some of my work quite how much was learned by interested children in the outdoor school garden with a keen-witted teacher.

PC   So the environment is important, and the adults, but what else? How can teachers really encourage learning? I've worked for a while in my time as a teacher with children with learning difficulties, some really keen but others, really disaffected, disinterested youths – they'd lost it along the way. What can early years education do about that?

SI   I think Jean [Piaget] would say that it is the development that is important; damaged development in the early years will set up these difficulties. And, yes, but whatever is happening – even where children are struggling – If we return to the idea that teachers need to observe children carefully to establish what the next step is in this process of learning independently – we can support their learning. This goes for any learner, whatever the age – you have first to understand what the learner can do, what interests them, and then teach them from that point, not some assumed point according to their age.

PC   This seems to bring us back to the idea of teachers being a sensitive 'guiding hand', much like that gardener nurturing growth from a small seed …

SI   Absolutely. Once a child begins to feel confident or, to put it another way, has established themselves in the social environment of school, the skill of promoting independence in learning becomes a very high priority in my mind. Perhaps somewhat controversially, I would advocate giving young children a relatively high degree of freedom to satisfy their curiosity and express themselves in the context of broad learning experiences. But there must still be teaching … Child Development theories seem to be sadly lacking in the training courses in the twenty-first century in England. I do not fully agree with Monsieur Piaget's position on developmental stages and their prescribed ages, and we have corresponded at length on these ideas, and

[18] 'In general, our aim should be to give children as many opportunities of free movement as possible, and to make use for social purposes of their love of doing things.' (Isaacs, 1929: 71).

spoken of it when he visited Malting House. But I do agree that teachers – indeed all who work with young children – must have a sound knowledge of child development theories and be able to draw on these theories to develop high quality and challenging teaching and learning encounters with young children.

PC   Say some more, would you, about the degree of freedom you think children should have? There have to be limits, don't there? What does your version of 'freedom' in early education look like?

SI   Freedom, yes. Well, first of all, freedom comes with good behaviour. The teacher should not condone anti-social and aggressive behaviours that run counter to the 'pleasant' atmosphere that we have agreed is important for young children. I do believe, however, that young children should be allowed to express themselves fully, and if such behaviour leads to conflict with other children or adults then it is the teacher's responsibility to address such behaviour constructively. That is an opportunity for children to learn something too. In my view, such things as aggressive behaviour should be seen in the context of, and at the same time as part of, a young child's emotional development.

PC   This makes sense, but you seem to be saying that your position on 'freedom' in the early years classroom is somewhat controversial? It's not that liberal is it? Isn't this something that Charlotte Mason has also pioneered?

SI   That's true, she has; but 'freedom for learning'[19] is a source of controversy because many would say that too much freedom for the young child is either physically or morally dangerous, or at least an abdication of responsibility on the part of the teacher. Some religious leaders who have had a hand in the development of schoolrooms for the poor children take the attitude that discipline is a pathway to morality.

PC   'Spare the rod and spoil the child' …

SI   That is an ethic of some establishments, but not mine. Indeed, some foresighted individuals like Robert [Owen] also had this belief that physical punishment was not helpful to the development of citizenship. However, I would prefer not to set limits on children's impulses that are governed by adult expectations of respectability and pedagogical purpose. I would prefer instead to set sensible rules for the safe and social behaviour of children which do not inhibit learning.

---

[19] Mason, C. (1923) *An Essay Towards a Philosophy of Education*. Oxford: Scriwener Press.

PC   You really have tested the boundaries of what is acceptable, though, haven't you? For example, in that famous account from the Malting House School where you seem to have allowed – even encouraged – a group of children who were curious to find out if the rabbit was really dead. You let them test a theory about whether it was really dead or not by letting them put it into water to see if it floated. The following day, after a discussion with two boys, you actually encouraged them to dig the rabbit up to see if it was still there! I recall a conversation about this observation in early 2000 when the practitioners I was working with were aghast at this practice! Some were quite appalled. How far would you push the bounds of acceptability to satisfy children's curiosity? What would you say to those practitioners who say that your rabbit stunt was a step too far?

SI   It wasn't a step too far! Absolutely not! And it was not a stunt; it was a serious attempt to respect and develop young children's genuine interest and to research with them their very genuine and serious questions. They had a theory that the rabbit was not there – I wanted them to use the evidence available to research the answer to that question. Firstly, I would argue that such examples of allowing young children greater freedom to learn will lead them to discover the truth for themselves and not some 'sanitised' version that we adults often try to satisfy them with. What is equally important though is that as teachers we are at the same time fully exposed to young children and therefore more able to make informed and accurate assessments of their all-round development.[20] And those who work with young children must be knowledgeable and grounded enough to be able to take such questions from children and work with them to find the answers; if that means digging up dead rabbits, then that's what it requires!

PC   Can you say a bit more about why this notion of 'freedom' is so important in young children's motivation to learn? It's fascinating ...

SI   My view is that everything young children do springs from the deep desire within them to learn from and understand the world in which they find themselves.[21] It goes without saying that this will sometimes lead them into behaviours that will challenge not only

---

[20] '... I myself happen to be interested in everything that little children do and feel.' (Isaacs, 1933: 19).

[21] 'The thirst for understanding springs from the child's deepest emotional needs, a veritable passion.' (Isaacs, 1932: 113).

their boundaries of knowledge but also some people's view of what is acceptable for young children to do. That we must live with ...

PC   But you draw the line in the sand though, don't you. You don't accept anti-social behaviour. What boundaries did you draw for the Malting House teachers when they observed behaviour which we might call 'unacceptable'?

SI   OK, well, to repress such behaviour – purely because it does not 'fit' with our adult understanding of how to behave – to me demonstrates a failure to try and fully understand young children. Young children long to explore, to discover and to understand, and as teachers we should be accepting the challenges that it will bring to our relationships with those we teach. Only by working in this way can teachers honestly say they are being responsive and reflective educators engaged in motivating and encouraging independence in young children's learning. But yes, there are boundaries which have to be drawn in the interests of acceptability and the good of all.

PC   Some would say that freedom in learning needs to be handled carefully as it has its pitfalls as well as its obvious advantages. One person's freedom is another person's prison.

SI   There will never be agreement on that, but what I am certain about is that these observations now speak for themselves. Readers can now decide if what the children in Malting House were learning was useful, honest, true scientific understanding. That is one thing I hope to have achieved. Let the records speak for themselves.

PC   I think that they do – but ... if you don't mind me saying – they do for a certain period in history, for a certain context and culture ... And the other thing is that – if you don't mind me saying – you are ... remarkable ... and not every practitioner has your skill, your confidence, your belief ...

SI   You flatter me! I was not so remarkable ... but I had a strong conviction of how things should be ... and, I think, a real understanding of how children learn ...

PC   And such understanding is what all who work with young children should strive for ...

SI   Indeed!

Conversation 4

How Do Young Children Learn?

In conversation: Johann Heinrich Pestalozzi (JHP), Jean Piaget (JP), and Friedrich Froebel (FF)

(Biographies: JHP p. 27, JP p. 59, FF p. 31)

It is a winter afternoon and three men meet in a small smoke-filled café overlooking the Schaffhausen Falls in Northern Switzerland, on the Swiss/ German Border on the Rhine. A waiter ensures that their cups are filled with hot coffee from time to time and the three men talk and talk…

In this imaginary conversation Johann Heinrich Pestalozzi, Jean Piaget and Friedrich Froebel are talking together about how young children learn.

FF   So, Mr Pestalozzi, I know you are convinced that 'learning through activity' is essential for early education; tell me more about your work which I so admire …

JHP Definitely sir! My experience with young children leads me to appreciate the necessity of allowing learners to discover the world through activity rather than through direct instruction. I don't accept that young children should be given answers to satisfy their curiosity, but they should be encouraged to arrive at them for themselves. Mrs Isaacs would agree with this!

FF   Mmm … So how do you see this working out in practice? What do you tell those teachers of young children in your schools to do?

JHP Well, in my view, learners, especially young children, are not able to assimilate words as a primary means for understanding a particular concept. What they need is plenty of opportunity to use their own senses to see, to touch and to feel in order to begin to discover what meaning things have for them.

FF   So words or talk of any kind are secondary to practical handling of objects. Is that how you would see it?

JHP To a degree, Froebel, yes; but not altogether. My ultimate goal is the education and well-being of the whole child, and so to neglect language completely at any stage would be quite ridiculous! However, my studies have led me to adopt a method or doctrine that seeks to ensure that there is some form of sequence to the process of learning.

FF   Go on …

JHP   You know the German word 'Anschauung' meaning 'sense per-
      ception' … this implies that direct concrete observation precedes
      any form of verbal description of an object.

FF   Many would not disagree with you. Some would put it in terms of
      'from the simple to the complex' or from the 'concrete to the abstract'.

JHP   Yes, and furthermore, as we progress and mature as learners and as
      human beings we discover that our experiences and learning are
      less and less based in physical or 'concrete' realities. I believe that
      encouraging young children to begin their learning through the
      senses is in keeping with their desire to discover and will ultimately
      produce a balanced learner or – to put it another way – learning
      through the hands, the head and the heart.

FF   From what I understand of the work of [Rudolph] Steiner, he
      would not disagree with you there; it's certainly something that
      I feel is very important, as you know.

JHP   Yes, teachers must have a reflective attitude if they are to encourage
      such a valuable quality in the process of children's learning. This is
      not always easy and some of the teachers in my own schools found
      this difficult too. Imaginative teaching situations must be reflected
      upon, explored and evaluated, first mentally and then verbally. But
      tell me, Froebel – you used the term 'Kindergarten', the 'garden of
      children'; it will doubtless become a common enough term one
      day, used all over the world and attributed to your work with young
      children. How do you see the role of the teacher and the teachers'
      relationship with young children in this 'garden'?

FF   I firmly believe that children should be 'nurtured' as are plants in a
      garden. As you have already said, they need a sensitive and respon-
      sible 'guiding hand' to help them flourish. In addition, I take the
      view that learning is a natural part of a young child's character.

JHP   Paint me a picture of this 'garden' … Tell me how the teacher in
      the kindergarten is 'sensitive' and nurturing?

FF   Well, I have drawn on your work first and foremost, and I also think
      that it is vital to act on Comenius' view that every child is absolutely
      an individual – each child develops at their own individual rate and
      it is most important that the teacher is not only aware of this, but
      does everything possible to take it into account when helping young
      children to learn. In my view this begins by acknowledging that edu-
      cation is a process … and the learning that a child goes through is like
      the process of growth that happens to a seed in fertile ground.

JP   Can I come in there? I must say that I find all this fascinating,
      Froebel, I'm sure, and the Reverend Comenius would be pleased to

hear you say these things. So would you say that this growth must be cultivated but not artificially forced, or, as some might say, rushed?

FF   Exactly Jean, exactly! You and I may not entirely agree on everything here, but I say that each child, like each seed, has the potential for growth inside, and just as it is not natural to force growth upon a seed, in the same way it is not natural to impose learning on a child from the outside. I know that this imagery is very strong too in Comenius' writings about the development of young children.

JP   But you don't surely mean therefore that … that the teacher is a 'passive' participant in her relationship with the child? Surely you are not suggesting that teachers just … what? Stand back? Wait for the 'sun' to come out and then watch the flowers grow in the garden?

FF   No, of course not! And you know I'm not saying that, Jean. Because – to stay with the metaphor – seeds need more than merely sunshine to grow. They need water in sufficient quantity and a suitable environment – including opportunities for shade from too much sunshine at times. As I said earlier, each child, like each seed, needs to be given individual attention, and this work of teaching is such a difficult job to get right for each individual child.

JP   Right, but Pestalozzi here asked you to paint him a picture of this garden – what would I find – what would I actually see – if I were to visit this Froebel Kindergarten of yours? What is this 'suitable environment' for teaching young children?

FF   Well, let me put it this way, and I will read to you, here … What I wrote in 1826 – so long ago! – was that simple playthings are important … things that allow children to feel … and experience… to act and represent, to think and recognise. Listen:

> Building, aggregation, is first with the child, as it is first in the development of mankind, and in crystallization. The importance of the vertical, the horizontal, and the rectangular is the first experience which the child gathers from building; then follow equilibrium and symmetry. Thus the child ascends from the construction of the simplest wall with or without cement to the more complex and even to the invention of every architectural structure lying within the possibilities of the given material. [22]

So you see, the environment is perhaps the most significant factor in the healthy growth of any natural, created being. Food, water and warmth are all necessary, but so too is the provision of physical space and adequate time. In my experience children take time to develop, sometimes slowly and in certain respects, sometimes quite rapidly, but always it is a process that unfolds from within. Now, I consider it the teacher's role to identify this 'unfolding' and neither to rush nor hold back its development. Yes … and each one will have required a different

[22] F. Froebel (1826) *The Education of Man*, p. 281.

type of relationship with the teacher in order to develop as much as possible while they are being taught.

JP   I can see that, and as we have been discussing the importance of relationships, it has brought to the surface something that Mrs Isaacs put to me in a letter from her Malting House School. It made me think that … in a sense the teacher/child relationship is the 'ultimate environment' if you like, in which growth of the individual takes place. Vygotsky would doubtless have something to say here … as I interpret his work, he would argue that learning has to take place with the teacher and the child quite in tune with each other – this 'Zone of Proximal Development' of his is where he says the real learning happens. Now Malting House has all the attributes of a carefully planned and richly stocked physical environment, and these are – if Mrs Isaacs' observations are anything to go by – these are obviously important. I saw for myself the way the richness of the school environment led children to ask questions that they were then encouraged to find answers to.

JHP   I'm going to interrupt you because I have to say … I must say that so much more significant than the physical space is the 'space' for the relationship that the teacher is able to establish with the learner. Froebel here is right on this …

FF   Yes, without that important relationship a teacher can't be expected fully to grasp a young child's individual needs and what the next step in their development requires for the learning process to move forward. For instance – going back to the analogy of the growing seed again – it would be considered unnatural … well, ultimately destructive if the gardener opened a tender bud with his fingers just so that he could see the beauty of the flower inside.

JP   You two keep talking about the importance of teachers being sensitive and 'nurturing' an individual child's natural impulse to learn. But tell me, Froebel, what do you think of the view that this impulse – the young child's natural desire to learn – can have both positive and negative outcomes?

FF   Well, you know of course that this is an issue that is rooted in our perception of whether young children are fundamentally 'good' or 'bad' … Jean, pass me the book again; here, listen:

The purpose of education is to encourage and guide man as a conscious, thinking and perceiving being in such a way that he becomes a pure and perfect representation of that divine inner law through his own personal choice; education must show him the ways and meanings of attaining that goal. [23]

---

[23] Friedrich Froebel (1826) *Die Menschenerziehung*, p. 2.

JP   So you say that children must 'become' pure and perfect, but are they just naturally 'good'? Do they need your 'guidance' in this respect?

FF   Well, I could ask, does the existence of serious psychological problems for a young child make them any less fundamentally 'good' than those that at least appear to conform to 'reasonable' behaviour expectations? Children are made in the image of God – though all men have sinned – and I believe that … I believe that all human beings seek harmony with God and his world – they seek 'goodness'. Children are born with a need to play and explore, and this they should do. But Piaget – you will have your own observations on what we have been discussing – you have particular views on what young children are capable of learning before they are 6 years of age …

JP   I do indeed – but I have to say first of all that I'd prefer to set God aside in this discussion; we can have this discussion without reference to any God, it seems to me … No, Friedrich, let's not get sidetracked …

FF   How can you possibly call our relationship with our maker a sidetrack, how can you …

JP   Anyway, let that pass for the moment, please? For me knowledge does not come from the 'outside', in some ready-made form that can be impressed upon the receptive learner like a stamp is stuck on a letter before it is posted … But I will tell you my position … My observations of young children learning, as well as those who are older, confirms for me that learners must actively construct knowledge for themselves. Human beings are not born with knowledge and they do not gain it by being passive recipients. In my opinion, all forms of intelligence, even abstract thought, have their origins in actions of various degrees. Learners tend to 'incorporate' or 'assimilate' new experiences in a way that provides some form of continuity to their existing structures of understanding. At the same time they also 'accommodate' new ideas in a way that expands their understanding and works for change and growth in cognitive development. The term I have used in my work to describe the interrelationship between these two aspects of learning is 'Adaptation'.

FF   I'm following you but I need you to tell me what this looks like for the teacher.

JHP   What Piaget means is …

JP   I think I'd prefer to utter my own words myself Johann, if you don't mind! I will tell you what it means … A good example is the imaginative play we often see young children engaged in, although it is rather more an example of the tendency to incorporate or 'assimilate' than 'accommodate'. Nevertheless, a child playing imaginatively with an object like a cardboard box clearly shows that young children can play according to their needs at that moment. The box can become a house, a car or a bed, regardless of the actual characteristics of the box itself. The box fits and 'reinforces' the child's current knowledge base, as opposed to imaginative play in a 'home corner' of a classroom. Such play would be more an example of a child wanting to accommodate their understanding of an adult domestic scene at home, into their own personal life with friends at school. In this instance a child's development is being 'stretched'; although, I should say that both examples contain elements of these two components that enable learners to construct knowledge.

FF   So when you raise the question of what young children are capable of learning at certain ages or stages of development, what would you say to others – Comenius, Vygotsky, Isaacs, Mason – who hold the view that up until the age of 6 young children can, in the right environment, learn a great deal?

JP   My conviction is that there is a pattern of development in human cognitive processes that follows a sequence and the main stages of that sequence follow one another. Each stage builds upon the previous one and can only begin to do so once the previous one is fully developed within the learner. These stages are generally visible at certain ages in a child's life, but of course I'm not saying that they are rigidly fixed – and indeed there are likely to be exceptions to any general 'rule' that I propose.

JHP   And Froebel's 3–5-year-olds – where would they fit into your scheme? Where do they come in your sequence?

JP   Well now, let me explain … I have termed the period from 18 months to 11 years as the 'Concrete Operational Period', and within that long period I see two distinct phases. I consider a child of the age you are referring to as being within the first of these two phases, the one that generally finishes at the age of 7.

JHP   Rudolf [Steiner] would perhaps share a modicum of agreement there – he believes that 7 is an important age too, but his reasoning isn't the same as yours. And what would be the implications for their learning in this phase according to your views?

JP   Right, well … let me see … I have termed this the 'Pre-operational Period'. This phase follows the 'Sensori-Motor Period' and it is characterised by evidence that a child is able to represent things for himself. For example a child of less than 2 or 3 who is asked to put some objects in a row, and then move them before rearranging them back into a row will think sequentially about the practical processes involved. One will follow another. This is evidence that the early processes of 'internalisation' are going on in the child's mind.

FF   But how does this relate to your understanding of what young children of this age are capable of learning in the way that Isaacs suggests they can?

JP   I see ... Well, my studies lead me to the conclusion that this process of internalisation is not sufficiently developed until the age of about 7 or 8 for the child to begin to show evidence that he can think other than subjectively about things.

JHP   But there is evidence to the contrary – surely you see that, Jean? Are you implying that you consider that children before the age of 7 or 8 are basically egocentric? And unable to consider another person's point of view? Preposterous!

JP   That is precisely what I'm arguing ... certainly. I would argue the case that a child in the 'Pre-operational Period' is not capable of the mental 'flexibility' that older children and adults bring to their learning. And there is nothing 'preposterous' about it! It follows that an egocentric view of the world is, in my view, a limiting factor in a young child's ability to 'construct' knowledge in the way I describe.

FF   Now, let me see if I fully understand what you're saying here ... In one important respect what you have said supports Comenius' view that young children need to experience the world in which they live on a 'first-hand' or concrete level – OK, well that fits with my own position which draws on Pestalozzi's own work. Actually I doubt if anyone would argue with that ... My own experience, too, supports the view that giving young children concrete experiences to learn through makes a powerful contribution to their development. Mrs Isaacs' work shows the same, in my view.

JP   Yes we can agree so far ... But we have to be clear about the theoretical basis on which we make decisions about young children's learning, and not waste the time of the teachers who try to have children do things which are currently beyond them.

FF   This is fascinating, but very annoying at the same time ... I have another question ...

JP   There will always be another question. And we shall not entirely agree, but this is good because those who work with young children should know whose ideas, whose theories, which practices, which ideals they base their work on. We don't have time now, we must talk again soon.

Conversation 5

A Policy of Creativity

In conversation: Alec Clegg (AC) with Peter Clough (PC)

(Biographies: AC p. 69)

> Summer 2013. Sir Alexander Bradshaw Clegg (more often known as Alec Clegg) and Peter Clough are sitting on a sunny afternoon on the grass hill at the Yorkshire Sculpture Park, in West Bretton; nearby is one of Barbara Hepworth's large brass sculptures that make up the Family of Man, and also a huge Henry Moore piece.
>
> It is a fitting setting in so many ways for this imaginary conversation, as they look down on the grand building that was once Bretton Hall College of Education, where generations of teachers were trained (and which holds the Sir Alec Clegg Collection: his notes, lectures, letters and children's art).

PC Tell me a little about you, what spurred you to take up the sorts of educational issues that you did: comprehensive schooling ... the centrality of art, music, drama .... Education of the 'human being'.

AC Where to start? Well ... I was born in 1909, in Derbyshire ... Long Eaton. My dad was a teacher, and I suppose you could say that I followed in his footsteps. I taught French and some PE for about five years in London. I came to the West Riding – it was one of the biggest local Education Authorities in Yorkshire at the time – in 1945 when I was 34.

PC So that was just after the end of the war ...

AC It was and I was amazed by these big sprawling and – in many cases – bombed cities: Bradford, Leeds, Halifax, and the efforts that were being made to improve lives and education. You know at this time we'd just had the 'Butler Act'[24] (1944) and whilst it was good in many ways, I didn't think it did enough for children's learning – for learning itself. It got the buildings in place but the curriculum was still lacking. And my strong interest was children as learners. I tried to keep that central in all I did in the West Riding.

PC Can you give me an example?

---

[24] The Butler Education Act 1944.

AC There had been some emergency teacher training during the war … and there were some good teachers … but I felt there was a lot to do to get teachers beyond … just the skills – d'you know? To get them to think about things like … creativity, and how that can open up children's learning. And that meant that the continuing education of teachers was important too … courses for them were, I believe, a strong influence on the quality of their teaching – our job was to keep them excited in what they did in their classrooms and in how children learned.

PC Tell me some more about those courses for teachers …

AC We established vacation courses – they usually lasted about three days and were residential, and I liked them to work in pleasant surroundings. That's so important, you know, and I believed that classrooms too should be pleasant places. There were – you'll marvel at this! – over 60 years of summer courses for teachers – quite something don't you think?[25]

PC An incredible achievement – and they must really have made a difference to the quality of children's experiences.

AC To see teaching genius at work has been my constant refreshment in inspiration and excitement,[26] and teachers needed encouragement to do that, to keep their teaching vibrant. I remember telling some young teachers who were on a course called 'The Creativity of Children' to take warning from the past – try to learn from our failures, and also to remember that education is for the mind and the spirit. Too often in education the focus is on things that can be measured, rather than things of the spirit that defy measurement. Children – and their teachers just as much – need both.

PC You also pioneered excellent initial teacher education, didn't you? Looking at those windows, glinting in the sunlight down there, do you recall the day Bretton Hall College opened?

AC Well, I do, indeed, and I can play it like a film in my memory … You know of course our focus here was always in training teachers in art and in music and drama. It's that thing – that central thing – about creativity again, creativity and the life of the spirit.

---

[25] http://sites.google.com-site/teachchoice/siralecclegg Sir Alec Clegg, West Riding Vacation Course – Bingley College of Education, Closing Session: Thursday, 3 August 1972.

[26] Ibid.

PC   That must have seemed innovative at the time ...? When was that precisely?

AC   1949 ... I was keen to see teachers taught to teach so that they would light fires in their pupils rather than fill them with facts much as one would fill a pot. There are those who say that the main aim of education is not just to prepare for something that is to come in the future, but to promote healthy growth and development now. The best way of doing this is to place the child in a stimulating environment, give him a wealth of experience rather than a welter of facts, and let his training and technique come through the activities into which he is guided by a wise and sympathetic teacher.[27]

PC   Your work had a profound impact on the place of the arts in schools, how they were taught and their importance in the curriculum ...

AC   Kind of you to say so .... I was Chief Education Officer for the West Riding of Yorkshire and I did that job for almost 30 years. I think it is true that in that period the place of the arts changed; teachers, and others too, saw their importance and influence on children's education. I always felt it important to attend to the senses, the aesthetics, and to children's emotional needs through the arts.

PC   And how did you do it? Were you able to take people along with you? Inspire teachers ... to use art – to inspire children to make art?

AC   No, I think we all inspired each other, we all took each other along ... We were a team: the inspirational HMI[28] in the West Riding was Christian Schiller – and he, together with the artist Robin Tanner and advisory teachers, spent much of their time in classrooms and nurseries working alongside teachers ... and they'd talk... and you know we all had so much to learn from each other.[29]

PC   And what guided you? Where did this importance of balance come from, your own education? Your own childhood?

---

[27] Peter Newsam (2008) 'What price hyacinths? An appreciation of the work of Sir Alec Clegg', *Education 3–13: International Journal of Primary, Elementary and Early Years Education* 36(2): 109–116.

[28] *Her Majesty's Inspectorate.*

[29] Tim Brighouse (2008) 'Sir Alec Clegg' *Education 3–13: International Journal of Primary, Elementary and Early Years Education*, 36(2): 103–8.

AC   Well ... my aunt had a poem hanging on her sitting room wall ...

If thou of fortune be bereft

And of thine earthly store hath left two loaves,

Sell one and with the dole

Buy hyacinths to feed the soul.[30]

PC   Say more ...?

AC   Mind and spirit ... Children need both. I do stress with all the urgency at my command that however much we digress from the orthodox, however much we endeavour to evolve methods of education which we believe have an effect on the emotions and the temperament, our approach to this difficult problem should be strictly intellectual. Let us know what we are doing, let us know very clearly what we are doing, and let us avoid everything which might be considered as stunting or quackery or window-dressing in our education.[31]

PC   So, learning, education, teaching – is about – what is it? – 'bread *and* hyacinths' ...

AC   Bread and hyacinths ...

PC   Alec, thank you – your vision of the place of the arts remains an important reminder of their importance in our lives.

---

[30] http://www.ysp.co.uk/page/sir-alec-clegg-collection/es

[31] Peter Newsom (2008).

Conversation 6

Looking back to 'Education' and 'Care' ... Challenging Current Policy through History

In conversation: Susan Isaacs (SI), Maria Montessori (MMon) and Margaret McMillan (MMc)

(Biographies: SI p. 53, MMon p. 48, MMc p. 46)

Go to www.sagepub.co.uk/nutbrownclough for a downloadable recording of the conversation.

> It is 9 May 2013, this past year the media has carried headline after head-line highlighting government policy on early years issues, and not least the debate around 'education' and 'care'. The Nutbrown Review was pub-lished on 19 June 2012 and the Coalition Government announced new policies, including its response to that Review, on 29 January 2013. Strong views have been expressed by many with an interest in early years provi-sion, including parents, professionals and politicians. An 'Urgent Question' about 'child care ratios' was asked in the House of Commons on 9 May, and in this conversation, we imagine the reactions of Susan Isaacs, Maria Montessori and Margaret McMillan. These three influential women, whose work stands as an important legacy in early childhood education, talk about current issues and ponder on how to construct policy so as to inte-grate education and care and ensure quality in both. We imagine them standing in Parliament Square, beneath the statue of Lloyd George, whose government in 1916 passed legislation to establish nursery schools for 2–5-year-olds. The three have just left the House of Commons, where they listened to the Minister for Children and Families answer the Shadow Minister's question about the Government's policy.

SI   Well, there is something missing in this debate ... I'm shocked that the issue under discussion is how many chil-dren should be under the sole charge of one person. I heard little about the quality of teaching, or the need for observation, and allowing children to set themselves chal-lenging questions. I wonder if my work at the Malting House[32] still has anything useful to offer teachers in 2013?

MMc   What I am worrying about – having heard the politicians' questions and the responses – is the seeming separation of 'education' and 'care'. It is as if these two things are distinct.

---

[32] The Malting House was an experimental school run by Susan Isaacs. The Malting House School (also known as the Malting House Garden School) was an experimental educational institution that operated from 1924 to 1929, founded by Geoffrey Pyke.

They are not – they are two sides of the same coin – inseparable. Good teaching is caring and good care is essential for children to learn. What is happening to the examples of multidiscipli-nary provision for the under fives? Rachel and I fought hard in the early 1900s to establish the importance of health, education and social welfare for very young children and we lobbied politicians hard to make changes. We both worked with Katharine Glasier, to campaign for school meals, and eventually the House of Commons passed the School Meals Act in 1906. You have to lobby hard to get messages across, and to bring about good change. It seems the lobbying of governments must continue – is early education slipping back? Is multi-agency working being lost? And what hap-pened to Sure Start?

SI   It is worrying – and the papers are full of strong arguments about the need to be clear about good early education – but it seems this policy is focusing only on 'care' while parents go to work. Did you hear the Minister just now say 'If we do not do something about this by reforming the supply of child care, it will become prohibitively expensive and many parents will not be able to afford to go out to work'?[33]. I say that whatever the reason for children being away from their parents, it is the quality of learning experiences that is important. And I agree the care needs to be good, but those who are caring need to understand how children learn, the importance of play, child development …

MMc   … and the importance of the outdoors, fresh air, wholesome food, clean clothes … Hungry children can't learn – they are too focused on the pain in their belly, our nursery schools have made a difference to so many children, and I'm proud of the work Rachel and I did to train nursery teachers to work with children from 2 to 5 years – until they enter elementary school. And work with parents is so important too; they also benefited from our explanations of how their children learn.

MMon   The environment is crucially important, the planned envi-ronment, set out so that even very young children, can learn life skills – and independence in learning. It seems some who work with young children today don't fully understand the importance of their role – how activities can be presented, how children learn, indeed. The training of nursery teachers is so important.

---

[33] Elizabeth Truss, *Hansard*, 9 May 2013: Column 142.

SI   Perhaps it is the case that people training to work with young children no longer read our writings, or maybe they don't consider that our work is relevant ... I read recently that young children just need to be loved. Well, I'm sure that love is important – but love alone is not enough. They need more than mother love, they need to develop enquiring minds – explore and ask questions – like young scientists! [34] And so they need creative, bold and knowledgeable, observant teachers!

MMon   And skills for living. ... There is much that is good, but perhaps the pace of policy change is just too fast. It does seem to be undoing much of the work that people have built using our ideas.

MMc   ... and what will happen to nursery teachers?

SI   ... we shall have to wait and see.

Note

Following considerable campaigning and effective lobbying the (Liberal Democrat) Deputy Prime Minister Nick Clegg announced on Thursday 6th June 2013, that the policy to allow fewer adults to work with more young children was to be halted. Controversy over aspects of the Coalition Government's policy on early years qualifications continued, and a two tier system of teacher qualification was introduced in September 2013 giving those working with the youngest children a different status (and different pay and conditions) to those teachers working with children over five.

---

[34] Issacs, S. (1952) *The Educational Value of the Nursery School*. Headly Brothers, London.

Conversation 7

Literacy in the Early Years – a Pedagogy of Patience?

In conversation: Rudolf Steiner (RS) with Cathy Nutbrown (CN)

(Biography: RS p. 37)

> It is May 2013, around the country 16-year-olds are taking their GCSE exams against a background of concerns over literacy and the employability of some young people for whom GCSE was not a realistic proposition. Worries persist over literacy levels and the reading habits of boys. Government policy continues the trend of beginning the formal teaching of literacy earlier and earlier. Children begin school at the age of 4 years and are tested in their knowledge of phonics when they are 6 years old (some are still only 5). In the early years a new curriculum has been issued for the Early Years Foundation Stage. There remains a lack of agreement about when, and how, it is best to teach young children to read and write. In this imaginary conversation, Cathy Nutbrown talks with Rudolf Steiner about what constitutes appropriate literacy pedagogy in the early years.

CN   Let me start, Mr Steiner, by saying thank you for making time to talk with me about literacy pedagogy. I've been thinking recently about what a 'hot potato' literacy has always been – it's always caused controversy. There is perpetual disagreement about what should be taught, when it should be taught, and how. In my own research I've always subscribed to the 'put a book in their hand before they can walk or talk' approach; I believe that immersing young children in books, inculcating in them a love of books and stories, is a fundamental building block to later literacy learning. But I know the approach taken in Steiner-Waldorf schools, particularly in the kindergarten, is different: you don't encourage the use of books or the formal teaching of reading and writing in the kindergarten, do you?

RS   Well, this is an opportunity for me to explain some of our thinking in the Steiner-Waldorf schools. What I must say first of all is that teachers must understand why human beings need certain circumstances at particular times in their life. The time before the child's second teeth come, at about 7 years, is different from the next phase of life. And so teachers need to teach with this view of child development in mind. Before the adult teeth come, children learn through their bodies ... they are 'physical selves'. I believe that the most important aspects of body, soul and spirit, must be thought about to give direction to education and teaching[35]. I would direct you to my lectures for more detail, on why teaching reading too early is dangerous and counterproductive.

CN   Well, many would not disagree about the dangers of formal learning too early ...

RS   In the first seven years of life a child learns to walk, to speak, and to think ... If you try to arouse curiosity in a child about some particular word, you will find that you thereby entirely drive out the child's wish to learn that word[36]. Children should come to school around 7 years old, around the time their second teeth appear. Before that, the home with their mothers and then the kindergarten is the place for them. But when they come to school, your teaching must not be made up of isolated units, but a coherent unity ... If they are taught to read and write as two separate things it is just as though the milk they drink was separated chemically into two parts – it would no longer be milk – no longer pleasant to drink. Reading and writing must form a unity. You must bring this idea of unity into being for your work with the children when they first come to school.[37]

CN   So you think that children should not begin school at five (or four as it is for many children in England now), and your rationale, if I can put it simply, is that their bodies and souls are simply not ready yet and that is something that cannot be hurried. Is that a fair way to summarise what you are saying?

RS   In short, that is what I am saying, but I think teachers must understand why children are not ready, they must understand what lies behind this, and they should be able to share this knowledge with the child's parents.

CN   And reading and writing, you see as two sides of the same coin? I think this would echo what was once called a 'whole language approach' where meaning in reading and expression in writing were the focus above accuracy and separate skills[38], which would be taught and acquired later.

---

[35] R. Steiner (1995) *The Kingdom of the Child: Introductory Talks on Waldorf Education.* Hudson, NY: Anthroposophic Press, p.5. (Originally published 1924.)

[36] Ibid., p. 12.

[37] Ibid., p. 15.

[38] K. Goodman, (1967) 'Reading: a psycholinguistic guessing game.' *Journal of the Reading Specialist*, 6: 126–135. And also N. Chomsky (1993) *Language and Thought.* Wakefield, RI and London: Moyer Bell.

RS   I think we are not quite on the same wavelength here, and this is why … You are seeking to make sense of what I say by matching my ideas, partially, to your own experience – just as children do! But of key importance is the rationale for what is done in the classroom – and not done in the kindergarten. This is not so much about repeating particular practices but of understanding why those practices are important and then knowing how to respond in the classroom with the children according to their needs. Let me explain … The calligraphy of today is quite foreign to children both in written or printed letters. They simply do not relate, say, to the letter 'A' – for example. Nevertheless, when children come to school they are taught these things, even though the child has no meaningful connection with what he is doing.[39] And if they are made to do tasks such as to stick letters onto paper, before the time is right for them, they are asked to work against their nature. It is difficult for them and they are at odds with their learning.

CN   I think this fits with the work of Bredekamp on developmentally appropriate practice,[40] but again – the rationale is different from your own.

RS   What you should appeal to is what the children possess; their artistic sense, and ability to create imaginative pictures … You should avoid a direct approach to teaching conventional letters of the alphabet too early[41].

CN   This notion of readiness is an issue whatever form of pedagogy or whatever particular approach to early education is taken. But literacy is so important, and there is this climate now of young people struggling with literacy. Employers sometimes complain that new employees are not fit to work because they cannot read instructions, write a letter, or add up accurately. There is a fear that starting too late can cause literacy difficulties and many of us who have carried out research in early literacy have met this concern. We have to keep trying to reassure people that starting too young is not necessarily the way to ensure a grasp of literacy early, but there are some things that are appropriate for very young children such as sharing books and beginning to make their own marks on paper.

---

[39] Steiner (1995: 23).

[40] S. Bredekamp (ed) (1987) *Developmentally Appropriate Practice in Early Childhood Programs Serving Children from Birth throught Age 8*. Washington, DC: NAEYC.

[41] Steiner (1995: 23).

RS   People will object that the children learn to read and write too late, but this is only because they do not realise how harmful it is when children learn to read and write too soon. Reading and writing are really not suited to human beings until a later age – the eleventh or twelfth year – and the more a child is blessed with not being able to read and write well before this age, the better it is for the later years of life.[42]

CN   I think I would have a problem with that – 11 or 12 seems very late, certainly if a child can't read reasonably fluently by then they would be considered to have learning difficulties. And wouldn't these children struggle with the rest of the curriculum? Literacy is the key to the whole curriculum, struggling with literacy throughout the school years means struggling with the whole of schooling.

RS   But perhaps then it is the nature of the schooling that is wrong, not the child.

CN   Ah! OK, so I'm perhaps not allowing myself to think sufficiently radically in this conversation. I need to imagine a system of education and pedagogical practices which are truly based on what we know of children, child development and humanity. And then I need to imagine a society which is similarly constructed.

RS   Well, naturally you really wouldn't be able to proceed as I suggest because children have to pass from school into adult life,[43] so there has to be some accommodation, but it is important to know these things. The child who struggles, is not struggling with reading but struggling because the time when he is being asked to learn these things is wrong for him.

CN   So what can I take from the Steiner-Waldorf approach that can realistically be transposed into an early years setting or a Key Stage One classroom? Can it be possible to have a part-Steiner-Waldorf approach?

RS   I would prefer things were done properly rather than piecemeal; as I said earlier, things fit together as a whole with the child in terms of body, soul and spirit. But let's think about how letters can be taught. Go to a Steiner-Waldorf school and you will see teachers teaching letters in all kinds of ways: forming the shapes with string, painting different shapes and forms from which letters eventually arise, letting children 'dance' the forms of the

---

[42] Ibid., p. 27.

[43] Ibid., p. 27.

letters round the room – experiencing the shapes with their whole bodies. There is freedom for teachers to be creative, but there is not chaos, because the spirit that is appropriate for each child is active in every class.[44]

CN   These are echoes too of the multisensory approach to literacy teaching which is popular with some early years teachers, and also used with pupils with learning difficulties.[45]

RS   And why do they have difficulties? Maybe because they were asked to learn these things too early! For some children it is what they are asked to do in school that creates their difficulties, it is important to realise that the problem is not always with the child.

CN   Well, there are many reasons why children struggle. I do agree that too much too soon can be detrimental, but it depends what it is. I believe that early literacy experiences, like other aspects of young children's learning, a lot of literacy, in the early years, can be learned through play. My colleague Peter Hannon[46] and I have shown how parents can provide 'Opportunities', 'Recognition', 'Interaction' and 'Models of literacy'. We've shown that parents really value the chance to learn more about how their young children learn literacy.[47] We've also looked at how important the role of stories and talking together are in families and in early years settings. In fact it was Gordon Wells' work which showed that listening to stories has an impact on later reading achievement[48]. It is important, won't you agree, that children are told stories, made-up stories, again and again ...

RS   It is of course important, but I don't attach this importance to later reading success. I see it as important because it is what the young child needs. Indeed in Steiner Schools you will hear

[44] Ibid., p. 29.

[45] J. Taylor, (2001) *Handwriting: A Teacher's Guide: Multisensory Approaches to Assessing and Improving Handwriting Skills.* London: David Fulton and also Helaine Schupack and Barbara Wilson (1997). *The 'R' Book: Reading, Writing & Spelling: The Multisensory Structured Language Approach.* Baltimore, MD: The International Dyslexia Association's Orton Emeritus Series.

[46] C. Nutbrown, P. Hannon and A. Morgan (2005) *Early Literacy Work with Families: Research, Policy and Practice.* London: Sage.

[47] P. Hannon, A. Morgan and C. Nutbrown (2006) 'Parents' experiences of a family literacy programme', *Journal of Early Childhood Research*, 3(3): 19–44.

[48] G. Wells (1987) *The Meaning Makers: Children Learning Language and Using Language to Learn.* London: Hodder and Stoughton.

teachers telling stories right through the school. Telling stories, often with a large picture, which they have drawn, on the blackboard.

CN Gosh! That really takes me back to my own infant school days; sometimes we would come in from lunchtime play and find a huge picture filling the board and the teacher ... Mrs Condon, would say ... 'If we get our work done I will tell you the story that goes with this picture before you go home'. I loved her stories, and I was amazed that she could draw those huge pictures in coloured chalk ...

RS That is not uncommon in Steiner classrooms, but you will often find that the story is a way to begin the day, rather than to end it. Steiner-Waldorf teachers must be good story-tellers and good illustrators! But I must make a point here about the stories told to young children – we must not just tell them any story. Different kinds of stories are fitting for different ages of children according to their needs of body, soul and spirit. This is important, not until the age of 9 do children see themselves as separate from their environment. For this reason, everything around little children should be spoken of as if it too were human. Plants, animals, stones, should be spoken of as if they too can speak, love, hate. Anthropomorphism should be used in the most inventive ways.[49] Treat all things as if they were human, and allow trees and stones, sun and rain and wind to talk – everything you bring to a child of this age is like a fairytale.

CN So the fittingness of anthropomorphism would, if we subscribe to your theory, explain why I loved *The Velveteen Rabbit* and the Beatrix Potter tales of Peter Rabbit and others.

RS These are the proper things for young children to hear. Children can hear the other difficult tales of human strife and love and hate later (such as the Greek myths and legends, the Old Testament stories), when they are ready in their bodies and souls to take them. You must teach and educate out of the very nature of the human being,[50] and, for this reason, education for moral life must run in parallel to the process of teaching which I set out.

CN From my experience of visiting Steiner schools, it seems all the teachers are such good story-tellers – they tell such compelling stories ...

---

[49] Steiner (1995: 31).

[50] Ibid., p. 52.

RS   Everything depends on the art of telling, and telling cannot be replaced by reading[51]. The teachers must learn how to tell stories, and know the stories in their hearts, and tell them as if they really believe the truth of them.

CN   Your focus is education for life, isn't it; part of a process of learning to be human? I can see this, but many policy-makers would not be content with this view. We inhabit a world of targets, success, failure, achievement, and so on, and because of that, success in early literacy learning is crucial. Can the Steiner-Waldorf approach really be successful in this kind of policy context?

RS   The teacher must come into the classroom in a mood of mind and soul that can really find its way into the children's hearts,[52] any other approach will be damaging. It is, however, extraordinarily difficult, in view of what is demanded of children today by the authorities, to succeed with an education that is really related to life itself. One has to go through some very painful experiences. Once, for instance, because of family circumstances, a child had to leave the Steiner-Waldorf school when he was about 9 years old. He had to continue his education in another school. We were then most bitterly reproached because he had not got so far in arithmetic as was expected of him there, nor in reading or writing. They said that the painting and other things he could do were of no use to him at all.

CN   But if he could not read at 9 years old he surely was at a disadvantage in the state school, yes?

RS   Professor, let me put it this way ... If we want to educate children out of knowledge of the human being and also in accordance with the demands of life they will need to be able to read and write to the standard expected of them. So the curriculum will have to include things because they are demanded.

CN   Do you think the gender of the child was significant in his later development in literacy? There has been growing concern that boys take longer to achieve certain aspects of literacy,[53] though in some of my own work boys were involved in literacy at home. At the age of 5, the boys in our study were active in literacy, even if studies and national testing raise concerns about literacy not

[51] Ibid., p. 25.

[52] Ibid., p. 62.

[53] DfEE (1997) *Excellence in Schools*. London: The Stationery Office.

being a masculine pursuit and boys' lower achievement in literacy later.[54] Working-class boys seem to be the group that struggle.[55]

RS   Boys and girls are different. Girls grasp things more easily than boys and with greater eagerness too.[56]

CN   So how about giving boys different, more boy-friendly, reading material, about football, cars, that kind of thing, online texts. The boys in our study really enjoyed their books, the illustrations, talking about them with their fathers. I can't see that this is harmful, but this emphasis of yours on only telling stories, and not reading or encouraging reading in the kindergarten doesn't fit with my experience as a nursery teacher or as a researcher.

RS   Professor, we shall disagree on some things, but I hope we shall not disagree on this. However we decide to fulfil the policies of the country and of the time we work in, we must still try to relate the children to real life as much as possible and for little children we must awaken a delight in them, liveliness, and a happy enjoyment of story.[57]

---

[54] C. Nutbrown and P. Hannon (2003). 'Children's perspectives on family literacy: methodological issues, findings and implications for practice', *Journal of Early Childhood Literacy*, 3(2): 115–45.

[55] P. Connolly (2004) *Boys and Schooling in the Early Years*. London: Routledge Falmer.

[56] Steiner (1995: 119).

[57] Steiner (1995: 25).

Conversation 8

Children's Rights and Early Learning

In conversation: Charlotte Mason (CM) with Cathy Nutbrown (CN)
(Biography: CM p. 35)

> It is a rainy day; summer in the Lake District was often punctuated with rainy days. Imagine them sitting in the Library of the House of Education at Ambleside, Charlotte Mason and Cathy Nutbrown looking at photo-graphs of past cohorts of student teachers who have trained there. The women who made up the class of 1890 are sitting on the lawn, beneath a large tree, looking elegant in their long skirts and white blouses, their badges with the college motto clear on their blazer pockets. They would have talked, while walking on the fells, something Charlotte did often for she was a strong believer in the benefits of the outdoors to life and learning, but the rain kept them indoors as they discussed children's rights and early learning.

CN   I wanted to talk about your 20 principles[58]... which some now call a Children's Bill of Rights ...

CM   My 20 principles are what underpin my philosophy; I set these out as clearly as I could because in order to understand my meth-ods it is important to know what they are built upon. First and foremost I see children born as 'people', neither good nor bad, but with the potential to develop either of those tendencies. Authority and obedience are important, and so too is the respect due to children as individuals.

CN   The notion of respect is important, I think, because it allows nursery teachers, parents and other educators, to design cur-ricula with the *capabilities* as well as the *needs* of children in mind.[59] I think that if we can ensure that young children are respected in their education, we have come a long way towards ensuring good quality experiences for them and proper training for their teachers. The UN Convention on the

---

[58] C. Mason (1923/1989) *An Essay Towards a Philosophy of Education*. Wheaton, IL: Tyndale House Publishers, Preface.

[59] C. Nutbrown (1996) *Respectful Educators – Capable Learners: Children's Rights and Early Education*. London: Sage.

Rights of the Child[60] establishes children's rights to education, to the arts, to decision making in matters that affect them. These are important building blocks for early childhood education …

CM …. As I was saying *authority* and *obedience* are important, alongside the respect due to children as individuals; that's why the principles of education being an *atmosphere*, a *discipline* and a *life* are crucial … we can talk about these later. We need to think of a child's mind as a spiritual organism with an appetite for knowledge, and therefore parents and teachers need to give the child a curriculum full of nourishment for their minds. The mind is not a receptacle for teachers to pour things into; teachers need to guard against over-preparation but also against the serving up of small 'morsels'. Children can deal with a great deal of knowledge from a full and generous curriculum, if they are offered what is relevant to them.

CN Give them multiple opportunities and trust them to take their own ideas from what is provided?

CM … and to do so naturally as they relate to things, thoughts and people. They experience the discipline of physical exercise, they learn from nature, handcraft, science, arts, and worthy, living books written by authors with a passion for the topic. And the business of parents and teachers is not to 'teach' but rather to help children make connections in their experiences, which appeal to their ideas and instil knowledge and thinking.

CN So there would be no syllabus? Rather an open curriculum based on your 20 principles? Have I got that right?

CM Three things are necessary in a syllabus: children need much knowledge (just as they need proper bodily nourishment); children need variety in the curriculum to promote their curiosity; good language, and high quality literature is essential, nothing oversimplified. And children need opportunities to recall and recount – to narrate their learning or write about it – so as to make their learning their own, and this is important for all children, whatever their social class or capabilities.

CN A rich curriculum indeed, and you believe that children need to be able to 'self-manage'…

[60] UNICEF, United Nations Convention on the Rights of the Child, http://www.unicef.org.crc/

CM Children need to develop a maturity in learning that will enable them to take quite a lot of responsibility for their own learning – choosing to accept and reject ideas.

CN And to do that they need good teachers.

CM Indeed and the motto of the student teachers at the House of Education here at Ambleside is *'I am, I can, I ought, I will'*, and they learn how to inculcate these things in the children they teach.

CN You promoted a universal right to education long before it was a popular idea. And in the late nineteenth century you were advocating the education of girls and women too; that mission of yours was almost an idea before its time ...

CM I saw no reason why education should be denied to anyone – rich, poor, male, female, all have the right to learn and to contribute to their society as well educated human beings. God created all human beings equal in his sight ... their intellectual and spiritual growth are as one ... and all children, whatever their backgrounds, whether girls or boys, should learn the interests, duties and joys of life, with the help of their God our Maker and Continual Helper.

CN So was it your belief in equality in God's sight that led you to push at so many boundaries? Not only did you promote education for the hitherto uneducated, but also you championed something that was still only receiving scant attention in the 1970s and 1980s, and that was work with parents on children's learning. Now I know you were also committed to helping parents support their children's learning, even teaching them at home. You gave lectures to parents too I believe?

CM Parents can teach their children very well ... You know, my ideas form the basis of a strong home education movement, even today – particularly in the United States of America, and there are many websites that seek to convey my educational philosophy and practices in the language of the twenty-first century! But I began the lectures for parents in 1885, when my vicar asked me for a donation towards the parish room fund. I offered instead to give a series of six lectures on education, which were later published in a book called *Home Education*.[61] I wrote five volumes in all between 1885 and 1905. And they were much welcomed by parents who wanted to teach their children – especially their girls – at

---

[61] C. Mason (1886) *Home Education: The Education and Training of Children Under Nine*. Oxford: The Scrivener Press.

home, and they were later very helpful in training governesses as well. Though I must say that I wanted all children to benefit – not just those born into privilege and wealth.

CN And you set up an educational group for parents? This was Bradford, wasn't it?

CM I sought advice from several knowledgeable people in the field of education and the Parents' Educational Union was established around 1886, with branches around the country. A monthly magazine began in 1890, called the *Parents' Review*. It was a busy time and there was much to do. I was trying to establish the House of Education to train teachers, and that happened in 1892, and we moved to Scale How (which was once Wordsworth's home) in 1894. Working in the training college and on the *Parents' Review* journal became my life's work. My parents taught me at home and I think it was that experience that fostered my conviction that children could and should learn at home and that parents needed guidance on how to create an education for their children; an education that was true to Pestalozzi's ideas and which also drew on Rousseau. I wanted children to learn in the world, from the real world – to use their senses, to move and to experience living things.

CN Going back to your 20 principles, you had three key ideas I think, Education is an atmosphere, a discipline, and ...

CM ... and a *life* ... When I say '*Education is an Atmosphere*' I make the point that children should learn by living in the world ... The child's own home and those people and things in that home are hugely influential in children's learning. And I am sorry to say that I disagree with Froebel's Kindergarten and also with Montessori's Children's Houses ... these thoughtful educators mean well but they cut the world down to a scale to fit the children – and this takes away freedom, and gives a somewhat false perspective on the world. Children should be free as much as possible to learn from nature. It is a wise parent who allows their child to be outdoors in nature as much as possible.[62] A mother's first duty to her children is to secure for them a quiet growing time, a full six years of passive receptive life ... the waking part of it spent for the most part out in the fresh air[63] with little interference from adults, free to learn through their senses.

---

[62] Ibid., p. 186.

[63] Ibid., p. 42.

CN You move on from exhorting 'freedom' to play and exploring outdoors uninterrupted to the idea that the discipline of habit is important. How do these two ideas fit together?

CM So, in saying *Education is a Discipline* I am saying that children need to learn good habits and discipline as well as being free to learn from nature. So it is important that only good behaviours are allowed to take root in children's brains, and these good behaviours need to become habit. And all this is possible. I am an Anglican, though I do not believe that children are born 'good' or 'bad' – for children can be helped to form good habits, starting as babies ... and this applies to all children – working and educated classes – for education is stronger than nature.[64] So discipline, cleanliness, routines for mealtimes and exercise – these are all important for infants. And later, things like table manners and politeness are essential for building good character. Now you ask where does this fit with freedom to learn from nature? Self-discipline is an important contributor to freedom.

CN I see, but it could be a tricky balance to achieve – especially when children are very young ...

CM Well they come together with my third thesis that *Education is a Life* and by that I mean that children need intellectual and moral sustenance as well as physical nutrition.[65] Our minds feed on ideas and so therefore it stands to reason that children should encounter lots of ideas in their home or school curriculum. It is not a case of giving children knowledge – but rather, as Plato might say, to be able to deal with ideas, children need a natural appetite for knowledge, which is informed with thought.[66]

CN So in their curriculum, nature plays a strong part, but you advocate learning to read and good books too, so you do see the need for balance in terms of nature and of reading books ... I mean, it's not a total outdoor classroom that you advocate is it?

CM Children should read good books, worthy books;[67] they should be read to, they should read, recount and narrate. But I do not approve of the watering down of story and language to what some think of as the 'child's level'; many 'children's books' are twaddle that leave out much of the world. Children have a right

[64] Ibid., p. 158.

[65] Mason (1923/1989: Preface).

[66] Ibid., p. 10.

[67] Ibid., p. 13.

to the best we possess; therefore their lesson books should be, as far as possible, our best books.

CN Many children's books are now of very high quality, covering a host of topics; would you keep these out of the classroom?

CM My point is that we should not limit children's learning to what adults think is fit for them at their age; we should not water it down. Living books, rather than dry textbooks, make a subject come alive for a child.

CN I have wanted to talk with you for many years, and I am so grateful to you for giving me some time today. This has been a fascinating conversation, thank you.

CM It is always interesting to talk over ideas and to invite questions that lead me to explain my beliefs and philosophy – talking over ideas helps to refine one's thoughts ...

CN You achieved so much – and it seems you never took 'no' for an answer – always found ways through. Can I ask you one more thing? It might seem trivial but I'm intrigued ... The badge on the blazer pockets that the students wore bore the words 'For the Children's Sake' – I can see that this was your guiding philosophy. But it also features a plant, what was that symbolising? Why did you choose it?

CM Ah! The humble *L'umile pianta* ... it is of the *juncus* species and on my walks in the damp fells around here I took a lesson from it. Pick it and another grows in its place, you can bend it – but it will never break ... that is why I chose it as our emblem.

Conversation 9

From God and Church to Awe and Wonder: Spirituality and Creativity in Early Childhood Education

In conversation: Cathy Nutbrown (CN) with Peter Clough (PC)

It is June 2013 – though you wouldn't know from the weather! We have spent the last few months finalising the revisions for the new edition of this book (which first appeared in 2008). This has been exciting in many ways; but perhaps less exciting are those moments when we've taken stock of developments during those five years, and realised how much there is still to secure in early years education and care. Perhaps more particularly, we have been dismayed by some of the EYEC policies that the current UK government – a coalition of Conservative and Liberal Democrat politicians – is pursuing.

We decided to keep Conversation 9 more or less in its original form – as something of an artefact in a time capsule, perhaps – and we'd encourage you to read it. We have added something of an update on developments and our responses to them. We hope that together these will give some sense of the fluidity and rapidity of social and political change ...

In this conversation we reflect on some of the motives of historical figures and of organisations and institutions which provided education in the past. We are in Cathy's office in Sheffield, surrounded by piles of history books, biographies, papers, archive material and notes. In this conversation we trace education as part of religious conviction and identify key elements which seem to them to be important lessons, and perhaps legacies, for early childhood education in the twenty-first century.

PC   I think that you can't separate the origins of education in England – early, secondary, whatever – from the motives of the church ... to provide education. That goes back to ... when? The ... 1700s? But it wasn't just about philanthropy or good works for poor people. There was a distinct enterprise on the part of the established Church to teach religion. It's here, in this note about the formation of the National Society, 1811:

> That the National Religion should be made the foundation of National Education, and should be the first and chief thing taught to the poor, according to the excellent Liturgy and Catechism provided by our Church.[68]

---

[68] http://www.churchof england.org/education/national–society.aspx# NS% 20History

CN   You can't get clearer than that! And the start of Church of England Schools, the beginning of nation-wide education … these were only picked up and supported by the State in 1870. In the UK the church was a key player in developing early education through Sunday Schools and the like … and the need to teach people to be able to read the Bible … That's a pretty big legacy, because there are now around 5,000 Church of England schools alone – I mean there are all the Roman Catholic and other faith-based schools – in England and Wales … most of them provide education for children up to 11 years … that must be around a million children just in the C of Es …

PC   Well, quite a number of organisations and movements made a real impact on faith schools, but there were some noisy individuals as well; individuals with a religious conviction or belief were also active in providing for young children. The McMillans, for example …

CN   … the McMillan sisters were surely driven by their Christian Socialist convictions – religious and political drive I think, as well as their own education and 'mission' to do something for young children in difficult home circumstances. And even Florence Nightingale had her say in her letters about what young children should be taught … where's …? Here's the copy of her letter from the archive … it's to Alice Hepworth a teacher, or 'little mother of the infants' as Nightingale puts it. She was 66 when she wrote this … listen … the whole letter, about 14 handwritten pages is about the importance of religious instruction for the 'infants' at Lea School in Derbyshire; she asks if they are going to introduce to the children 'the nice lessons practised in Thomas Street. … the little moral tales which you used to give your scholars once a week at Thomas St'. And she says:

> And would there be time now for giving the religious morning instruction in talk? Perhaps you always do this. I do not know exactly what the Infants' religious instruction is. It may be necessary to give a good deal of learning Scripture by heart. But then if Scripture is really to tell on the children's lives – the only thing that Christ cares about & that Christ came to live & die for – & still lives for – the little 'mother' must explain a good deal by little tales & illustrations"[69]

PC   Have you got the Burton one there? There's another letter to the School Master …

---

[69] Letter to Alice Hepworth, dated 9 March 1886, Clendening History of Medicine Library: http://clendening.kumc.edu/dc/fn/2hpwrth1.html

CN   To William ... it's here... to William John Prinsep Burton – his wife Mrs Adeline Burton, was the infants' Mistress, I think.[70]

I am delighted to hear the result of the School Scripture Examination – not that a Scripture Exam ensures an earnest life necessarily among the children, any more than a Grammar Exam. But it is a Master's (or a Mother's) daily Scripture lesson, from which the children learn whether he (or she) means it for their life or no – whether it is to bring in 'the kingdom' into our lives, or whether it is merely a lesson in words.[71]

PC   Fascinating ... I didn't know anything beyond the ... the medical Nightingale until you sent me that stuff; but I guess it's obvious that all her work – schools, soldiers, whatever – was all about serving God ... But this idea of religious instruction, and learning passages by heart being the most likely form of lesson for the infants, we wouldn't do that now ... and it wouldn't be wholly Christian ...

CN   It takes me back to my own days in Sunday School, learning texts by heart. But we didn't do that in school. There would be little of Nightingale's form of religious instruction now, if anything in the early years ... it would really be more about encouraging the children to develop a sense of awe and wonder about the world. Stories, moral tales ... I think that's probably true of the C of E and the RC schools up to a point ... but not the New Christian Schools, of course. The accounts in *The Love of God in the Classroom*[72] here point to an ethos and a ... a curriculum for the youngest children which works so that ...'Infants' as they call them here should 'know God through His word and His creation.'[73] Reading this – and this is ... 2005 – it's not so far away from those fundamantalist aims of Wesley.[74]

---

[70] Derbyshire transcripts of *Kelly's Directory* from *Kelly's Directory of the Counties of Derty, Notts, Leicester and Rutland* (London, May 1891), pp.183–4: http://digitalcollections.library.ubc.ca/cdm/landingpage/collection/florence

[71] Letter to Mr Burton, dated 30 August 1897.

[72] S. Baker and D. Freeman (2005) *The Love of God in the Classroom: The Story of the New Christian Schools*. Ross-Shire, Scotland: Christian Focus.

[73] Ibid., p. 93.

[74] Charles Wesley (18 December 1707–29 March 1788) was a leader of the English Methodist Church. Known for his hymn writing, Wesley travelled the country preaching to and converting thousands.

The Christian Schools have been forces for good in their neighbour-hoods in that they have often been able to help families with needy children, for whom the other schools are not working for one reason or another. Often what is needed is the loving atmosphere that a Christian school is uniquely able to provide. What better environment for any child than one where the love of Christ is known and felt? ... The lord Jesus promised that, where his people were meeting in his name, he would be present in a special way, and that is the testimony of the schools and of those who visit them.[75]

CN   And these new Christian Schools are actually very different, aren't they, from the more traditional 'faith schools' like the Church of England or the Roman Catholic schools ...

PC   That's what I was saying ... they're often worlds apart as far as the religious commitment of pupils, parents and staff is con-cerned, however explicit the traditional 'faith' schools might be about their mission ...

CN   Perhaps the point is that it's more than a curriculum, it's a mis-sion to teach children about how to live, to have a belief, a set of values ... based on a religious doctrine.

PC   But this is a long way from Nightingale's letters about scripture lessons and the pioneers of Church schools of the 1800s. I've been thinking quite a bit recently about this element of faith – well, Christianity mainly – that is so central to a lot of the think-ing of our pioneers ...Well, for some of them – and perhaps Comenius is the best example – a belief in God is absolutely central to their pedagogy ... No, more than that: for someone like Comenius you couldn't even start to talk about ECE as some-thing independent of a theology ... an expression of a Divine scheme ... the rearing of children in godly ways, yes?

CN   Yes ... he stressed the purpose of education as making humans fit to become ... like God, in a sense ... There's the bit here ... where he writes ...

[That] Children ought to be dearer to parents than gold and silver, than pearls and gems, may be discovered from a comparison between both gifts of God; for ... Gold and silver are fleeting and transitory; children an immortal inheritance.

PC   Exactly! That's what I'm saying ... God is central to the pedagogy that is being put forward. But ... suppose you don't believe in

---

[75] Baker and Freeman (2005: 16).

God – and let's face it most, well many of our students don't – then is the Comenius stuff any use? I mean if you strip out the core wiring – as it were – that carries the religious current, does his work truly have any contemporary appeal?

CN   Is there still an important pedagogy without an appeal to God? Well there must be – I've worked with countless brilliant teachers – I mean really brilliant – who are not remotely interested in religion – in fact some who were vehemently opposed ... Sort of 'Keep God out of the Classroom!' But they would all accord with Comenius' views about play and learning, about the importance of nature, his idea of 'opening up their understanding to the outer world' ... The rationale might be different, the philosophy which drives the pedagogy, but the belief in the importance of an holistic approach to pedagogy, a respect for the child, those things would be recognisable, and I think it's important in the twenty-first century to take the ideas of the past, like Christian Schiller said, and make them our own, forge new paths ... and I don't mean throw away the old stuff, but in a world where for many, many people, God is not the reason for life and living, we have to find different points of reference ... well we have to be free to do that ...

PC   Yes, I see that, and agree, I think – but perhaps some of the teachers you talk about would acknowledge something more like spirituality ... if not God and faith ...

CN   But if I think about little children, for me, it's not so much Nightingale's urge that they should learn passages of the Bible by heart, or the catechism. Although, having said that, I still recall some of the words I learned in Sunday School! For me, in present times, early childhood education should be about teaching children to wonder, to experience awe and wonder in the world, yes, a kind of spirituality in themselves, that's why I like the opening words of Blake's poem ...

To see a world in a grain of sand,

And a heaven in a wild flower,

Hold infinity in the palm of your hand,

And eternity in an hour.[76, 77]

[76] W. Blake (1917) 'Auguries of Innocence,' in C.W. Eliot (ed.) (2001) *English Poetry II from Collins to Fitzgerald*. New York: P.F. Collier and Son.

[77] And Comenius has much the same view: 'The proper education of the young does not consist in stuffing their heads with a mass of words, sentences, and

Little children can do that, they really can see a world in a grain of sand, they really can be open to the world, like leaves, and flowers ... And we interrupt them all the time ... 'hurry up, come on ...' we say. Rushing them on, when what they want to do is peer long and hard into the grass to watch an ant in the soil, or watch waves crashing on a rock ... I have a photo of a little girl holding a leaf and there's a ladybird on the leaf ... in her 3-year-old's face you can see puzzlement, intrigue, but ... yes awe and wonder ... That's what I think we need to make sure is so very present in early years provision, and it's one of the reasons why I worry so about the downward pressure of curriculum for older children which seems to have the effect of squeezing out the arts ...

PC   Hang on ... don't leave the faith thing for one moment ... Is there ... I mean whether or not we believe in God – or gods or whatever – we shouldn't throw babies out with bathwater ... there's all the aspects of culture that go with religion, and that we need to ... expose children to ... learning about different communities ...

CN   You mean the distinction between teaching a faith, and teaching about faiths? Sure ... many of those teachers who'd be opposed to any notion of God-in-the-classroom would be wholly committed to multi-culturalism ... multi-faith education, celebrating Eid or Holi or whatever ... teaching respect for different cultures ... And the importance of people, children, families of all faiths and none being informed about the practices and traditions of different faith groups. But spirituality ... that's different isn't it?

PC   It is, and there's an important point here I think. Now I know some faiths worship in very simple surroundings, in simplicity and silence in some cases. But many faiths make their places of worship awesome! Even if that is at the expense of people in the community who live in real poverty. Look at some of the cathedrals, mosques, synagogues, temples ... they are ... beacons of beauty, art, craft ... Why does the Church invest in the best of choral music? Huge organs with the most accomplished of organ scholars! Stained glass, ancient and modern, wonderful works of art, using colour and light to make you gaze, kneel in wonder ... And the vestments – the clergy adorned in gold, red, purple, heavily

ideas dragged together out of various authors, but in opening up their understanding to the outer world, so that a living stream may flow from their own minds, just as leaves, flowers, and fruit spring from the bud on a tree'. *The Great Didactic of John Amos Comenius.* Translated and edited, with biographical, historical and critical introduction by M.W. Keatinge. London: A. and C. Black, 1896.

embroidered ... So the church, high church, knows how to use colour, words, sound, music, art, touch, light and dark, scents even, to create a sense of wonder.

CN   Yes, but ... art doesn't equal spirituality... What I'd say is that building up and encouraging young children's sense of awe and wonder and creativity is a way of helping them to think and wonder and puzzle about other amazing things later ... which might be God, for that matter, but also ... other beliefs and commitments ...

Look at all the people who visit some of the famous cathedrals in the world – light candles even – many of whom declare themselves as non-religious. But what does this mean? Apart from being able to say 'I've been to Notre Dame'? The architecture, music, paintings, stained glass, sculpture – for those who created these buildings, stone by stone, year after year after year ... great monuments to the glory of God. For me, spirituality and creativity go hand in hand. That's why the arts are so important – a sort of channel of expression of what's in one's soul ... And yes, spirituality, awe and wonder can be about and connected with belief in God but they don't have to be ... And it's important that whatever a family's religious faith or non-belief might be, whatever that might be, it's important that every child's early years give them opportunities to wonder and gaze and take in amazing things ... That quote of Socrates ... 'Wisdom begins in wonder'.

PC   Learning begins with ... little children being fascinated with their world?

CN   I think what matters most of all is that we be aware of some reason for doing what we do; not 'Well, we do it this way because that's how it's done here ...', or 'because that's how I was taught to do it in college... ' – but 'We do it this way because we believe that children learn better if ...' or 'We do it this way because research shows that children ...'. You know? You should be able to justify everything – I mean every single thing – you do when you work with children ...

PC   You mean like a ... a fully-worked out theory? A philosophy?

CN   Yes ... and for Christian-based education it's underpinned by 'Jesus said: Suffer the little children to come unto me, for of such is the Kingdom of Heaven'; and then there's St Paul: 'When I was a child I spoke as a child ... But when I became a man I put away childish things'. These two texts collide really ... Christ saying children are perfect ... Paul saying that the aim is to get through childhood and grow up! But I can see how approaches to teaching young children could be based on views of childhood such as these. And how you see children, no matter how that view is derived, will determine (to some extent) the shape of provision and practice, and research for that matter.

PC   You mean it could be based on a political view of childhood?

CN   Well, any view must be! But rather the need for a distinct way of looking at things and a means of justifying one's thinking and practice. Practice has to be based on something, belief in some-thing and for some it's belief in God, for others, social justice ... for some it's both ...

PC   So, how do you get, in your thinking, from God and church to your position on 'awe and wonder' being the approach to devel-oping ... or perhaps I should say supporting ... young children's spirituality?

CN   Well, I was reading about Van Gogh and Hepworth the other day and ... Van Gogh's famous words about creativity when he said: 'I can very well do without God both in my life and in my paint-ings, but I cannot, ill as I am, do without something which is greater than I, which is my life, the power to create'. And then Hepworth who wrote of the importance of her childhood to the development of her ideas: 'Perhaps what one wants to say is formed in childhood and one spends the rest of one's life trying to say it'. If I put these two things together I come up with a view of how important creativity, the arts are to the human spirit.

PC   And you wouldn't be alone there ... Steiner's writing ... here 'A sense for what is noble and beautiful awakes love for what is worthy of love. But what strengthens the will is religion; it must permeate the teaching of every subject'[78]. He goes on to say ... 'We enter earthly existence through birth and there a creative and productive spirituality takes over the formative material of heredity before we can develop concepts. Only later is the conscious soul added'.[79]

CN   Well, maybe I'm trying to put too many things together, but I do think that spirituality is not necessarily dependent on belief in God or in holding a religious faith. Many would not disagree with me ... What I'm trying to get at in terms of the arts is the way they offer opportunity for young children to experience 'creation' ... Those who have pioneered the arts in education haven't done so

---

[78] Steiner, *The Kingdom of Childhood*, 1995, p.69.

[79] Ibid., p. 112.

on an 'Arts for Arts sake' pitch. They've pointed to learning, to self-confidence, to the capacity of the arts to open up young minds to a different kind of thinking. But I want to say *without art we die!* Yes *'Without art we die'*. Human beings have to make their mark, draw, dance, sing ... and it's inside us ... some are better at it than others, but all children (unless they have damage or difficulty in their lives), all children want to dance, paint, sing, make noise, make marks – it's only adults who sometimes suppress this very natural urge. I recall being in the Ulster Museum in Belfast in 2005 with Elliot Eisner and we were looking at some beautifully crafted Egyptian hair ornaments and other jewellery, and he said to me, 'Why do you suppose people make these things?' I didn't realise what he was getting at immediately ... then he said, with that very thoughtful tone of his ... 'Because it reminds them that they are human beings'. Human beings must create ... Early education needs to adopt a pedagogy of the arts.

PC   A pedagogy of the arts ... and part of your rationale for that is to foster spirituality ...?

CN   To foster awe and wonder, and within that, support the development of children as spiritual people yes ... HMI,[80] the 'old' pre-Ofsted HMI – the real Her Majesty's Inspectors were so good at promoting the arts ... Think of Christian Schiller ...

PC   And the work of Robin Tanner ... 'If those we teach are potentially creative they deserve to be taught by artists and craftsmen ...' (Tanner, 1989). And Sir Alec Clegg, when you start to think about it all it's quite incredible, the things that were achieved only a few decades ago ... And how regimes and policies can shift emphases in education so rapidly, and even make us forget those deeply significant contributions to teaching and learning ... So how would you sum this up, Cathy? How do we achieve an approach to early childhood education which builds on the best of its roots, adapts to modern times and needs, and still gives children a sense of humanity, awe, wonder, helps them to become spiritually aware people?

CN   I think it is important that people who work with young children, really understand pedagogy. They need to understand theories of learning, the important role of the arts, child development, and they need also to be creative and thoughtful human beings themselves.

PC   Creative pedagogy leads to creative classrooms as Alec Clegg would say ...

---

[80] Her Majesty's Inspectorate (of Schools).

CN   Yes – yes, exactly that – and really well qualified, well educated and well supported early years practitioners and nursery teachers.

PC   And beginning to develop, in children a simplicity of faith and belief, so that we can really talk about respect for young children's approach to understanding the world ... and I could quote more of Blake's 'Auguries of Innocence'(if I could remember it!):

> *He who respects the infant's faith*
>
> *Triumphs over hell and death.*
>
> *The child's toys and the old man's reasons*
>
> *Are the ... [Something ...] fruits...*

PC/CN   'Are the fruits of the two seasons'.

Part 4

Linking the Past with the Present

In this final part of the book we bring together the present with the past and look at the relation of contemporary issues and policies with their historical precedents. We reflect on some of the important contemporary issues of the early twenty-first century which affect early childhood education and care and the nature of the concerns that affected earlier generations.

Navigating policy and remaining aware of multiple policy developments is a full-time task, and unravelling the complex policy connections to reach the heart of an issue, and then relate it to practice, is a challenge of a scale that has never before existed. Our predecessors did not have the weight of policy that exists now and neither did they have instant access to numerous and frequently changing policy statements and guidance that are now available through government websites. In the twenty-first century policy shifts and communication of those policies are faster and more detailed than ever before.

We identify eight themes that we see as recurring, in differing forms and with differing emphases, throughout the book; these are:

1. Children's rights
2. The arts and creativity
3. Literacy
4. Play, learning and pedagogy
5. Early intervention
6. Home learning and parents
7. Inclusion
8. Professional development and training

In the pages that follow we take each of the above issues in turn and reflect on some recent events, research and policies. These reflections are followed by another look back to the less recent past to identify the work of those who might be seen – however anachronistically – as having been motivated by those issues.

1. Children's rights

Current policy and practice in children's rights in the early years

The UN Convention on the Rights of the Child (UNCRC) lists 54 Articles of Rights which are designed to prevent illness and neglect; provide education; protect children from abuse and exploitation; and ensure participation in decisions that affect them.

Issues of children's rights have gained currency in the last 50 years, beginning with the *Declaration of Rights of the Child* by the General Assembly of the United Nations on 20 November 1959. Subsequently, the United Nations Convention on the Rights of the Child was established by the United Nations in 1989. The 1959 Declaration established 10 principles which laid down rights to which the UN said children should be entitled:

The right to:

1. Equality, regardless of race, colour, religion, sex or nationality
2. Healthy mental and physical development
3. A name and a nationality
4. Sufficient food, housing and medical care
5. Special care if handicapped (sic)
6. Love, understanding and care
7. Free education, play and recreation
8. Immediate aid in the event of disasters and emergencies
9. Protection from cruelty, neglect and exploitation
10. Protection from persecution and to an upbringing in the spirit of worldwide brotherhood and peace.

The language of the Declaration of 1959 is somewhat changed in the Convention of 1989, where 54 detailed Articles define the range of children's rights under four categories. The Convention states children's rights to:

1. *Prevention* (of illness and neglect)
2. *Provision* (of education with specific references to children who are disabled)
3. *Protection* (from abuse and exploitation)
4. *Participation* (in decisions which affect them)

The issues covered under the theme of 'children's rights' are very wide ranging and, internationally, focus on issues which include such topics as: corporal punishment, child poverty, legislation, child labour, child health (including immunisation, food and the environment). Children whose families are refugees or asylum seekers also have these rights when in a country which is a signatory to the Convention, and thus controversy arises when children in such circumstances are not treated according to their rights. Recently, disputes over hospital treatment, allocation of school places and housing have been brought to court on the basis of contravention of the UNCRC.

Recent policy in the UK has addressed issues of rights in relation to protection through the *Every Child Matters* initiative (DfES, 2005), the *National Childcare Strategy* in 1998, *Sure Start* (DfEE, 1999), *The Ten Year Childcare Strategy* (DfES, 2004), integrated services of protection, health and education, and the *Early Years Foundation Stage* (DfES, 2007) which was revised in 2012 (DfE). Within these wide-ranging policy initiatives many issues of rights are addressed but concerns about rights are also perpetuated.

Of course, issues of 'rights' have been variously embraced and disputed and different countries take a range of views, as do institutions and individuals. However, where a country is a signatory to the UNCRC, it is required to adhere to, promote and report on progress in implementing the Convention. Despite the almost global ratification of the Convention, and the responsibility of governments to enshrine children's rights in legislation, there remain difficulties and, as UNICEF points out:

> Despite the existence of rights, children suffer from poverty, homelessness, abuse, neglect, preventable diseases, unequal access to education and justice systems that do not recognize their special needs. These are problems that occur in both industrialized and developing countries. ... The task, however, must engage not just governments but all members of society. The standards and principles articulated in the Convention can only become a reality when they are respected by everyone – within the family, in schools and other institutions that provide services for children, in communities and at all levels of administration. (UNICEF, 2005)

In December 2010, the then Minister for Children and Families, Sarah Teather, pledged, in a written statement, that the government would give 'due consideration' to the Convention whenever making new law and policy. The Ministerial Code refers to the 'overarching duty on Ministers to comply with the law including international law'. Governments must report on their progress on children's rights to the Committee on the Rights of the Child every five years. The UK government reported to the Committee in 1995, 2002 and 2008; concluding observations in the 2008 report said that income poverty is strongly associated with a range of other disadvantages and noted that children in poverty are more likely to have poor educational and health outcomes than other children. In October 2008 the UNCRC made 118 recommendations for improving the promotion and protection of children's rights in England.

Having signalled the ill effects of living in poverty in 2008, the 2011 midterm report on progress in children's rights, from the UK Children's Commissioners, reiterated their concerns that children in poverty are:

> ... more likely to live in areas where they have limited access to services and to play and leisure opportunities. Their parents are more likely to be experiencing poor mental health, poor physical health, to be disabled or caring for a disabled relative, and to be out of work or in poorly paid work. These issues are both causes and outcomes of poverty, and impact both on children's lives in a very immediate way, as well as on the future life chances of children experiencing persistent poverty. (UK Children's Commissioners, 2011: 29)

The report (2011) also signalled a new area of concern around the policy of 'Payment by Results', a policy that has surfaced again from the depths of history.

A Save the Children study of young children's rights (Alderson, 2008) examined children's involvement in decisions which affected them. Based in the UK, the study showed how children's contributions were often unrecognised by adults – and how many adults, due largely to their desire to protect children from danger – denied children basic freedoms to play, to be with their friends and play in the park, for example. Alderson (2008) gives many examples of young children participating in decisions about their lives such as: suggesting ideas for the development of play facilities, buildings and menus and getting involved in strategies to resolve bullying. Considering children's rights in the twenty-first century, Alderson (2008: 215) writes:

> With greater respect for children, there will be greater justice, care that is more deeply informed by children's views and interests, and awareness of the major contributions children can make.

There are examples of practice where children's rights are a fundamental and guiding principle of curriculum and pedagogy. Such an example can be found in the infant-toddler centres and preschools in Reggio Emilia in Northern Italy. Central concerns expressed by its founder Malaguzzi, are:

> The rights of children: the fact that the rights of children are recognised as the rights of all children is the sign of a more accomplished humanity;

> The rights of teachers: for the teachers, each and every one of them, it is a condition that enhances communication and the comparison of ideas and experiences, all of which enrich the tools of professional evaluation;
>
> The rights of parents: participation and research are, in fact, two terms that sum-marise much of the overall conception of our educational theory. These two terms might also be seen as the best prerequisites for initiating and maintaining a cooperative understanding between parents and teachers, with all the value that is added to the educational prospects of the children. (Malaguzzi 1996: 2)

A second example is found in daily practice; that is to say, that although governments which have signed the UNCRC thus formally declare their commitment to it, much of the reality of putting children's rights into practice lies in the hands of individual practitioners. This draws attention to the fact that whilst there are obligations on governments, 'there are responsibilities for every adult citizen too' (Nutbrown, 1996: 108).

Such arguments continue to be made, with concerns that too great a focus is still being placed on the principles of the UNCRC, and too little on development and progress at a more local level (Veernam and Levine, 2000). The responsibility of government and of citizens was stressed by the Children's Commissioners in their most recent report on progress in children's rights in the UK (2011).

Some roots of children's rights

Some may imagine that the idea of rights for children is a new and modern concept. But if we look back through time we can see how, using different forms of expression, the idea that children should have rights is not new.

Perhaps Comenius' position, in the 1600s, on how children should be educated could be viewed as an issue of 'rights' because, for him, the child was God-given and therefore should be treated as such; in this sense the child's rights were God-given. Rousseau's notion of the protection of Emile until he was able to think for himself carried underpinnings of this 'ideal' state of education for young children, and whilst he views the education of girls as different from that of boys (because they were being educated towards different 'ends'), he nevertheless held the view that girls too should receive education.

A clear example of education as a matter of social justice is to be found in the work of Pestalozzi, who, between 1804 and 1806, established schools for underprivileged and abandoned boys and girls, in the belief that education was a key component in improving conditions in society. His direct work with children, including those with learning impairments, is paralleled with another significant achievement in terms of his approach to early education generally: he advocated an education of the 'whole' child where teachers were 'sympathetic' towards young children and where children were not forced to conform to adult wishes or ideals. His ideas were developed by Froebel, who also stressed appropriate ways of working with children, and he could be said to be a proponent of a child's 'right to play'.

Similarly, Robert Owen's approach, also in the early 1800s, was to see young children's education as something which formed a part of society as a whole, and fitted with concerns about housing, work and health care. His early ban on corporal punishment would perhaps amaze those who today still regard smacking by parents as an appropriate response to 'bad' behaviour. His insistence that teachers treat pupils well could be interpreted as a view that educators should 'respect' their pupils. A similar example of these concerns is found in Rachel and Margaret McMillan who worked in the early 1900s to combat ill-health and poverty. They provided clinics and centres for children living in the slums of Bradford and in London; their work was self-consciously politically driven, and based on a premise that children's success in education and good health were directly linked.

Of all those whose lives and work we have reflected on in this book, it is the work of Charlotte Mason, born in 1842, that carries the clearest connection to issues of children's rights; her 20 'Articles of Education' have also been referred to as a child's 'Bill of Rights'. Mason's work was based on the ideas of Rousseau and Pestalozzi and she developed her own distinctive philosophy of education in which she spelled out exactly how education should be for young children. She described education as 'an atmosphere', by which she meant that children should be part of the real world and not isolated or separated from adults and their daily work and routines. She argued that 'it stultifies a child to bring down his world to the "child's level"' (1923). This was in clear opposition to the work of Froebel and Montessori who were in favour of creating 'scaled-down' child-size environments in their Kindergarten and Children's Houses, and is also, no doubt, something which would challenge aspects of current policies and the practices of many in the Early Years Foundation Stage. Her view was that children should learn through living, that parents should play a central part in their children's early learning – including reading with them, and reading 'good' literature – and that the outdoor world was the best classroom. Her final publication, written in 1923, shortly before her death at the age of 81, includes these words:

> The claims of the schoolroom should not be allowed to encroach on the child's right to long hours daily of exercise and investigation.

> Children have a right to the best we possess; therefore their lesson books should be, as far as possible, our best books.

> They require a great variety of knowledge – about religion, the humanities, science and art.

Reading Charlotte Mason's writings leave the impression of a woman whose ideas were distinctly ahead of her time and, despite the different forms of expression, there is much here which can be clearly identified as a pedagogy of rights; her views anticipate contemporary calls for greater curriculum freedom and the opportunity to play outdoors.

2. The arts and creativity

Current policy and practice in relation to present understanding around the arts and creativity in the early years

If we look to developments in Europe, we can see in Scandinavia and in Northern Italy, for example, how a focus on the arts can enhance children's learning in all aspects of their development. The now familiar work of Reggio Emilia (Reggio Children, 1995) demonstrates how arts-based curricula and experienced support from artists can give rise to learning in all aspects of an early years curriculum. Such projects promote sustained shared thinking and foster children's learning 'in community'. In Sweden, a physical environment and adult involvement which stimulates and enables children's dramatic play has been shown to enhance young children's imaginations and involvement (Lindqvist, 2001).

Engaging in creative arts experiences is important for the sheer joy it can bring, part of which is the self- and shared expression that is enabled through creative processes. But although creative arts experiences have been shown to impact on cognitive, social and emotional development (Deans and Brown, 2005; Reggio Children, 1995; Nutbrown and Jones, 2006) the arts are suffering. In England we have seen reductions in funding for the arts, year on year, risking a narrowing of opportunities for children and their families to enjoy the arts in their leisure time. The arts are suffering in the early years (birth to 5) and in primary schools too, often being regarded as of lesser value than the sciences and mathematics and, perhaps, something to be kept for leisure time.

However, from a widely shared view of the arts as co-foundational of our humanity (Dissanayake, 1990, 1995, 2000; Eisner, 2002), we see them as an inalienable feature of young children's learning and development; as Dissanayake wrote:

> Viewing the species Homo sapiens as it evolves and expresses a behaviour of art is a way of understanding ourselves and the modern condition humaine. (Dissanayake, 1990: xi)

Discussing the inseparability of the arts from notions of human-being, Dissanayake (2001) suggests that infants are born with *aesthetic incunabula*, a sort of 'swaddling' which makes the emotional effects of the arts discernible from the earliest months. The human need to seek out and organise through the aesthetic is what Clough (2002) calls an 'aesthetic attending', the way in which, as a condition of being in the world, we attend – through the senses – to the 'objects' we encounter. So, the youngest of human beings engage with the world first through an innate aesthetic attending, through their senses, and because babies are sensory beings (Trevarthen, 1984; Goldschmeid and Jackson, 1999), they seek experiences which smell, or taste, or feel, or sound or look pleasing, because sense craves satisfaction.

Early education must pay due regard to the human need, in *all* young children, for aesthetics in the design of inclusive curricula. And this argument is not simply an academic or historical one – it is also a matter of rights. For the UNCRC, Article 31 states:

> That every child has the right to rest and leisure, to engage in play and recreational activities appropriate to the age of the child and to participate freely in cultural life and the arts.

> That member governments shall respect and promote the right of the child to participate fully in cultural and artistic life and shall encourage the provision of appropriate and equal opportunities for cultural, artistic, recreational and leisure activity. (United Nations, 1989)

One explanation of the decimation of arts curricula in many schools (NACCCE, 1999; Chapman, 2004) is the redistribution of timetabling in response to concerns about underachievement in English and maths (the so-called 'basics'). However, developments in Scandinavia (Barratt, 2006; Hopperstad, 2008a, 2008b; Pramling Samuelsson et al., 2009) in Northern Italy (Reggio Children, 1995) and in Melbourne, Australia (Deans and Brown, 2005) show how, far from inhibiting children's achievement in the 'basics', a focus on the arts positively and disproportionately enhances this and other aspects of their development. The work of Reggio Emilia (Filippini and Vecchi, 1996) has long demonstrated how an arts-based curriculum and the involvement of experienced artists, as well as teachers, can give rise to many forms and foci of learning in the early years; and in the UK, a number of arts-based learning projects have shown how the involvement of artists can enhance the early years curriculum (Gillespie, 2006; Brown et al., 2010; Hallowes, 2013). Such claims rest ultimately on the considered and life-long observations of scholars such as Gardner (1989; 1990) and Eisner (2002; 2004) who have shown how young children *need* the arts to help them learn central lessons in life; how, for example, to communicate ideas, collaborate with others, persist with a problem, deal with disappointment, and enjoy the support of peers and adults (Nutbrown and Jones, 2006).

Internationally, research into aspects of arts-based learning often focuses more specifically on the practice of elements of particular skills in the arts, rather than the experience and more holistic development and understanding of music per se (Young, 2008) for which they are 'wired from birth' (Trehub, 2003, 3). We know little about the place of dance in early years curricula (Bannon and Sanderson, 2000), and the use of the arts generally in the early years appears to be a 'means to ends'. Art forms such as poetry, dance and graphic arts are sometimes used as vehicles through which other things are taught, rather than experiences of learning in their own right (Brown et al., 2010).

Projects closer to home have confirmed that the youngest children can respond to, and enjoy, involvement in the arts. Work at Tate Britain for children under 3 and their parents has shown how artist involvement can open up new avenues for parents to explore and enjoy the arts with their young children (Hancock and Cox, 2002). We know also of the importance of talk in early years settings, and recent research demonstrates the centrality of oracy and storytelling in the early years curriculum (Harrett, 2001). Arts-based learning projects, including work funded through the now disbanded Creative Partnerships, have shown that even short-term involvement of artists can enhance the early years curriculum (Gillespie, 2006), and current policy acknowledges the place of the arts in young children's learning (EYFS, DFE, 2012). However, many practitioners are ill equipped and under resourced to offer truly inspiring arts experiences for young children to enjoy and learn from.

What policies have brought us to our current situation? During the 1990s the place of the arts and of creativity in schooling generally suffered in favour of a notion of education founded on the 'basics', which were given prominence by the introduction of the National Curriculum (1989) and later by the Foundation Stage (2000) and Baseline Assessment (1997). Together these policy initiatives had the effect in many settings of squeezing out (or seriously limiting) children's experiences of the arts – even in the early years. Alert to the difficulties this was causing and aware of the potential dangers which may occur as a result of a narrow curriculum, the National Advisory Committee on Creative and Cultural Education was set up in May 1999 to make recommendations to government on:

> ... the creative and cultural development of young people through formal and informal education: [and] to take stock of current provision and ... make proposals for principles, policies and practice. (NACCCE, 1999 p.iv)

The report recommended arts provision in education, formal and informal, for young people to the age of 16 and a wider national strategy for creative and cultural education. Importantly, the report said:

We are not advocating creative and cultural education as alternatives to literacy and numeracy, but as equally relevant to the needs of this and of future generations. We support the need for high standards of literacy and numeracy. These are important in themselves. They can also enhance creative abilities: equally creative teaching and learning can enhance literacy and numeracy. These are complementary abilities, not opposing objectives. The Government and the vast majority of people in education recognise this. (NACCCE, 1999: 13)

Recommendations included: raising the priority given to creative and cultural education; revising the National Curriculum from 2000; and ensuring 'that teachers and other professionals are encouraged and trained to use methods and materials that facilitate the development of young people's creative abilities and cultural understanding' (NACCCE, 1999: 197).

It was arguably the recommendation for partnership that led to a more embedded approach to the arts and creativity in recent years:

... the development of partnerships between schools and outside agencies ... are now essential to provide the kinds of creative and cultural education that young people need and deserve (NACCCE, 1999: 199)

This, among other initiatives, led to the development with the Arts Council of the Creative Partnerships[1] initiative which successfully promoted creativity and the arts in education settings and beyond.

It is not yet the case that the place of arts and creativity is secure in the early years, even though policy currently promotes the arts alongside more traditional 'academic' subjects such as literacy, numeracy and the sciences under the heading 'Expressive arts and design'. This is the curriculum for this specific area of learning:

Exploring and using media and materials: children sing songs, make music and dance, and experiment with ways of changing them. They safely use and explore a variety of materials, tools and techniques, experimenting with colour, design, texture, form and function.

Being imaginative: children use what they have learnt about media and materials in original ways, thinking about uses and purposes. They represent their own ideas, thoughts and feelings through design and technology, art, music, dance, role-play and stories. (DfE, 2012: 9)

This is a somewhat narrow view of 'expressive arts' and though further non-statutory guidance is given, the importance of experiencing the arts is missed.

---

[1] Creative Partnerships was the Labour Government's creativity programme for schools and young people, managed by Arts Council England and funded by the DfES and DCMS. http://www.creative-partnerships.com/

Some roots of present understanding around the arts and creativity in the early years

Of course, seeing the possibilities of song, dance, music, drama, paint, sculpture and story-telling for enhanced teaching and learning is not a new phenomenon. Valuing the aesthetic can be traced in the work of Comenius, Rousseau, Froebel, Pestalozzi and Owen, where rhyme, verse, song and story-telling were regarded as important to young children's development. It has been recognised by many that inclusion of the arts in curricula also helps young children to develop vital aesthetic appreciation which is so much part of their humanity (Dewey, 1902; Gardner, 1989; Dissanayake, 1995; Eisner, 2002).

The Creative Partnerships initiative did, without doubt, achieve great success in promoting the arts and creativity, but it is difficult to see what tangible increments remain. There *is* a legacy of vision and purpose to inherit, however, and a secure platform on which to rebuild the arts in early education. Between 1895 and 1909 three boys were born who were, in their adult lives, to affect education and the arts in England in a way that no one had done before. Informed, no doubt, by the work of Rousseau, Pestalozzi and Froebel, from the 1920s onwards Christian Schiller, Robin Tanner and Alec Clegg promoted a radical change to include the arts in primary education.

From around 1930, Alec Clegg emphasised the importance of creativity in education, and pioneered in-service courses for teachers. Between 1930 and 1974 he personally visited many hundreds of schools, talking with teachers about their work and developing an extensive collection of children's artwork. He noted that:

> ...there are two kinds of education: the education of the mind by imparting facts and teaching skills, and the education of the spirit, and the material to be worked on here is the child's loves and hates, his hopes and fears, or in other terms, his courage, his integrity, his compassion and other great human qualities. (After-dinner speech, Making the Whole World Wonder, Bingley College of Education, 3 August 1972)

In his book *Excitement of Writing* (1964), Alec Clegg wrote:

> Children learn mostly from that which is around them, and from the use of the senses. These impressions so gained will depend a great deal on interests which will vary considerably. If children are interested they will listen more carefully, look more closely and touch more sensitively. With interest there is created the element of wonder, the most precious element of life. (Clegg, 1964: 33)

Clegg's innovative and less constrained outlook on learning situations for children inspired many teachers. Similarly, HMIs Robin Tanner and

Christian Schiller worked from the 1930s onwards, promoting creative and undoubtedly 'progressive' approaches to education, often through residential courses for teachers which were at the time run by HMI and funded by the Department for Education and Science. In a lecture given to the Plowden Conference in 1977, Tanner describes his partnership with Schiller:

> ... at a course for teachers in Chester I met and listened to a colleague who was to teach me more than any other – indeed, who has taught England more about Primary Education than anyone else in this century – Christian Schiller ... To him it seemed obvious that the education of children should be centred upon them ... Schiller insisted that in order to learn and grow children must move, try out their powers, explore and find out for themselves. (Tanner, 1977: 7)

Perhaps it was Schiller's influence that led Tanner to argue so strongly for a curriculum which allowed children to create. He wrote:

> If we need scientists and technologists we need also gardeners, and carpenters, tailors, artists, postmen, writers, dancers, clerks and booksellers. Man cannot live by bread alone! ... I would emphasise that in young children there is a timeless, primitive, elemental simplicity that it would be folly to try to pass by. And it is children's sense of awe and wonder at the phenomena of the natural world that should be at the root of their scientific investigations. The other world will all too quickly teach them the rest!... In every school education should be primarily through the arts. (Tanner, 1977: 13)

These voices are part of a chorus, heard variously throughout this book, which promotes creativity and discovery as inalienable to young children's learning.

3. Literacy

Current policy and practice in literacy in the early years

Until the 1970s early literacy development was effectively overlooked and Nursery education tended to focus simply on oral language and story-telling. Literacy only properly became part of the early years curriculum during the 1980s with the growth of research in *emergent literacy*, and a shift from a belief that literacy learning at too young an age could be harmful; this gave way to the development of practices which incorporated meaningful literacy activities – based on children's everyday lives – into the curriculum. New ways of teaching literacy were developed during the 1980s as researchers and teachers became more aware of *how* children learned about writing and reading. These changes were also incorporated (to some extent) in the new English National Curriculum in 1988 (DES, 1988). Since then, developments have been rapid and now it would be difficult to find settings where literacy is not a key element of the curriculum. Children are also encouraged to use reading and writing in many aspects of their play. The Foundation Stage (QCA, 2000) promoted the incorporation of aspects of literacy learning through play and required the assessment of literacy according to elements on an assessment scale for *Communication, Language and Literacy* which measured: language for communication and thinking; linking sounds and letters; reading; and writing. Assessed elements included: phonic knowledge to read simple regular words; understanding of the elements of stories, such as main character, sequence of events and openings; and writing for a variety of purposes, using features of different forms (DfES/QCA, 2003).

The most recent curriculum for early years, the Early Years Foundation Stage in England (DfE, 2012: 6–7), sets out *Communication and Language* as a *Prime Area of Learning*, with literacy as a *Specific Area of Learning*.

The objectives are thus:

Educational programmes must involve activities and experiences for children, as follows.

• **Communication and language** development involves giving children opportunities to experience a rich language environment; to develop their confidence and skills in expressing themselves; and to speak and listen in a range of situations. (DfE, 2012: 6, para 1.6)

This involves:

Listening and attention: children listen attentively in a range of situations. They listen to stories, accurately anticipating key events and respond to what they hear with relevant comments, questions or actions. They give their attention to what others say and respond appropriately, while engaged in another activity.

Understanding: children follow instructions involving several ideas or actions. They answer 'how' and 'why' questions about their experiences and in response to stories or events.

…

Speaking: children express themselves effectively, showing awareness of listeners' needs. They use past, present and future forms accurately when talking about events that have happened or are to happen in the future. They develop their own narratives and explanations by connecting ideas or events. (DfE, 2012: 6–7)

Literacy is described thus:

> **Literacy** development involves encouraging children to link sounds and letters and to begin to read and write. Children must be given access to a wide range of reading materials (books, poems, and other written materials) to ignite their interest. (DfE, 2012: 6)

This involves:

> **Reading:** children read and understand simple sentences. They use phonic knowledge to decode regular words and read them aloud accurately. They also read some common irregular words. They demonstrate understanding when talking with others about what they have read.

> **Writing:** children use their phonic knowledge to write words in ways which match their spoken sounds. They also write some irregular common words. They write simple sentences which can be read by themselves and others. Some words are spelt correctly and others are phonetically plausible. (DfE, 2012: 9)

There is little here to indicate the importance of excitement and pleasure in the written word.

All around children in much of the world print abounds, on clothing, buildings, packaging, household equipment, mobile phones, Ipads, laptops, and so on. It may be temporary and ever-changing, as with electronic billboards and digital screens in shopping centres, cars and transport depots (bus and rail stations and airports, for example). Context-based print, such as that found on household packaging and shop signs, is meaningful to young children and has a place in their reading development as children draw meaning from familiar symbols in their environment (Goodman et al., 1978; Hiebert, 1981). It has been suggested that reading begins the moment young children become aware of environmental print (Smith, 1976), and many children develop a sense of such print awareness long before going to school (Goodman, 1980; Burke, 1982). Environmental print can stimulate talk about literacy as children ask questions such as 'What does that say'? It also prompts children, at times, to pick out and identify from signs, some letters that are familiar to them, perhaps in their own name. Environmental print can stimulate some children to write, with children often imitating the writing they see, such as notices or notes left for others.

Access to good quality books, both children's fiction and non-fiction material, is essential if children are to build an adequate foundation of reading in their early years. Aspects such as the quality of illustration or the overall quality of the story and look of a book are matters for personal judgements, but if children are introduced to books that represent the best in children's publishing they are more likely to want to use them, to turn the pages, to look at the pictures and listen to the story, and to return to the book again later.

Children absorb messages very quickly, both positive and negative, and so the literature offered to children and taken into homes needs to be selected so that it offers positive images of all members of society, of a variety of cultures and of both male and female protagonists. The first encounter with a particular book is important, and the cover, the feel, size, shape, as well as content, make a difference to whether children and parents are attracted to read it or not. Meek (1982) argued that children and parents reading books and stories *together* is the fundamental cornerstone of reading. In recent years there has been a growth of literature for children based on the popular culture of the time. Books related to children's television programmes and films abound and numerous related comics for children are available in most newsagents. Marsh (2005a) has argued that literacy related to children's popular culture should be valued and children's use of texts in comics, film- and TV-related story books, television and other multi-media literacies should be a part of children's literacy repertoires.

Some studies (Bissex, 1980; Baghban, 1984; Payton, 1984; Schickedanz, 1990) have provided useful insights into the fine detail of children's early literacy achievements and patterns of learning. Research into children's early mark-making (Goodman, 1980; Harste et al., 1984; Ross and Brondy, 1987; Ferrerio and Teberosky, 1989) challenged the earlier belief that children could not and should not write until they went to school. As more was understood about 'emergent' or 'developmental' writing, teachers in the early years began to watch what children were doing and incorporate provision and support for such writing behaviours and interests into the pre-school curriculum. Ferrerio and Teberosky's (1989) work focused on the hypotheses about writing which children generated for themselves as they tried to understand writing rules and conventions. The children in their study explored various ideas and hypotheses about writing: writing, they argue, does not depend on graphic skill – the ability to make letters look conventional – but on the level of conceptualisation about writing; that is, the set of hypotheses they have explored for the purpose of understanding writing.

Three aspects of oral language appear to be key to children's literacy learning and development: story-telling, phonological awareness and 'talk about literacy'. Goswami and Bryant (1990) and Maclean et al. (1987) have identified the importance of *phonological awareness* in children's literacy development. Goswami and Bryant (1990) suggested that the important thing for children to be aware of is what they call *onset* and *rime* in spoken words, 'onset' being the beginning sound and 'rime' being the end sound of a word. Their work highlights this importance of *alliteration* and *rhyme*, thus showing the role of nursery rhymes in early literacy development. Goswami and Bryant (1990) showed that children who are aware of onset and rime find learning to read easier. Maclean et al. (1987) found that preschool children's knowledge of nursery rhymes predicted later reading success in school.

Wells' (1987) longitudinal study of children's language in the home identified key experiences. He found that the best predictor of children's reading attainment in school was a measure of what he termed 'knowledge of literacy' at school entry. Foremost of all of the activities found to be important to later literacy achievement was *listening to stories read aloud*. Wells suggested that this was because it extended experience and vocabulary; increased conversation with adults; validated the children's own 'inner storying'; and enabled children to use language to *create worlds*.

The place of new media and popular culture in children's early literacy development has attracted interest in the last decade. Television programmes often have accompanying merchandise: dolls, figures, books or comics, lunch boxes, t-shirts, bed covers, wallpaper, and so on (Kenway and Bullen, 2001). The force of popular culture in the development of children's literacy was highlighted by Dyson, who shows how television 'superheroes' can fuel children's writing (Dyson, 1997, 2002), while Marsh (2005b) has demonstrated the skill of children who use digital texts of all kinds.

Some roots of early literacy

In 1658 Comenius published *Orbis Sensualium Pictus*, believed to be the first picture book for children. Robert Owen from 1816 placed an emphasis on books and reading. Charlotte Mason, working from around 1860, believed that books had a central role in the education of young children but that they should be the best books, not 'twaddle' (her word!) which reduced the world to a simple form, but books which told stories of life and told them well. She might even be seen as the first to champion the cause of the 'real books' movement which became popular in the 1970s.

Religion played a large part in teaching reading and Sunday Schools were set up for the education of the poor, mainly to teach them to read the Bible (though not to write, since it was not desirable for the poor to be able to express their ideas). Robert Raikes is widely acknowledged for his work in establishing Sunday Schools in the 1780s, for adults as well as children. Raikes was editor of the *Gloucester Journal*, and following an article in 1783, the number of Sunday Schools grew, supported in 1785 by the national Sunday School Society. By 1784 there were some 1,800 Sunday School pupils in Manchester, Salford and Leeds (Kelly, 1970).

But perhaps a lasting legacy in terms of promoting literacy and providing regular and free access to books of all kinds comes from William Ewart, a politician who, in 1850, introduced a Bill to parliament which paved the way for 'free libraries' funded by local council rates. Libraries have, over the decades, suffered threats of closure – and this continues at the time of writing with Coalition Government cuts in spending leading many Local Authorities to close some library services. Whilst the free status of libraries remains, their role in providing books and other sources of (and access to) information continues to support study and leisure reading. Public libraries and children's librarians have done much to foster young children's love of books and reading.

There have been other identifiable points of influence on the teaching of literacy over the years. Marion Richardson was an HMI of Art who developed in 1935 the eponymous system for teaching handwriting in primary schools (Richardson, 1935). Later, in the 1960s, attempts were made to make the teaching of reading to infants less difficult through the development of the 'Initial Teaching Alphabet' (ita) by Sir James Pitman, grandson of the inventor of Pitman shorthand. Whilst some schools used this system, it never became an established method of teaching.

Because literacy is so important to learning it remains inseparable from many concerns of early learning.

4. Play, learning and pedagogy

Current policy and practice in learning and pedagogy in the early years

Defining play is problematic, though the word 'play' is used liberally and with the assumption that its meaning is understood. Play has, in turn, been heralded as the essential means through which children learn (Hutt et al., 1983), and then reprioritised in favour of ensuring that young children should 'work' in school. In the introduction to their book *Structuring Play in the Infant School* Manning and Sharp (1977: 7) explain the purpose of the project on which they report:

> The idea of the project first arose because of the difficulties which many teachers were experiencing in using play in the classroom. Although

accepting that children learn and develop through play, and that play is a motivating force for children's learning, many teachers are pressurised by the very full first school curriculum and large classes to neglect play as a means of teaching. They leave children to play on their own. In addition, many parents' expectations are that children will 'work' when they come to school, not 'play'.

Over 35 years later many teachers continue to struggle to 'fit' play into their pedagogic repertoire, and, though it is recognised that play has a place in the early years, some practitioners still lack the necessary skills, support and confidence to make children's play an integral part of learning and pedagogy. There remains a need to understand play as something children do in their own right and the ways in which adults seek to manipulate children's play to encourage specific learning objectives. In 2003 a Working Party of the British Educational Research Association (BERA) reviewed research on early years pedagogy, curriculum and adult roles. The Review noted that:

> Several key studies have provided an evidence base on the quality of play, its educational benefits, and the pedagogy of play, in the contexts of preschool and school settings (Tizard et al. 1975, Sylva et al. 1980, Wood et al. 1980, Meadows and Cashdan, 1988, Hutt et al. 1989, Bennett and Kell, 1989, Cleave and Brown, 1991, Bennett et al. 1997). Most of these studies did not focus specifically on play, but on broader curriculum and pedagogical processes, of which play was an integral part. Their findings were critical of the quality of play; the dislocation between rhetoric and reality of play; the extent to which play and learning were linked; the role of the adults in children's play, and how play was utilised towards educational outcomes. The consistent picture to emerge from these studies is that play in practice has been limited in frequency, duration and quality, with teachers and other adults too often adopting a reactive 'watching and waiting' approach. (BERA EYSIG, 2003: 14)

Whilst research evidence is inconclusive, the natural, irrepressible instinct and capacity of children to play, and the perceived benefits of play to children's holistic development provide a strong case for the professional exploration of the role of play in supporting children's well-being, development and learning.

In recent years increasing attention has been paid particularly to the play of children from birth to 3. Manning-Morton and Thorp (2004) examine the importance of play for children under 3, and identify the crucial role for adults in such play in supporting and developing play experiences. Play is seen in relation to all aspects of a child's day, integral to and part of an holistic approach to early education and care for very young children.

Research continues to focus on definitions of play, children's roles and interests in play and how play is supported in various forms of early years provision in a variety of international contexts. But questions about the efficacy of play as a pedagogical tool remain, and successive governments have shown varied commitment to play in the early years and schools curriculum. The implementation of the National Literacy and Numeracy strategies, for example, promoted the importance of the basic skills and threatened play. Teachers became anxious that, as standards were raised, play was increasingly sidelined (and in some cases eliminated). Christmas (2005) asked the teachers and other staff in her small village school for their views on play and found that whilst people generally thought it was 'OK to play', significant worries over the play/work balance remained.

Themes of children's play are mostly influenced by their experiences – either first-hand or secondary, as gleaned from television or stories – and practitioners faced with war and gun play vary in their responses from 'zero tolerance' to a strategy of embracing and seeking to enhance the play. Holland (2003) argues that war, weapon and superhero play properly supported with sensitive adult guidance, can be generally positive experiences for children and practitioners, resulting in imaginative play and social development. Hyder (2004) explored the importance of play for young refugee children's development. She considered the implications of war and conflict on young children and notes how opportunities for play are often denied them. Hyder's work with young refugee children is set in the context of the UNCRC and she argues that play is a healing experience for young children affected by war and conflict.

Discussing the difficulties of defining, and the uses and purposes of, play in early childhood settings, Wood (2008: 27) says:

> One of the fundamental principles in early childhood education is the importance of play to children's learning and development. The commitment to play can be traced through theory and ideology into early childhood programmes in many different countries (Saracho and Spodek, 2002; Wood and Attfield, 2005). While there is substantial evidence on learning through play, there has been less evidence on teaching through play. Linking play and pedagogy has long been a contentious area, because of the ideological commitment to free play and free choice (Wood, 2008). However, contemporary theoretical and policy changes have shifted the focus to better understanding the distinctive purposes and nature of play in education settings, and the role of adults in planning for play and playfulness in child-initiated or teacher-directed activities.

This gives a strong sense of the complexity of the play/learning relation, and perhaps explains how it is that play has been differently positioned in early education policy over the years.

Some roots of present-day approaches to play, learning and pedagogy

Of course, the prominent names which come to mind when a history of play is discussed include Rousseau, Pestalozzi and Froebel. But a number of others, such as Robert Owen and James Buchanan, made significant attempts to forge a pedagogy away from the direly routine and fear-inducing 'Dame' schools and towards making coming to school something which children might enjoy. An experimental kindergarten was opened in 1902 by Catherine Isabella Dodd which developed such 'new', play-aware teaching methods; Maria Montessori, of course, is renowned for her work on using play in a 'controlled environment' and her work was introduced to England by Edward Parnell Culverwell who published *The Montessorian Principles and Practice* in 1913. John Dewey is perhaps more notable among many who sought to promote a new pedagogy which was more child-centred, less prescriptive and not punishment-based (Dewey, 1897).

A key contributor to current understandings of the importance of play and learning is Susan Isaacs. Her meticulous observations of children making use of a richly stocked environment are still inspiring, and the accounts of teaching and learning in the Malting House School remain central to the archaeology of present-day work on the pedagogy of play.

As far back as 1911 – and six years after becoming Chief Inspector for elementary schools in 1905 – Edmund Holmes resigned his position and wrote a forceful critique in *What Is and What Might Be: A Study of Education in General and Elementary Education in Particular*. Holmes was alarmed by the prescriptive nature of education in schools at the time and felt it imperative to point out the damaging effect it was having on children and teachers alike. Holmes stated that the real function of education was

> ... to foster growth. The end which the teacher should set before himself is the development of the latent powers of his pupils, the unfolding of their latent life. If growth is to be fostered, two things must be liberally provided – nourishment and exercise. (Holmes, 1911)

Given all that we know of the work and thinking of so many of the pioneers of early childhood education, it would be hard to disagree with such things and, indeed, Holmes' subsequent writings were taken as an early statement of 'progressive' and 'child-centred' positions. It is therefore not surprising that he was highly critical of those who emphasised education's utilitarian role or who saw education as an agent of institutional preservation. Holmes argued that one of the most dangerous aspects of such beliefs was to attach high importance to visible 'results': the tendency to measure inward worth by outward standards and to judge progress in terms of 'success'. Opposing such beliefs, Holmes wrote of

> ... that deadly system of 'payment by results' which seems to have been devised for the express purpose of arresting growth and strangling life, which bound us all, myself included, with links of iron, and which had many zealous agents, of whom I, alas! was one. (1911)

and again:

> The real 'results' of education are in the child's heart and mind and soul, beyond the reach of any measuring tape or weighing machine. (1911)

This remains a concern in the pressurised climate of the early twenty-first-century marketplace where the currency of external appearance is treasured above the value of inward realities, and 'results' seem to matter more than 'quality'. Such trends are no less true for teachers today than they were for Holmes at the beginning of the twentieth century. The imperative for success and achievement has too often de-humanised the learning process to the point where teachers can find themselves teaching merely with a specific end in sight, and pupils passively learning with a prescribed result to achieve. The concepts of 'nourishment' and 'exercise' that Holmes espoused become hidden in a system designed to 'deliver the goods' while the deeper, even spiritual, qualities of human beings engaged in learning together are neglected and allowed to waste away.

Undoubtedly the creative response to a mechanical pedagogy is built on the work of Holmes, Dewey, Pestalozzi, Froebel and Comenius (to name but a few) and involves adopting practices which privilege learning and play in the early years. Pestalozzi reported that:

> My children soon became more open, more contented and more susceptible to every good and noble influence than anyone could possibly have foreseen ... I had incomparably less trouble to develop those children whose minds were still blank than those who had already acquired inaccurate ideas ... The children soon felt that there existed in them forces which they did not know ... they acquired a general sentiment of order and beauty ... the impression of weariness which habitually reigns in schools vanished like a shadow from my classroom. They willed, they had power, they persevered, they succeeded, and they were happy. (Pestalozzi, 1801: 6)

For Pestalozzi, and so many of the other pioneers, education was important for society as well as for the individual. Education was seen – particularly by Rachel and Margaret McMillan – as a means by which the social regeneration of humanity might be achieved. What these people put forward was a conviction that education is more than just growth for growth's sake but rather growth as a means to a richer quality of life, both now and in the future.

5. Early intervention

Current policy and practice in early intervention

In 1998 the Labour Government launched the National Childcare Strategy (NCS), at that time a milestone in policy development and a key marker in terms of government investment in early intervention. A central aim of the NCS was to ensure: 'Good quality, affordable childcare for children aged 0 to 14 in every neighbourhood' (DfEE, 1998: 5). Issues of work–life balance, and particularly of women contributing to the economy rather than refraining from paid work until their children were over 5 years old, were a main determinant of this policy; additionally, concerns about child protection – following high-profile cases of abuse, neglect and child killing – were highlighted.

A further strategy was launched in 2004 with *Choice for Parents, the Best Start for Children: A Ten Year Childcare Strategy* (DfES, 2004). Again, a commitment to support parents in balancing their work life with family needs and child care was central to the national policy. The issue of mothers returning to the workplace was explicit, as was the awareness of the need to address the difficulties suffered by parents living in socially and economically deprived areas of the country.

In 2013 the Conservative–Liberal Democrat Coalition Government made another controversial attempt to make childcare more affordable. The publication of *More Great Childcare* (DfE, 2013) in January 2013 met with huge opposition from childcare providers, who petitioned the government; they warned of the dangers of government proposals to increase the number of very young children that practitioners could work with. This initiative met with further difficulties when the Deputy Prime Minister, Nick Clegg, announced his concern over the policy, which led to the Minister for Children and Families, Elizabeth Truss, being called to the House of Commons on 9 May 2013 to answer an urgent question from the Labour opposition.

In parallel with the 'welfare to work' policy of the Labour Government's (1997–2010) agenda for raising the educational attainment of children, was a drive to streamline child-facing provision and child protection issues by requiring the various local authority agencies to work as integrated services for children and families. Every local authority in England was required to establish multi-agency partnerships (Early Years Development and Childcare Partnerships [EYDCPs]) to provide services – with clear emphasis on creating new childcare places, and addressing the need for provision for children under 3 (until recent years, a much neglected area).

A flagship policy initiative of these moves was the establishment of the Sure Start programme in the UK in 1999. Sure Start was set up to work with a range of agencies in health, employment and education to achieve its comprehensive aims to provide children with a 'Sure Start' and enable them to 'flourish'. Working within local communities to develop local projects, the key Sure Start aims are achieved by: helping services develop in disadvantaged areas alongside the provision of financial help for parents to afford childcare; and the 'rolling out' of the principles driving the Sure Start approach to all services for children and parents.

Key elements of the Sure Start programme were:

- *Early education for all*: free part-time early education for 3- and 4-year-olds in the Foundation Stage
- *Increased quality and quantity of childcare*: start-up grants for childminders, nurseries and after-school care, inspected by the Office for Standards in Education (Ofsted); help for working parents with their childcare costs; local Children's Information Services and a national information service for parents; information for parents and employment advice linked to information on childcare
- *Local programmes*: Children's Centres (with links with Sure Start Neighbourhood Nurseries *and* Early Excellence Centres) in the most disadvantaged areas – to offer families early education, childcare and health and family support with advice on employment opportunities.

Sure Start principles

Sure Start aimed to support families from pregnancy until children were 14 years old (16 if they were disabled). The following seven principles underpinned Sure Start work:

1. **Working with parents and children** Every family should get access to a range of services that will deliver better outcomes for both children and parents, meeting their needs and stretching their aspirations.

2. **Services for everyone** But not the same service for everyone. Families have distinctly different needs, both between different families, in different locations and across time in the same family. Services should recognise and respond to these varying needs.

3. **Flexibility at point of delivery** All services should be designed to encourage access. For example, opening hours, location, transport issues, and care for other children in the family need to be considered. Where possible families should have access to the health and family support services they need through a single point of contact.

4. **Starting very early** Services for young children and parents should start at the first antenatal visit. This means not only advice on health in pregnancy, but preparation for parenthood, decisions about returning to work (or indeed, starting work) after the birth, advice on childcare options and on support services available.

5. **Respectful and transparent services** These should be customer driven, whether or not the service is free and have well publicised ease of access.

6. **Community driven and professionally coordinated** All professionals with an interest in children and families should be sharing expertise and listening to local people on service priorities. This should be done through consultation and by day-to-day listening to parents.

7. **Outcome driven** All services for children and parents need to have as their purpose better outcomes for children. The Government needs to acknowledge this by reducing bureaucracy and simplifying funding to ensure a joined up approach with partners.

(Sure Start, 2003)

Much Sure Start-oriented research has been in the form of evaluation of programmes, and there is a wealth of reports available from the National Evaluation of Sure Start. Hannon (1999) suggested that there are four areas in which educational research can contribute to Sure Start research:

lessons from the past – drawing on evidence from effective preschool programmes; *relevant research findings* – about, for example, the effects of poverty on early educational attainment; *research into new programmes* – such as those involving parents in early literacy development; and *evaluation methods* – allocating resources for local projects to evaluate their own work through systematic, self-critical and clearly reported evaluation which becomes a means of sharing Sure Start work. (Hannon, 1999, p.3)

Hannon (1999) further identified the following questions to ask about Sure Start programmes:

• Are programmes relevant?
• How well is the programme documented?
• For what communities is it designed?
• For what age is it designed?
• Has it been adequately evaluated?
• Is it shown to be valued by families?
• Do claims go beyond evidence?
• Will potential benefits justify resources?
• What are the staff development implications?
• How can the community assess its potential?

Hannon suggested that local evaluations of Sure Start should consider how they articulate with the national evaluation; whether they use external or practitioner research; whether this research is formative or summative; what resources are needed; and whether they involved support from outside the project.

Overall Sure Start programmes were wide ranging, with a myriad activities which included: family support; work with teenage mothers; breastfeeding support; home safety; smoking cessation; play and learning programmes; language development screening; media literacy projects; reading projects; and community involvement. Many of these were identified through community surveys.

Early Intervention Programmes

The belief that the early years are crucial to children's later educational achievement has prompted the widespread development of intervention programmes which target young children who are 'at risk' in some way (Field, 2010; Allen, 2011). Early intervention programmes are based on the premise that 'beginning early' means a greater chance of being successful and they are often designed to prevent difficulties as well as to overcome or minimise any difficulties which young children already experience.

Of course, it is important that those working on early intervention programmes are well equipped and appropriately qualified (Jackson, 2012; Nutbrown, 2012). Making it possible to attend some form of preschool provision does not necessarily reach the most vulnerable groups, and can fail to provide the necessary support for children who are at risk of later school failure.

Educational disadvantage is clearly structurally linked to other factors such as housing, poverty, parents' educational qualifications, and so on. The Sure Start programme in the UK can be seen as a large-scale early intervention programme which sought to address multiple factors threatening children's development. Such programmes seek to provide something specific and additional to usual mainstream provision, and are often targeted at groups likely to benefit most.

The National Child Development Study (NCDS) began with data from 15,000 children all born within the same week in the UK in 1958. In the seven-year follow up it was found that the children's teachers judged far more children whose parents were unskilled or semi-skilled manual workers to have special educational needs (24% and 17%) than children whose parents were in professional groups (4% and 7%) (Davie et al., 1972). The same NCDS sample was studied at age 11 and found that 6% of the 11-year-olds were 'disadvantaged' – that is, living in single parent or large families and in families with low income and poor housing. This 6% were some three and a half years behind their peers according to reading tests and more likely to be receiving additional teaching support due to learning difficulties (Wedge and Prosser, 1973).

Since the 1960s there have been several well-known international early intervention programmes, such as the High Scope Perry Preschool Project (Schweinhart et al., 1993, 2004; Whitehurst et al., 1994). How can we know that early intervention programmes and strategies will achieve their aims? Such questions require funded studies and can be complex and costly. Bronfenbrenner (1974) reviewed the findings of 26 experimental early intervention studies and reported on the findings from two types of programme: 'group' and 'parent-child'. Bronfenbrenner's review showed that programmes involving parents had longer lasting effects than those which only provided for or worked with the child. He concluded that in the future programmes which addressed all the factors contributing to educational failure should be developed. It is such a strategy that underpinned the Sure Start programmes to support children's learning and development *alongside* strategies to tackle the difficulties in families and their communities which militate against healthy progress in childhood.

The Field Review (2012) on the effects of childhood poverty noted that:

> ... the early years (age zero to three in particular) are crucial and that interventions early in a child's life are most effective in improving outcomes and life chances. (Field, 2012: 90)

Further, the Allen Review of Early Intervention (2011) set out key recommendations after the observation that: 'All who care about realising the potential of our babies, children and young people need to work together and take the pathway to a long-term Early Intervention culture in the UK' (Allen, 2011: i). This review recommended that:

> ... the nation should be made aware of the enormous benefits to individuals, families and society of Early Intervention – a policy approach designed to build the essential social and emotional bedrock in children aged 0–3 and to ensure that children aged 0–18 can become the excellent parents of tomorrow. (2011: xvii)

and:

> ... the nation should recognise that influencing social and emotional capability becomes harder and more expensive the later it is attempted, and more likely to fail. (2011: xvii)

and stressed the importance of:

> ... proper co-ordination of the machinery of government to put Early Intervention at the heart of departmental strategies, including those seeking to raise educational achievement and employability, improve social mobility, reduce crime, support parents and improve mental and physical health. (2011: xviii)

Providing the best bespoke support, early in the lives of children, can enhance life chances, promote social mobility and reduce inequalities.

So, the collective advice to government in this second decade of the twenty-first century is clear: high quality work with very young children and their families is a worthwhile and necessary investment.

Some roots of early intervention

Looking back, we can again see the contributions of many pioneers. The work of Pestalozzi and his wife demonstrates a commitment to intervene with an effective programme in the life of young children to make a difference to their futures. Although Maria Montessori began her work by developing a programme to work with 9- and 10-year-old street boys in Rome, her success led her to revise this programme – based on the development and practice of life skills – for use with preschool children. And Robert Owen's work is similarly based on an insight into preventive rather than remedial measures: his New Lanark project was designed to intervene not merely in the education but in the lives of workers and their families to the betterment of the community and of society.

Arguably, the most significant contribution to the historical development of early intervention as a theme in education, is that of Rachel and Margaret McMillan. These two women were committed to improving living conditions for young children, preventing disease and providing play space and nourishment for them in the slums of London and Bradford. Their passionate commitment is demonstrated in the fact that they were not wealthy women; indeed Margaret McMillan's biography of her sister *The Life of Rachel McMillan* (published in 1927) contains several references to their struggles for funds. Writing about Rachel's funeral Margaret says:

> We laid her to rest in Brockley Cemetery... It was a small funeral. But the children were all there – all our older camp children. They stood around her grave, wistful, astonished, and laid offerings of spring flowers at her feet. I found no word to put upon her gravestone. In this book and on this page, written for her students, who will often speak her name, it seems I must say for them some word of faith and reassurance. I said it to myself, when the first terrible months were over: 'The works of the just are in the hands of God.' There was nothing more.

> We had been straitened for money. On the day after her funeral a friend left her a legacy of £1,200. It seemed a new bitterness – but this also passed, and with this money I rebuilt the shelter for the four-year-olds. (McMillan, 1927: 186)

The work of the McMillan sisters is a rich reflection of those who, throughout history, have tried to make a difference to the lives of children who are disadvantaged.

6. Home learning and parental involvement in early education

Current policy and practice in home learning and parental roles in the early years

Research in the past three decades has shed light on parents' roles in their own children's learning and prompted the development of programmes to involve parents more systematically in their own children's education. During the 1960s programmes to involve parents began to be developed largely as a way of addressing poor home experiences. However, a more recent understanding of parental involvement can be more properly traced back to the Rumbold report *Starting with Quality* (DES, 1990); this championed the idea that parents are their children's first and most important educators. Current government policy makes it clear that involvement with parents is an expected part of early childhood education and care in all settings:

> Parents are children's first and most enduring educators. When parents and practitioners work together in early years settings, the results have a positive impact on the child's development and learning. Therefore, each setting should seek to develop an effective partnership with parents. (QCA, 2000: 9)

There are many examples of parental involvement in children's learning, but recent examples emphasise a more directly participative role for parents (Whalley et al., 1997; Draper and Duffy, 2001; Nutbrown et al., 2005).

Throughout the 1990s, Sheffield LEA, like many others, promoted partnership with parents in schools throughout the city and these 'partnerships' took many forms, with workshops, open days, opportunities for adult learning and special events being offered in many schools across the whole age range from nursery to secondary. In one school, for example, the 'Parents in Partnership' project led to the development of an award-bearing programme designed to help parents better support their children. This programme had four units: sharing your child's school; sharing your child's reading; sharing your child's maths; and sharing your child's science. Parents' evaluative comments confirmed the usefulness of the project (and, indeed, the aspirations of many to continue lifelong learning). Comments included:

> I've got a greater awareness of child-centred learning and primary education.

> I think that it is easy to sit back and let school and teachers get on with doing their jobs but when I think back to when I was younger and how easy it was not to do any work I want to help my child realise that learning could be fun.

Just being involved helps children because it shows your interest in what they do and helps them to understand it is worthwhile. (Firth, 1997: 266)

The headteacher reported:

A key aim is to raise achievement of pupils. Through being involved in the project parents can learn alongside their children and develop better understanding of the expectations of school learning and there is shared understanding of where children's education is coming from and going to. Parents are continuing on their paths of *lifelong* learning too and many have yet to discover where those paths will lead. The potential is tremendous. (Firth, 1997: 267)

Another example of a study involving parents in their children's early literacy development is the 'Raising Early Achievement in Literacy' (REAL) project (Nutbrown et al., 2005). This study (which took place between 1995 and 2003) brought together the University, the Local Education Authority and many Sheffield schools with the aim of promoting family literacy through work with parents of preschool children. From the outset the project had six main aims:

1. To develop methods of working with parents to promote the literacy development of preschool children (particularly those likely to have difficulties in the early years of school).
2. To meet some of the literacy and educational needs of the parents so involved.
3. To ensure the *feasibility* of methods developed.
4. To assess the *effectiveness* of the methods in improving children's literacy development at school entry and afterwards.
5. To disseminate effective methods to practitioners and to equip them with new skills.
6. To inform policy-makers about the effectiveness and implications of new practices.

The most promising methods developed in Phase 1 were used to develop an 18-month 'long duration, low intensity' early literacy programme of work with families. Based on the ORIM framework[1], the programme had five main components: home visits by programme teachers; provision of literacy resources (particularly books); centre-based group activities; special events (e.g. group library visits); and postal communication between teacher and child. The core of the programme was similar at all schools but shaped by local community circumstances and teachers' styles. A

---

[1] www.real-online.group.shef.ac.uk/orim-network.html

total of 80 families from 10 schools (eight families working with each teacher) participated in the programme. Teachers were funded for release one half day per week to work with the families in their group. Adult learning opportunities were also developed and offered to parents. Outcomes in terms of measures of children's literacy showed that the programme was effective in making a difference to children's literacy, with children in the programme scoring more highly than children in control groups. Nutbrown et al. (2005) reported that the programme was highly valued by parents who were involved in their children's literacy and by programme teachers. They also reported on children's enhanced achievement in literacy, especially for children whose mothers had no formal educational qualifications. Children reported that their parents, mothers and fathers were involved in their home literacy (Nutbrown and Hannon, 2003).

Hurst and Joseph (2003) viewed the coming together of parents and practitioners as 'sharing education'. They argued for understanding of the complex cultural differences and shifts which children, parents and practitioners experienced when they entered each other's worlds and examined the opportunities for each to 'share' the other's domain. However,

> The sharing of intentions and perspectives between parents and practition-ers is not easy in a busy classroom. There has to be a rationale for it, and it needs links with a curriculum model which sets a value on children's experi-ences at home with family and friends. It requires just as much commit-ment as sharing intentions with children does. Contacts with the home should be seen as a part of the curriculum, and a part of the practitioner's responsibility to provide for children's learning in ways that suit them. The first step is to consider what kind of contact with parents is most valuable, and to find out what kind of contact with the setting is needed by the parents. (Hurst and Joseph, 2003: 89)

Specific initiatives to involve parents in the early years have often focused on young children's learning or aspects of curriculum and helping parents learn more about their children's ways of learning. In the late 1980s the 'Froebel Early Learning Project' (Athey, 1990) identi-fied ways of helping parents to understand their children's learning interests so that they could better support them. This theme was fur-ther developed by Nutbrown (1999), who argued that the more parents know about how children's learning developed, the better position they are in to understand what their children are doing and how they might further enhance learning opportunities for them. More recently, the 'PEEP' project in Oxfordshire, has developed ways of involving parents with babies and young children in several aspects of their learning and development.

Key issues for research continue to be how to involve parents in ways which are inclusive, participative, respectful and meaningful. Some settings have developed an international reputation for their work in involving parents in their children's learning, for example the Penn Green Centre (Whalley et al. 1997; Arnold, 2001; Whalley, 2007), the Coram Children's Centre in London (Draper and Duffy, 2001) and the Sheffield Children's Centre. Sure Start projects have involved parents in a range of programmes to support them in promoting babies' and young children's health, and their physical, social, emotional and cognitive development. Many settings develop their own specific projects to help parents learn more about their children's learning, such as that reported by Parker (2002), who explains how sharing work with parents on children's drawing and mark-making leads to enhanced understanding and enthusiasm from parents. Parker records the views of some parents who remarked:

> I have been able to enter her imagination and see the world through her eyes.

> Now I'm fascinated by the way she develops a drawing, rather than just looking at the end result.

> I have learnt that Brandon is more capable of mark making than I first thought. (Parker, 2002: 92)

Parker notes:

> The parents learned from observing their children and developed an appreciation of their children's high levels of involvement, discussing their children's achievements at home with confidence, clarity and joy … The children have been the primary beneficiaries of this collaboration between parents and practitioners. We all had valuable knowledge and understanding to share. This was a group which enjoyed mutual respect, shared understandings, political awareness and a commitment to extending learning opportunities for young children. (Parker, 2002: 92–3)

In some cases initiatives have been targeted specifically at minority groups, including families for whom English is not the language of the home. Karran (2003) describes work with parents who are learning English as an additional language and the importance of bilingual support for such parents who want to understand more of education systems and how to help their young children. Siraj-Blatchford (1994) has argued that in some cultures 'education' and 'home' are distinct and separate, and time may need to be given to explaining how home–school partnerships can support young children's learning and development. Baz et al. (1997) have discussed the importance of bilingual early childhood educators working bilingually with parents and young children using books, early writing, rhymes and poems in families' homes and in group settings.

Some roots of home learning and parental roles in early education

Though it is difficult to identify precisely when parental involvement in their children's learning became an important topic as such, it seems that this has for some time been part of working with young children. We find early examples in *The Mother's Manual* or *The Guide to Mothers in Teaching their Children how to Observe and Think* written by Pestalozzi's teaching staff in 1803, or in the example of Edith Mary Deverell, who in 1900 joined five other women in the 'Women's Inspectorate' responsible for inspecting girls' and elementary schools, and urged the promotion of parental interest in their children's education. It is also known, for example, that around 1915, Margaret McMillan gave 'lectures' for parents whose children attended her nursery schools. In 1885 Charlotte Mason gave a series of lectures to the parishioners of St Mark's in Manningham on the education of young children (later published as *Home Education*). The lectures were attended by a Mrs Francis Steinthal, who, in 1886, helped Mason to form the Parents' Educational Union in Bradford.

Again, looking back, we can see that recent projects to involve parents in their children's learning are not so much born of new and innovative ideas but are deeply rooted in a view that, as Vygotsky might have said, children's learning is social and the first social group in which most children learn is their immediate family.

7. Inclusion

Current policy and practice in inclusion in the early years

The term 'inclusive education' has come to mean many different things so that it is often a source of confusion for students in this area. It is, in fact, a contestable term used to different effect by politicians, bureaucrats and academics. 'Inclusion' is not a single *movement*; it is made up of many strong currents of belief, many different local struggles and a myriad of practices (Clough, 2000: 6).

In the UK of the twenty-first century there is increasing demand for inclusive practices, and equality of opportunity and access to educational provision. But this has not always been the case and the origins of inclusive education lie in a history of exclusion, segregation and inequality.

Clough (2000) traces the roots of inclusion through the last half of the twentieth century (Figure 4.1), from the psycho-medical legacy of the 1950s through the sociological response of the 1960s, the curricular approaches which dominated the 1970s, and school improvement

1950s ↓	The psycho-medical legacy				
1960s ↓		The sociological response			
1970s ↓			Curricular approaches		
1980s ↓				School improvement strategies	
1990s ↓					Disability studies critique

Figure 4.1 An historical interpretation of the development and interaction of ideologies leading to present thinking in inclusive education (Clough, 2000: 9)

strategies and programmes of the 1980s, to the disability studies critique and the challenge of the disability movement to the state education system of the 1990s. Whilst acknowledging that this perspective is not the only way of viewing historical developments, Clough suggests that it is these different 'eras' and developments that help us to understand the movement towards the current 'era' of inclusion.

It is perhaps because of such recent policy roots that inclusive education is sometimes viewed as the latest term to describe the education of children with Special Educational Needs in mainstream education settings. However, this is not how advocates of inclusive education (or of a broader social inclusion) necessarily define the term. As Booth has it:

> Some continue to want to make inclusion primarily about 'special needs education' or the inclusion in education of children and young people with impairments but that position seems absurd ... If inclusion is about the development of comprehensive community education and about prioritising community over individualism beyond education, then the history of inclusion is the history of these struggles for an education system which serves the interests of communities and which does not exclude anyone within those communities. (Booth, 2000: 64)

As provision for education and care for children of all ages considers ways of meeting education targets, together with wider social challenges, the 'broad' view of inclusion seems to be gaining currency. Lingard (2000) similarly emphasises the larger structures of inclusion in diversity:

What I want to do is to hold to a broader definition which links across the whole social justice, equity and citizenship issues. The concept of inclusion might also encourage an across-government approach to social and economic disadvantage. (2000: 101)

The development of inclusive education raises many research issues, including:

1. The practicalities of fully inclusive education
2. Conflicting understandings and definitions of what is meant by 'inclusion'
3. The impact of inclusion and exclusion on the lives of young children
4. Parents' views and responses to the inclusion and/or exclusion of their own and other children.

Some argue that children with particular needs are difficult to include in mainstream settings, and attempts to include children who experience, for example, emotional and behavioural difficulties, can be detrimental to some children unless managed with the utmost knowledge and skill (Angelides, 2000; Visser et al., 2003; Clough et al., 2004). Others take the view that there is no justification for the segregation of children in 'Special Schools' because they have a particular impairment (Herbert, 1998). Further research is needed to understand the relationship between inclusion and Special Educational Needs and between inclusion and other issues of social justice. Mairian Corker put it this way:

I don't like using the term 'special needs' – it's paradoxical to 'inclusion'. I worry that it is increasingly part of a labelling process that is used to pick children off or as a justification for a lack of or a redistribution of resources in a way that is not in the child's interests. These labels are very dehumanising – they really get to the nub of why we are disabled people and not people with disabilities. (Corker, 2000: p. 77)

As Booth (2000) and Lingard (2000) illustrate, definitions of inclusion are contestable. What is meant by 'inclusion' varies from culture to culture, society to society, institution to institution and individual to individual. For example, in some parts of the world (perhaps particularly in the southern hemisphere) the inclusion of indigenous children in education is a key issue in terms of education and social policy and for research (Fleer and Williams-Kennedy, 2001). In other parts of the world inclusion of refugee and asylum-seeking families is an issue. Some Traveller families find that they are excluded from educational services or that attempts to include them threaten to violate their cultural heritage and ways of living (Lloyd et al., 2003).

The impact of inclusion and exclusion on the lives of young children is a further area for study; we need to know more about the human impact of decisions about young children's early education and care and how pedagogy and learning communities affect their lives and well-being. Parents' views and responses to the inclusion and/or exclusion of their children is a further critical area for research. Berry's study of four young children's experiences of inclusion (Berry, 2002) demonstrates how important it is that parents have their say in the education of the children they know best, and Murray uses poetry and narrative to give voice to parents' experiences of fighting for inclusive education as a right for their children (Murray and Penman, 1996).

Inclusive education is as much about helping children to behave inclusively as it is about including particularly marginalised groups of society. Gussin Paley's work (1992) provides one profound example of pedagogy which helps children to include everyone in their play; Gussin Paley's well known book *You Can't Say You Can't Play* (1992) documents the development and agreement of this 'rule' for the kindergarten which led to complex understandings and negotiations within an emotionally supportive setting. Gussin Paley's work is not specifically about children with impairment or a particular identified need, but focuses on helping children voice their own stories and demonstrates her pedagogy of inclusion of all children's contributions in the learning setting.

Addressing unfairness and discrimination is recorded by Babette Brown (1998) in her book *Unlearning Discrimination in the Early Years*. Brown describes how children were supported by their parents and teachers to challenge discrimination and bias:

> Children can become active, enthusiastic and independent learners if, as their educators, we value their cultures and communities, and understand how racism and other social inequalities influence their lives. With our guidance and support children can, as this example illustrates, actively challenge unfairness:

> A group of 6-year-old children were looking through a toy catalogue. They told their teacher that they thought that it wasn't fair because there were no pictures of Black children or any showing girls building or climbing. It was agreed that they should write a letter to the manufacturer. They got no reply so they wrote again. This letter was also unacknowledged. The disappointed children enthusiastically agreed with a parent who suggested that they should draw up a petition. Children, staff and parents signed and it was sent off. To the children's delight the company replied that in future pictures in the catalogue would be more carefully chosen. (Brown, 1998: 3)

The above example shows how children can, with support, challenge exclusive practices and learn strategies to argue for social justice.

The *Index for Inclusion* was first published in 2000 (Booth et al., 2000) and issued to all schools in the UK. A second edition was published in 2002 (Booth et al., 2002) followed in 2004 by a specially adapted version for use in early years and childcare settings (Booth and Ainscow 2004). In the words of the introduction, the *Index for Inclusion: Developing Learing, Participation and Play in Early Years and Childcare* is:

> ...a resource to support the inclusive development of early years and childcare settings which include: nurseries; playgroups; parent and children centres; crèches; childminding; homecare; clubs and playschemes. The *Index* is a comprehensive document that can help everyone in these settings to find their own next steps for increasing the participation in play and learning of the children and young people in their care. The materials are designed to build on the knowledge and experience of practitioners and to challenge and support the development of any setting, however 'inclusive' it is thought to be currently. (Booth and Ainscow, 2004: 1)

In the *Index*, inclusion is an approach to education and childcare according to inclusive values, rather than a concern with a particular group of children and young people. Inclusion is often seen to be associated with children and young people who have impairments or are seen as 'having special educational needs'. However, in the *Index* inclusion is concerned with increasing the participation of all children as well as adults. 'We recognise that some children may be more vulnerable to exclusionary pressures than others and argue that settings should become responsive to the diversity of children and young people in their communities' (Booth and Ainscow, 2004: 1).

The *Index* takes a broad definition of inclusion, stressing the participation of *all* children and not just the inclusion of a single group (such as children identified as having Special Educational Needs). The *Index* seeks to support practitioners in developing their own responsiveness (and the responsiveness of the systems in place in the setting) to the diversity of children in those learning communities.

Using the *Index* is itself an inclusive process to ensure that the processes of review, planning for change and putting plans into practice are themselves inclusive. Young children, parents, staff and others associated with the provision are included in the process. All of these aspects of the *Index* provide many avenues for research. Key, of course, is the question as to if and how using the *Index* makes a difference and how that difference is identified in practice.

The following examples are taken from the *Index for Inclusion: early years and childcare* (Booth and Ainscow, 2004) and illustrate how people who have and are using the *Index* have used the process to understand more of what young children think about the setting they attend.

Learning to listen

We wanted to find out what our children thought about what we were doing for them. We showed some of our five year olds how to use a digital camera and one at a time, asked them to take pictures of things they liked and things they did not like. One girl came back with a picture of the sensory room [a room where children can control experiences of light, sound and touch]. We were very pleased with that room and so I said 'Oh that's something that you really like?' and she said 'No, I don't like it at all'. She said it 'frightened' her. I learnt my lesson, and was careful, from then on, not to jump to conclusions about what the children thought. We also discussed how we could introduce children to the room so that they could choose the level of interaction with it that they felt comfortable with. (Booth and Ainscow, 2004: 29)

Learning how to consult with parents/carers

The practitioners in a playgroup, serving many families on very low incomes, attempted to consult with parents/carers by handing out an adapted questionnaire. Only those parents/carers who helped out regularly replied. The practitioners invited the others, a few at a time, for a cup of tea after a session, explained the purpose of the questionnaire and talked through the main points. With the parents'/carers' agreement they kept a note of opinions expressed. As a result, the practitioners realised that many parents/carers did not feel involved in the playgroup and did not read the information that was given out. They decided to pair practitioners with parents/carers and encourage them to stay behind for a while after sessions to build relationships and offer support. (Booth and Ainscow, 2004: 31)

Nutbrown (1998) has argued that early education – at its best – is *inclusive education* because of the emphasis, in practice, on identifying and meeting the individual learning needs of all young children. It is often the experience of those who work in early years settings that young children, whatever their learning needs, have a right to inclusion. Many such settings would argue that supporting children with learning difficulties is as much about an *attitudinal* response as it is about *practical* responses.

Studies are needed of the relationship between addressing learning difficulties, meeting special educational needs, inclusive education and how learning difficulties are variously 'constructed' by parents, policy–makers and practitioners. There are often diverse views on what 'special educational needs' are, and on how they should be met. Many such views are inferred from particular sets of circumstances, and, Clough (2000: 6) argues, give rise to the following questions which could well form part of a research agenda:

- Where do the various 'constructions' of difficulty come from?
- How are they evidenced?
- How are they communicated?
- How are they challenged? How do they change?
- Who changes constructions of educational need, of difference and of difficulty?

Reviewing a history of 'inclusion' Nutbrown and Clough (2013: 3) suggest that:

> ... the current phase of the history (of inclusion) is a properly radical one: a broadly-understood inclusion movement which seeks to realise a sociology that insists that it is primarily in the environment where we will discover the root cause of, and the root solution to, exclusive practices. In contrast to integration, the inclusion ideology looks to change not the individual – so that s/he can be 'brought in from the cold' – but, quite simply, to change the environment, the school, society, the world ... It is no less radical a task. And in this sense it is about eradicating prejudice, injustice, and inequality.

Some roots of inclusion

In recent years, in the UK, there has been massive expansion of provision for children whose families live in areas of deprivation and who have been targeted to receive additional help through government initiatives such as Sure Start.

If we try to find the roots of inclusive education in the early years we find that specific groups – previously effectively excluded – are often identified as in need of provision. Thus, Pestalozzi did not only provide education for abandoned children, but also made a point of providing schooling for girls; similarly Rousseau, though focusing on education as he thought it should be for boys, set out the principles of educating girls as well. A similar commitment can be seen in the drives of Charlotte Mason, the McMillan sisters and Sir John Newsom.

In 1890 Mary Humphrey began what might be seen as an early Sure Start programme, providing play hours, a social centre (and Bible teaching). She later set up a similar scheme for what she called 'crippled' children, paving the way for some recognition of the need for additional programmes of support for children with Special Educational Needs.

The education of 'the poor' was a focus for Joshua Watson who founded the *National Society for the Education of the Poor* in the Principles of the Established Church in 1811. The McMillan sisters in the early 1900s, developed nursery schools for the children of the poor and succeeded in developing provision that addressed children's health issues which inhibited their growth and development. They also successfully lobbied Parliament to provide free school meals so that children were properly fed whilst in school and could therefore attend to their play and learning; the School Meals Act was passed in 1906.

Though, in their times, not carried out as 'inclusion', the driving force of these pioneers was no less one of promoting social justice and combating exclusive practices. This is a set of values which would be recognised by many who advocate inclusive education and the development of an inclusive society in the twenty–first century.

8. Professional development and training

Current policy and practice in professional development and training

In the first years of this century, the quality of early years provision (Rahilly and Johnston, 2002; NICHD and Duncan, 2003), and the need for a well-trained and appropriately qualified workforce were key issues (Abbott and Pugh, 1998). There has for some time been recognition that a 'highly skilled workforce' is central to increasing the number of education and care places and that 'working with children is a demanding, skilled profession' (DfEE, 1999: 1). There have been several attempts to develop a single qualifications framework for the education and childcare profession, but in 2013 this remains a goal yet to be achieved. Workforce reform builds on recent history in policy and the (then) innovative recommendations of the Rumbold report (DES, 1989), which stressed the importance of highly qualified professionals who could provide what was needed for children and their families.

In July 2011, continuing the attempt to address the concern that has exercised several governments, the Conservative–Liberal Democrat Coalition Government commissioned an Independent Review of the Qualifications of the Early Education and Childcare Workforce. The Nutbrown Review (as it was known) made 19 recommendations on how to improve the quality of experiences for children from birth in home and group care and reported on 19 June 2012 (Nutbrown, 2012). This wide-ranging report began by setting out a new vision for the early years workforce where babies and young children must have the very best early education and care. The Nutbrown Review (2012) argued that if those working with young children have the necessary skills, knowledge and understanding, they have the potential to offer the formative experience all young children deserve. This, of course, would need to be supported by significant government investment in the early years. This means that the government and the early years sector need to prioritise the training and development of all early years practitioners.

Nutbrown (2012) set out her vision for early childhood education and care as one where:

- Every child is able to experience high quality care and education whatever type of home or group setting they attend.

- Early years staff have a strong professional identity, take pride in their work, and are recognised and valued by parents, other professionals and society as a whole.

- High quality early education and care is led by well-qualified early years practitioners.

- The importance of childhood is understood, respected and valued.

There are examples of excellent practice that meet these aims, but this is not the case in all settings, and the time is right to set our sights higher and demand excellent work with all young children across the sector. This requires:

- An increase in the number of qualified teachers with specialist early years knowledge who lead practice in settings, working directly with babies, young children and their parents, using their pedagogical expertise to support young children's learning, play and development.

- Early years teachers who lead, and are supported by, an effective team of early years practitioners, qualified at a minimum of level 3, with all staff taking professional pride in their work, and continually seeking to extend and develop their knowledge and skills.

- Those who are working towards early education and childcare qualifications to be taught and supported by qualified and knowledgeable tutors, who are experienced in the early years. Tutors, as much as the practitioners in the setting, must take pride in their professional development, and regularly engage in practice in settings, ensuring their skills and pedagogy are current.

- Only those candidates who are confident and capable in their literacy and numeracy are able to enroll on these level 3 courses. Level 3 qualifications must be rigorous and challenging, requiring high-quality experiences in placements and giving students time to reflect on and improve their own practice.

- A rigour of qualification such that employers can have confidence that those who hold a recognised qualification have the necessary depth and breadth of knowledge and experience to be ready for work in the setting.

- Employers who support new members of staff, and take the time to induct them into the setting and their role, and ensure they have good support and mentoring in place for at least their first six months.

(Foundations for Quality, 2012: 10–11)

The Review made 19 recommendations to government on how to improve quality provision for young children and raise the status of the workforce through improved qualifications and clarity of roles and responsibilities:

Recommendation 1

The Government should continue to specify the qualifications that are suitable for staff operating within the EYFS, and the Teaching Agency should develop a more robust set of 'full and relevant' criteria to ensure qualifications promote the right content and pedagogical processes. These criteria should be based on the proposals set out in this report.

Recommendation 2

All qualifications commenced from 1 September 2013 must demonstrate that they meet the new 'full and relevant' criteria when being considered against the requirements of the EYFS.

Recommendation 3

The previously articulated plan to move to a single early years qualification should be abandoned.

Recommendation 4

The Government should consider the best way to badge qualifications that meet the new 'full and relevant' criteria so that people can recognise under what set of 'full and relevant' criteria a qualification has been gained.

Recommendation 5

The EYFS requirements should be revised so that, by September 2022, all staff counting in the staff:child ratios must be qualified at level 3.

Recommendation 6

The EYFS requirements should be revised so that, from September 2013, a minimum of 50 per cent of staff in group settings need to possess at least a 'full and relevant' level 3 to count in the staff:child ratios.

Recommendation 7

The EYFS requirements should be revised so that, from September 2015, a minimum of 70 per cent of staff in group settings need to possess at least a 'full and relevant' level 3 to count in the staff:child ratios.

Recommendation 8

Level 2 English and mathematics should be entry requirements to level 3 early education and childcare courses.

Recommendation 9

Tutors should be qualified to a higher level than the course they are teaching.

Recommendation 10

All tutors should have regular continuing professional development and contact with early years settings. Colleges and training providers should allow sufficient time for this.

Recommendation 11

Only settings that are rated 'Good' or 'Outstanding' by Ofsted should be able to host students on placement.

Recommendation 12

Colleges and training providers should look specifically at the setting's ability to offer students high quality placements.

Recommendation 13

The Department for Education should conduct research on the number of BME staff at different qualification levels, and engage with the sector to address any issues identified.

Recommendation 14

Newly qualified practitioners starting in their first employment should have mentoring for at least the first six months. If the setting is rated below 'Good', this mentoring should come from outside.

Recommendation 15

A suite of online induction and training modules should be brought together by the Government, that can be accessed by everyone working in early education and childcare.

Recommendation 16

A new early years specialist route to QTS, specialising in the years from birth to seven, should be introduced, starting from September 2013.

Recommendation 17

Any individual holding Early Years Professional Status (EYPS) should be able to access routes to obtain QTS as a priority.

Recommendation 18

I recommend that Government considers the best way to maintain and increase graduate pedagogical leadership in all early years settings.

Recommendation 19

I am not recommending that the Government impose a licensing system on the early years sector. However, the Government should consider supporting a sector-led approach, if an affordable and sustainable one emerges with widespread sector support.

(Nutbrown, Foundations for Quality, 2012: 71–3)

Additionally, the Nutbrown Review (2012) set out a progression route from GCSE to degree level for those working with young children (Figure 4.2).

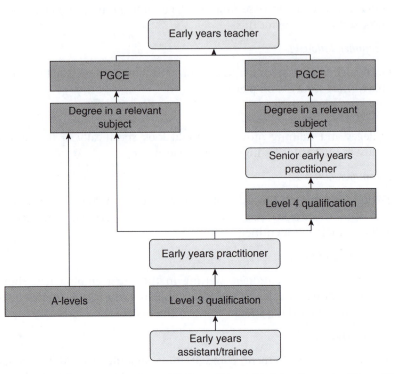

Figure 4.2   Progression routes from GCSE to degree level for those working with young children (Nutbrown, 2012)

Despite widespread support, the government rejected or adapted most of these recommendations in its policy document *More Great Childcare* published on 29 January 2013 (Nutbrown, 2013).

Whatever the policy commitment, until there is adequate funding for Further and Higher Education programmes and a political will to address issues of status, pay and conditions for early childhood practitioners of high quality early childhood provision for *all* children will not be fully realised.

Some roots of professional development and training

An overarching theme which brings together the eight issues and their histories discussed in this final part of the book is that of professional development and training. Often, the development of new initiatives was accompanied by a call for appropriate training. We can see this particularly, perhaps, in the work of Pestalozzi, Mason and the McMillans. This was not simply a solution to a practical problem of needing others to do the work they had pioneered, but was a deep recognition that no one can stand alone. And in their commitment to training for teachers these pioneers were committed to passing on their knowledge to others and thus giving others the tools with which to do their job. It also makes it clear how, even though we have drawn on the names and particular works of a small number of people, behind them and around them were countless hundreds: collaborators, partners, supporters and apprentices who were involved in developing and improving practice and provision for young children. None of them was an 'island' and their biographies testify to collaboration and co-operation as well as vision and mission. Those who currently work in early childhood education and care have an equal need for, and responsibility to develop collaboration and partnership.

Suggestions for further reading

G. Pugh and B. Duffy (2013) *Contemporary Issues in the Early Years*, 6th edn. London: Sage.

Issacs, S. (1952) *The Educational Value of the Nursery School*. Headly Brothers: London.

References

Abbott, L. and Pugh, G. (eds) (1998) *Training to Work in the Early Years: Developing the Climbing Frame*. London: Paul Chapman Publishing.

Aeppli, W. (1986) *Rudolf Steiner Education and the Developing Child*. Hudson, NY: Anthroposophic Press.

Alderson, P. (2008) *Young Children's Rights: Exploring Beliefs, Principles and Practice* (2nd ed). London: Jessica Kingsley Publishers.

Aldrich, R. and Gordon, P. (1989) *Dictionary of British Educationists*. London: The Woburn Press.

Allen, G. (2011) *Early Intervention: The Next Steps: An Independent Report on the Early Years Foundation Stage to Her Majesty's Government*. London: DfE. Available at: uk/docs/early-intervention-next-steps.pdf

Angelides, P. (2000) 'A new technique for dealing with behaviour difficulties in Cyprus: the analysis of critical incidents', *European Journal of Special Needs Education*, 15(1): 55–68.

Anning, A. and Edwards, A. (2003) 'Language and literacy learning', in J. Devereaux and L. Miller (eds), *Working with Children in the Early Years*. London: David Fulton/Open University.

Arnold, C. (2001) 'Persistence pays off: working with "hard to reach" parents', in M. Whalley and the Pen Green Centre Team, *Involving Parents in their Children's Learning*. London: Paul Chapman Publishing.

Athey, C. (1990) *Extending Thought in Young Children: A Parent–Teacher Partnership*. London: Paul Chapman Publishing.

Backstrom, K. (1997) 'The significance of the UN Convention on the Rights of the Child to children in preschool and school', paper given at the 22nd International Montessori Congress 'The Child and Communication', 22–27 July.

Baghban, M. (1984) *Our Daughter Learns to Read and Write*. Delaware, NY: International Reading Association.

Baker, S. and Freeman, D. (2005) *The Love of God in the Classroom: The Story of the New Christian Schools*. Ross-shire, Scotland: Christian Focus.

Bannon, F. and Sanderson, P. (2000) 'Experience every moment: Aesthetically significant dance education'. *Research in Dance Education*, 1 (1): 9–26.

Barratt, M.S. (2006) Inventing songs, inventing worlds: The 'genesis' of creative thought and activity in young children's lives. *International Journal of Early Years Education* 14(3): 201–20.

Barton, L. (1998) *The Politics of Special Educational Needs*. Lewes: Falmer Press.

Baz, P., Begun, L., Chia, K., Mason, G., Nutbrown, C. and Wragg, L. (1997) 'Working bilingually with families', in C. Nutbrown and P. Hannon (eds), *Preparing for Early Literacy Education with Parents: A Professional Development Manual*. Nottingham/Sheffield: NES Arnold/University of Sheffield School of Education.

Bennett, N. and Kell, J. (1989) *A Good Start? Four Year Olds in Infant Schools.* Oxford: Blackwell.

Bennett, N., Wood, E. and Rogers, S. (1997) *Teaching Through Play: Teachers' Thinking and Classroom Practice.* Buckingham: Open University Press.

BERA EYSIG (British Educational Research Association Early Years Special Interest Group) (2003) *Early Years Research: Pedagogy, Curriculum and Adult Roles, Training and Professionalism.* Nottingham: BERA.

Berry, T. (2002) 'Does inclusion work? Simon's Story' in C. Nutbrown (ed.), *Research Studies in Early Childhood Education.* Stoke-on Trent: Trentham.

Bertram, C. (2003) *Rousseau and the Social Contract.* London: Routledge.

Bettleheim, B. (1982) *Freud and Man's Soul.* New York: Knopf.

Bettleheim, B (1988) *The Uses of Enchantment: The Meaning and Importance of Fairy Tales.* London: Penguin.

Biber, G.E. (1831) *Henry Pestalozzi and his Plan of Education.* London: John Souter, School Library.

Birmingham (1869) *Report of the First General Meeting of the Members of the National Education League.*

Bissex, G.L. (1980) *GYNS AT WRK: A Child Learns to Write and Read.* Cambridge, MA: Harvard University Press.

Board of Education (1936) *Nursery Schools and Nursery Classes.* Education Pamphlet, No. 106. London: HMSO, pp. 39–53.

Booker, S. (1995) 'We Are Your Children': The Kushanda Early Childhood Education and Care Dissemination Programme. Zimbabwe 1985–1993 (extracts). *Early Childhood Development: Practice and Reflections*, Number 7, Bernard Van Leer Foundation.

Booth, T. (2000) 'Reflection: Tony Booth', in P. Clough and J. Corbett, *Theories of Inclusive Education.* London: PCP/Sage.

Booth, T. and Ainscow, M. (2004) *Index for Inclusion: Developing Learning, Participation and Play in Early Years and Childcare.* Bristol: Centre for Studies in Inclusive Education.

Booth, T., Ainscow, M., Black-Hawkins, K., Vaughan, M. and Shaw, L. (2000) *Index for Inclusion: Developing Learning and Participation in Schools* Bristol: Centre for Studies in Inclusive Education.

Booth, T., Ainscow, M., Black-Hawkins, K., Vaughan, M. and Shaw, L. (2002) *Index for Inclusion: Developing Learning and Participation in Schools.* (2nd edn). Bristol: Centre for Studies in Inclusive Education.

Bredekaup, S. (ed.) (1987) *Developmentally Appropriate Practice in Early Childhood Programs. Serving Children from Birth through Age 8.* Washington, DC: DHEW.

Brighouse, T. (2008) 'Sir Alec Clegg', *Education 3–13: International Journal of Primary, Elementary and Early Years Education*, 36(2): 103–8.

Bronfenbrenner, U. (1974) *A Report on Longitudinal Evaluations of Preschool Programs. Vol 2: Is Early Intervention Effective?* Washington, DC: DHEW.

Brown, B. (1998) *Unlearning Discrimination in the Early Years.* Stoke-on-Trent: Trentham.

Brown, E.D., Benedette, B. and Armistead, M. E. (2010) 'Arts enrichment and school readiness for children at risk', *Early Childhood Research Quarterly*, 25: 112–24.

Burke, C. (1982) 'Redefining written language growth: the child as informant', Paper presented at the 8th Australian Reading Association Conference, Adelaide.

Chapman, L.H. (2004) 'No child left behind in art?', *Arts Education Policy Review*, 106: 3–17.

Cholmondeley, E. (1960) *The Story of Charlotte Mason 1842–1923*. London: Dent.

Chomsky, N. (1993) *Language and Thought*. Wakefield, RI and London: Moyer Bell.

Christmas, J. (2005) 'Is it OK to play?', in K. Horst and C. Nutbrown (eds), *Perspectives on Early Education: Essays in Contemporary Research*. Stoke-on-Trent: Trentham.

City of Edinburgh Council/Early Education (1999) *Excellence from the Start: Edinburgh Nursery Schools from 1903 to the Present Day*. CD-ROM.

Clay, M. (1972) *Reading Recovery: The Patterning of Complex Behaviour*. Auckland, NZ : Heinemann.

Cleave, S. and Brown, S. (1991) *Early to School: Four Year Olds in Infant Classes*. Slough: NFER/Nelson.

Clegg, A. (1964) *The Excitement of Writing*. London: Chatto and Windus.

Clegg, A. (1972) *Changing Primary School: Its Problems and Priorities*. London: Vintage.

Clegg, A. (1973) *Enjoying Writing: Further Collection of Children's Poetry and Prose*. London: HarperCollins.

Clegg, A. (1980) *About Our Schools*. Oxford: Blackwell.

Clegg, A. and Megson, B. (1968) *Children in Distress*. London: HarperCollins.

Clough, P. (ed.) (1998) *Managing Inclusive Education: From Policy to Experience*. London: PCP/Sage.

Clough, P. (2000) 'Routes to inclusion', in P. Clough and J. Corbett, *Theories of Inclusive Education*. London: Paul Chapman Publishing.

Clough, P. (2002) *Narratives and Fictions in Educational Research*. Buckingham: Open University Press.

Clough, P. and Corbett, J. (2000) *Theories of Inclusive Education*. London: PCP/Sage.

Clough, P. and Garner, P. (2003) 'Special educational needs and inclusive education: origins and current issues', in S. Bartlett and D. Burton (eds), *Education Studies: Essential Issues*. London: Sage.

Clough, P. and Nutbrown, C. (2002) 'The Index for Inclusion: personal perspectives from early years educators', *Early Education*, 26 (Spring).

Clough, P. and Nutbrown, C. (2003) 'The "Index for Inclusion": perspectives of early years practitioners', in M. Nind, K. Sheehy and K. Simmons (eds), *Inclusive Education: Learners and Learning Contexts*. London: David Fulton.

Clough, P. and Nutbrown, C. (2004) 'Special educational needs and inclusive early education: multiple perspectives from UK educators', *Journal of Early Childhood Research*, 2(2): 191–211.

Clough, P., Garner, P., Pardeck J.T. and Yuen, F. (eds) (2004) *Handbook of Emotional and Behavioural Difficulties*. London: Sage.

Cohen, D. (1997) *Carl Rogers: A Critical Biography*. London: Constable.

Cole, M. (1997) 'Equality and primary education: what are the conceptual issues?', in M. Cole, D. Hill and S. Shan (eds), *Promoting Equality in Primary Schools*. London: Cassell, pp. 48–75.

Coles, R. (1970) *Erik H. Erikson: The Growth of His Work*. Boston, MA and Toronto: Little, Brown.

Collins, P. (1963) *Dickens and Education*. London: Macmillan.

Comenius, J.A. (1923) *The Great Didactic of John Amos Comenius* [1657]. Translated and edited by M.W. Keatinge. London: A. & C. Black.

Comenius, J.A. (1968) *Orbis Sensualium Pictus: A Facsimile of the First English Edition of 1659 [1658]*. Introduced by J.E. Sadler. London: Oxford University Press.

Comenius, J.A. (1956) *The School of Infancy* [1631]. Edited with an introduction by E.M. Eller. Chapel Hill, NC: University of North Carolina Press.

Connolly, P. (2004) *Boys and Schooling in the Early Years*. London: Routledge Falmer.

Cooper, L. (1999) *Rousseau, Nature and the Problem of the Good Life*. Pennsylvania: Pennsylvania State University Press.

Cordes, C. and Millar, E. (2000) *Fool's Gold: A Critical look at Computers in Childhood*. College Park, MD: Alliance for Childhood.

Corker, M. (2000) 'Profile: Mairian Corker', in P. Clough and J. Corbett, *Theories of Inclusive Education*. London: PCP/Sage.

Covell, K. and Howe, R.B. (1999) *Children's Rights Education Curriculum Resource*. Cape Breton, Nova Scotia: University College of Cape Breton Children's Rights Centre.

Cranston, M. (1982) *Jean-Jacques: The Early Life and Work of Jean-Jacques Rousseau, 1712–1754*. New York: Norton.

Croall, J. (1983) *Neill of Summerhil: The Permanent Rebel*. London: Routledge & Kegan Paul.

Damrosch, L. (2005) *Jean-Jacques Rousseau: Restless Genius*. New York: Houghton Mifflin.

David, T. and Powell, S. (1999) 'Changing childhoods, changing minds', in T. David (ed.), *Young Children Learning*. London: Paul Chapman Publishers/ Sage.

Davie, R., Butler, N. and Goldstein, H. (1972) *From Birth to Seven: A Report of the National Child Development Study*. London: Longman.

Deans, J., and Brown, R. (2005) 'Reflection, renewal and relationship building: An on-going journey in early childhood arts education', *Contemporary Issues in Early Childhood* 9, (4): 339–53.

Dent, N.J.H. (1988) *Rousseau: An Introduction to his Psychological, Social, and Political Theory*. Oxford: Blackwell.

Dent, N.J.H. (2005) *Rousseau*. London: Routledge.

DES (Department of Education and Science) (1978) *The Warnock Report*. London: HMSO.

DES (Department of Education and Science) (1988) *English for Ages 5–11: Proposals of the Secretary of State for Education and Science and the Secretary of State for Wales*. National Curriculum Council: London.

DES (Department of Education and Science) (1989) *Starting with Quality: The report of the Rumbold Committee*.

DES (Department of Education and Science) (1990) *Starting with Quality: Report of the Committee of Inquiry into the Quality of Educational Experience Offered to Three and Four Year Olds*. London: HMSO.

DfES (Department for Education and Skills (2007) *Statutory Framework for the Early Years Foundation Stage: Setting the Standards for Learning, Development and Care for Children from Birth to Five*. London: HMSO.

Dewey, J. (1897a) *Experience and Education*. New York, NY: Macmillan Publishing Co.

Dewey, J. (1897b) *My Pedagogic Creed*. Washington, DC: Progressive Education Association.

Dewey, J. (1897c) *How We Think*. New York: Dover Publications.

Dewey, J. (1899) *The School and Society*. Chicago: University of Chicago Press.

Dewey, J. (1902) *The Educational Situation*. Chicago, IL: University of Chicago Press.

Dewey, J. (1931) *The Way Out of Educational Confusion*. Cambridge, MA: Harvard University Press.

Dewey, J. (1938) *Experience and Education*. New York, NY: Kappa Delta Pi.

DfE (Department for Education) (2012) *Statutory Framework for the Early Years Foundation Stage*. Available at: https://www.foundationyears.org.uk/early-years-foundation-stage-2012.

DfE (Department for Education) (2013) *More Great Childcare*. London: HMSO.

DfEE (Department for Education and Employment) (1997) *Excellence in Schools*. London: The Stationery Office.

DfEE (Department for Education and Employment) (1998) 'Developing a more inclusive education system', in *Meeting Special Educational Needs: A Programme for Action*. London: DfEE, pp. 22–27.

DfEE (Department for Education and Employment) (1999) *Sure Start: Making a Difference for Children and Families*. London: DfEE.

DfES (Department for Education and Skills) (2001) *Code of Practice on the Identification and Assessment of Children with Special Educational Needs*. London: HMSO.

DfES (Department for Education and Skills) (2004) *Choice for Parents, the Best Start for Children: A Ten Year Childcare Strategy*. London: DfES.

DfES (Department for Education and Skills) (2005) *Every Child Matters: Change for Children*. London: HMSO.

DfES/QCA (Department for Education and Skills/Qualifications and Curriculum Authority) (2003) *Foundation Stage Profile Handbook*. London: QCA.

Dickens, C. (1994) *Great Expectations* [1861]. Harmondsworth: Penguin.

Dickens, C. (1999) *Nicholas Nickelby* [1839]. Harmondsworth: Penguin.

Dickens, C. (2003) *Bleak House* [1852]. Harmondsworth: Penguin.

Dickens, C. (2004) *David Copperfield* [1850]. Harmondsworth: Penguin.

Dickens, C. (2007) *Hard Times* [1854]. Harmondsworth: Penguin.

Dissanayake, E. (1990) *What is Art For?* Seattle, WA: University of Washington Press.

Dissanayake, E. (1995) *Homo aestheticus*. Seattle, WA: University of Washington Press.

Dissanayake, E. (2000) *Art and Intimacy: How the Arts Began*. Seattle, WA: University of Washington Press.

Dissanayake, E. (2001) Aesthetic incunabula. *Philosophy and Literature*, 25: 335–46.

Donaldson, M. (1978) *Children's Minds*. London: Fontana/Croom Helm.

Draper, L. and Duffy, B. (2001) 'Working with parents', in G. Pugh (ed.), *Contemporary Issues in the Early Years: Working Collaboratively for Children*. London: Paul Chapman Publishing.

Dyson, A.H. (1997) *Writing Superheroes: Contemporary Childhood, Popular Culture and Classroom Literacy*. New York: Teachers College Press.

Dyson, A.H. (2002) *Brothers and Sisters Learn to Write Popular Literacies in Childhood and School Cultures*. New York: Teachers College Press.

Edwards, C., Gandini, L. and Forman, G. (eds) (1993) *The Hundred Languages of Children: The Reggio Emilia Approach to Early Childhood Education*. Norwood, NJ: Ablex, pp. 305–12.

Eisner, E.W. (2002) *The Arts and the Creation of the Mind*. New Haven, CT: Yale University Press.

Eisner, E.W. (2004) 'What can education learn from the arts about the practice of education?' *International Journal of Education and the Arts*, 5(4): 12–7.

Erikson, E. (1950) *Childhood and Society*. New York: W.W. Norton.

Erikson, E. (1958) *Young Man Luther: A Study in Psychoanalysis and History*. New York: W.W. Norton.

Erikson, E. (1963) *Youth: Change and Challenge*. New York: Basic Books.

Erikson, E. (1964) *Insight and Responsibility*. New York: W.W. Norton.

Erikson, E. (1968) *Identity: Youth and Crisis*. New York: W.W. Norton.

Feldman, M. (ed.) (2004) *Early Intervention: The Essential Readings*. Oxford: Blackwell.

Ferrerio, E. and Teberosky, A. (1989) *Literacy Before Schooling*. Oxford: Heinemann.

Field, F. (2010) *The Foundation Years: Preventing Poor Children Becoming Poor Adults: The Report of the Independent Review on Poverty and Life Chances*. London: HMSO. Available at: http://webarchive.nationalarchives.gov.uk/20110120090128/ http://povertyreview.independent.gov.uk/media/20254/poverty-report.pdf.

Filippini, T. and Vecchi, V. (eds) (1996) *The Hundred Languages of Children: The Exhibit*. Reggio Emilia: Reggio Children.

Firth, R. (1997) 'Brunswick Primary School "Parents in Partnership" project', in C. Nutbrown and P. Hannon (eds), *Preparing for Early Literacy Education with Parents: A Professional Development Manual*. Nottingham/Sheffield: NES Arnold/ University of Sheffield School of Education.

Fleer, M. and Williams-Kennedy, D. (2001) *Building Bridges: Literacy Development in Young Indigenous Children*. Canberra: Department of Education, Science and Training.

Freire, P. (1972) *Pedagogy of the Oppressed*. London: Penguin.

Friedman, L.J. (1999) *Identity's Architect: A Biography of Erik H. Erikson*. New York: Charles Scribner.

Froebel, F. (1826) *The Education of Man (Die Menschenerziehung)*. Keilhan/Leipzig: Wienbranch.

Froebel, F. (1843) *Mother Songs (Mutter und Koselieder)*. Keilhan/Leipzig: Wienbranch.

Froebel, F. (1887) *The Education of Man*. New York: D. Appleton.

Frosh, S. (1987) *The Politics of Psychoanalysis: An Introduction to Freudian and Post-Freudian Theory*. New Haven, CT: Yale University Press.

Gardner, D.E.M. (1969) *Susan Isaacs*. London: Routledge & Kegan Paul.

Gardner, H. (1989) 'The key in the key slot', *Journal of Aesthetic Education*, 23(1): 141–58.

Gardner, H. (1990) Art education and human development: An essay commissioned by the J. Paul Getty Center for Education in the Arts, Occasional Paper 3. Los Angeles: The J. Paul Getty Museum.

Gattico, E. (2001) *Jean Piaget*. Milano: Bruno Mondadori.

Giardeillo, P. (2013) *Pioneers in Early Childhood Education: The Roots and Legacies of Rachel and Margaret McMillan, Maria Montessori and Susan Isaacs*. London: Routledge.

Gillespie, A. (2006) 'Children, art and artists', *Early Education*, (Summer): 3–7.

Goldschmeid, E., and Jackson, S. (1999) *People Under Three*. London: Routledge.

Goldson, B. (1997) '"Childhood": an introduction to historical and theoretical analyses', in P. Scraton (ed.), *'Childhood' in 'Crisis'?* London: UCL Press.

Goodman, K. (1967) 'Reading: a psycholinguistic guessing game', *Journal of the Reading Specialist*, 6: 126–35.

Goodman, K., Goodman, Y. and Burke, C. (1978) 'Reading for life – the psycholinguistic base', in E. Hunter-Grundin and H.U. Hunter-Grundin (eds), *Reading: Implementing the Bullock Report*. London: Ward Lock.

Goodman, Y. (1980) 'The roots of literacy', in M.P. Douglass (ed.), *Claremont Reading Conference 44th Yearbook*. Clarement, CA: Claremont Reading Conference, pp. 1–32.

Goodman, Y. (1986) 'Children coming to know literacy', in W.H. Teale and E. Sulzby (eds), *Emergent Literacy Writing and Reading*. Norwood, NJ: Ablex Publishing Corporation.

Goswami, U. and Bryant, P. (1990) *Phonological Skills and Learning to Read*. Hove: Lawrence Earlbaum Associates.

Griffin-Beale, C. (ed.) (1979) *Christian Schiller in His Own Words*. London: A. & C. Black.

Grunelius, E. Von (1974) *Educating the Young Child*. London: New Knowledge Books.

Gussin Paley, V. (1992) *You Can't Say You Can't Play*. Cambridge, MA: Harvard University Press.

Hallowes, A. (2013) Storytelling and Story Drawing. Unpublished EdD Thesis, University of Sheffield.

Hancock, R. and Cox, A. (2002) '"I would have worried about her being a nuisance": workshops for children under three and their parents at Tate Britain', *Early Years*, 22(2): 118.

Hannon, P. (1980) 'Preschool care and education: historical and psychological issues with implications for policy', Working Paper. Sheffield: University of Sheffield, Division of Education.

Hannon, P. (1999) *What Can Educational Research Offer Sure Start?* Briefing note commissioned by the NHS Executive (Trent Region) for a symposium held in Derby, 29 March.

Hannon P., Morgan A. and Nutbrown C. (2006) 'Parents' experiences of a family literacy programme', *Journal of Early Childhood Research*, 3(3): 19–44.

Hardy, L. (1999) *The Diary of a Free Kindergarten* [1912]. Edinburgh: The City of Edinburgh/Early Education.

Harrett, J. (2001) 'Young children talking: an investigation into the personal stories of key stage one infants', *Early Years*, 22(1): 19–26.

Harste, J.C., Woodward, V.A. and Burke, C.L. (1984) *Language Stories and Literacy Lessons*. Portsmouth, NH: Heinemann Educational Books.

Herbert, E. (1998) 'Included from the start? Managing early years settings for all', in P. Clough (ed.), *Managing Inclusive Education: From Policy to Experience*. London PCP/Sage.

Hesse, H. (1939) *Siddhartha*. Germany: New Directions.

Hickson, H. (2003) 'Developing the role of parents in early writing experiences of their children', in *Summaries of Action Research Reports*. Tameside LEA/ University of Sheffield School of Education.

Hiebert, E.H. (1981) 'Developmental patterns and inter-relationships of preschool children's print awareness', *Reading Research Quarterly*, 16: 236–59.

Hirst, K. (1998) 'Pre-school literacy experiences of children in Punjabi, Urdu and Gujerati speaking families in England', *British Educational Research Journal*, 24(4): 415–29.

HMI (1989) *The Education of Children Under Five: Aspects of Education Series*. London: Department of Education and Science, pp. 5–19.

Holland, P. (2003) *We Don't Play with Guns Here*. Buckingham: Open University Press.

Holmes, E.G.A. (1911) *What Is and What Might Be: A Study of Education in General and Elementary Education in Particular*. London: Constable.

Hopperstad, M.H. (2008a) Relationships between children's drawing and accompanying peer interaction in teacher-initiated drawing sessions. *International Journal of Early Years Education* 16, no. 2: 133–50.

Hopperstad, M. (2008b) How children make meaning through drawing and play. *Visual Communication*, 7(1): 77–96.

Hughes, J.L. (1900) *Dickens as an Educator*. New York: D. Appleton.

Hurst, V. and Joseph, J. (2003) *Supporting Early Learning: The Way Forward*. Buckingham: Open University Press.

Hutt, S.J., Tyler, S., Hutt, C. and Christopherson, H. (1989) *Play, Exploration and Learning: A Natural History of the Preschool*. London: Routledge.

Hyder, T. (2004) *War, Conflict and Play*. Buckingham: Open University Press.

Isaacs, S.S. (1929) *The Nursery Years*. London: Routledge & Kegan Paul.

Isaacs, S.S. (1930) *Intellectual Growth in Young Children*. London: Routledge & Kegan Paul.

Issacs, S. S. (1932) *The Children We Teach: Seven to Eleven Years*. London: University of London, Institute of Education.

Isaacs S.S. (1933) *Social Development of Young Children*. London: Routledge & Kegan Paul.

Isaacs, S.S. (1952) *The Educational Value of the Nursery School*, London: The Nursery School Association of Great Britain and Ireland.

Jackson, L. (2012) *National Education Trust. Securing Standards, Sustaining Success: Report on Early Intervention*. London: National Education Trust. http://www.nationaleducationtrust.net/SchoolImprovementServices/downloads/EarlyYearsReport.pdf

Jenkinson, S. (2001) *The Genius of Play: Celebrating the Spirit of Childhood*. Stroud: Hawthorn Press.

Jones, E. (1953–1957) *Sigmund Freud: Life and Work* (3 vols). New York: Basic Books.

Karran, S. (2003) '"Auntie-Ji, please come and join us, just for an hour." The role of the bilingual education assistant in working with parents with little confidence', in J. Devereaux and L. Miller (eds), *Working with Children in the Early Years*. London: David Fulton/Open University.

Keatinge, M.W. (1896) *The Great Didactic of John Amos Comenius*. Translated and edited, with biographical, historical and critical introductions, by M. W. Keatinge. London: A. and C. Black.

Kelly, T. (1970) *A History of Adult Education in Great Britain*. Liverpool: Liverpool University Press.

Kenway, M. and Bullen, E. (2001) *Consuming Children: Education – Entertainment – Advertising*. Buckingham: Open University Press.

Kilpatrick, W.H. (1916) *Froebel's Kindergarden Principles Critically Examined*. New York: Macmillan.

Kirschenbaum, H. (1979) *On Becoming Carl Rogers*. New York: Delacorte Press.

Kitchener, R. (1986) *Piaget's Theory of Knowledge*. New Haven: Yale University Press.

Kramer, R. (1976) *Maria Montessori*. Toronto: Longman Canada Limited.

Kraut, R. (1984) *Socrates and the State*. Princeton, NJ: Princeton University Press.

Lange, L. (2002) *Feminist Interpretations of Jean-Jacques Rousseau*. University Park, PA: Penn State University Press.

Laurie, S.S. (1904) *John Amos Comenius, Bishop of Moravians: His Life and Educational Works* (6th edn). Cambridge: Cambridge University Press.

Lawrence, E. (ed.) (1952) *Friedrich Froebel and English Education*. London: University of London Press.

Lindqvist, G. (2001) 'When small children play: how adults dramatise and children create meaning', *Early Years*, 21(1): 7–14.

Lingard, B. (2000) 'Profile: Bob Lingard', in Clough P. and J. Corbett, *Theories of Inclusive Education*. London: PCP/Sage.

Lissau, R. (1987) *Rudolf Steiner: Life, Work, Inner Path and Social Initiatives*. Stroud: Hawthorn Press.

Lloyd, G., Stead, J., Jordan, E. and Norris, C. (2003) 'Teachers and Gypsy Travellers', in M. Nind, K. Sheehy and K. Simmons (eds), *Inclusive Education: Learners and Learning Contexts*. London: David Fulton.

Lowenfeld, M. (1935) *Play in Childhood*. London: Gollancz.

Maclean, M., Bryant, P. and Bradley, L. (1987) 'Rhymes, nursery rhymes and reading in early childhood', *Merrill-Palmer Quarterly*, 33(3): 255–81.

Malaguzzi, L. (1996) 'The right to environment', in T. Filippini and V. Vecchi (eds), *The Hundred Languages of Children: The Exhibit*. Reggio Emilia: Reggio Children.

Manning, J. (1956) *Dickens on Education*. Toronto: University of Toronto Press.

Manning, K. and Sharp, A. (1977) *Structuring Play in the Early Years at School*. London: Ward Lock Educational.

Manning-Morton, J. and Thorp, M. (2004) *Key Times for Play*. Buckingham: Open University Press.

Marsh, J. (ed.) (2005a) *Popular Culture, New Media and Digital Literacy in Early Childhood*. London: RoutledgeFalmer.

Marsh, J. (2005b). 'Digikids: young children, popular culture and media', in N. Yelland (ed.), *Critical Issues in Early Childhood Education*. Buckingham: Open University Press.

Marsh, J. and Thompson, P. (2001) 'Parental involvement in literacy development using media texts', *Journal of Research in Reading*, 24(3): 266–78.

Martinez, L. (1998) 'Gender equity policies and early childhood education', in N. Yelland (ed.), *Gender in Early Childhood*. London: Routledge, pp. 115–30.

Mason, C. (1886) *The Home Schooling Series: Volume 1: Home Education. The Education and Training of Children Under Nine*. Oxford: The Scrivener Press.

Mason, C. (1896) *The Home Schooling Series:Volume 2: Parents and Children. A Practical Study of Educational Principles*. Oxford: The Scrivener Press.

Mason, C. (1904a) *The Home Schooling Series: Volume 3: Home and School Education. The Training and Education of Children Over Nine*. Oxford: The Scrivener Press.

Mason, C. (1904b) *The Home Schooling Series: Volume 4: Ourselves, Our Souls and Bodies. Book 1: Self knowledge. Book 2: Self Direction*. Oxford: The Scrivener Press.

Mason, C. (1905) *The Home Schooling Series: Volume 5: Some Studies in the Formation of Character*. Oxford: The Scrivener Press.

Mason, C. (1923/1955) *An Essay Towards a Philosophy of Education*. Oxford: The Scrivener Press.

Mason, C. (1923/1989) *An Essay Towards a Philosophy of Education*. Wheaton, IL: Tyndale House Publishers.

Mason, C. (1955) *The Home Schooling Series*. Oxford: The Scrivener Press.

McMillan, M. (1896) *Child Labour and the Half Time System*. London: George Allen and Unwin.

McMillan, M. (1900) *Early Childhood*. London: George Allen and Unwin.

McMillan, M. (1917) *The Camp School*. London: George Allen and Unwin.

McMillan, M. (1919) *The Nursery School*. London: George Allen and Unwin.

McMillan, M. (1920) *Nursery Schools: A Practical Handbook*. London: George Allen and Unwin.

McMillan, M. (1925) *Childhood, Culture, and Class in Britain*. London: George Allen and Unwin.

McMillan, M. (1927) *The Life of Rachel McMillan*. London: J.M. Dent.

Meadows, S. and Cashdan, A. (1988) *Helping Children Learn: Contributions to a Cognitive Curriculum*. London: David Fulton.

Meek, M. (1982) *Learning to Read*. London: The Bodley Head.

Menegoi-Buzzi, I. (1999) 'A critical view of inclusion in Italy', in M. Chaltin, I. Menegoi-Buzzi, S. Phillips and N. Sylvestre (eds), *Integrating Children with Special Educational Needs (Handicapped) in Ordinary Schools: Case Studies in Europe*. Milan: IRRSAE, Lombardia.

Merleau-Ponty, M. (1962) *Phenomenology of Perception*. London: Routledge.

Miller, P. (1983) *Theories of Developmental Psychology*. San Francisco: W.H. Freeman and Company.

Mills, R.W. and Mills, R.M. (1998) 'Child of our time: variations in adult views of childhood with age', *International Journal of Early Years Education*, 6(1): 75–85.

Molt, E. (1991) *Emil Molt and the Beginnings of the Waldorf School Movement*. Edinburgh: Floris Books.

Montessori, M. (1914) *Dr Montessori's Own Handbook*. New York: Schocken Books.

Montessori, M. (1962) *Education for a New World*. Wheaton, IL: Theosophical Press.

Montessori, M. (1963) *The Secret of Childhood*. Calcutta: Orient Longmans.

Montessori, M. (1964a) *The Absorbent Mind*. Wheaton, IL: Theosophical Press.

Montessori, M. (1964b) *The Montessori Method*. New York: Schocken Books.

Moss, P. (1989) *The United Nations Conventions on the Rights of the Child: Articles and Summary Commentary*. UNESCO/NCB.

Moyles, J. (ed.) (1994) *The Excellence of Play*. Buckingham: Open University Press.

Murphy, D.J. (1995) *Comenius: A Critical Reassessment of his Life and Work*. Dublin: Irish Academic Press.

Murray, P. and Penman, J. (1996) *Let Our Children Be*. Sheffield: Parents with Attitude.

Myers, R. (1993) Attention by International Organisations to Early Childhood Care and Development: An Analysis of United Nations World Reports, 1993. Early Childhood Care and Development website: http://www.ecdgroup.com

National Advisory Committee on Creative and Cultural Education (NACCCE) (1999) *All Our Futures: Creativity, Culture and Education.* London: Department for Children, Schools and Families.

Neill, A.S. (1916) *A Dominie's Log.* London: Herbert Jenkins.

Neill, A.S. (1939) *The Last Man Alive.* London: Gollancz.

Neill, A.S. (1960) *Summerhill: A Radical Approach to Child Rearing.* New York: Hart Publishing.

Neill, A.S. (1973) *Neill, Neill, Orange Peel!* New York: Hart Publishing.

Newman, F. and Holzman, L. (1993) *Lev Vygotsky: Revolutionary Scientist.* London: Routledge.

Newsam, P. (2008) 'What price hyacinths? An appreciation of the work of Sir Alec Clegg', *Education 3–13: International Journal of Primary, Elementary and Early Years Education,* 36(2): 109–16.

Ney, M. (1999) *Charlotte Mason.* Nottingham: Education Heretics Press.

NICHD Early Child Care Research Network and Duncan, G. J. (2003) 'Modeling the impacts of child care quality on children's preschool cognitive development'. *Child Development,* 74(5) 1454–75.

Nutbrown, C. (ed.) (1996) *Respectful Educators – Capable Learners.* London: Sage.

Nutbrown, C. (1998a) 'Managing to include? Rights, responsibilities and respect', in P. Clough (ed.), *Managing Inclusive Education: From Policy to Experience.* London: Paul Chapman Publishing/Sage, pp. 167–76.

Nutbrown, C. (1998b) *The Lore and Language of Early Education.* Sheffield: Sheffield University Papers in Education.

Nutbrown, C. (1999) *Threads of Thinking: Schemas and Young Children Learning,* 4th ed. London: Sage.

Nutbrown, C. (2012) *Foundations for Quality. The independent review of early education and childcare qualifications.* Final Report. London: Department for Education.

Nutbrown, C. (2013) *Shaking the Foundations of Quality? Why 'Childcare' Policy Must Not Lead to Poor-quality Early Education and Care.* Available at www.shef.ac.uk/polopoly-fs/1.263201!/file/shakingthefoundationsofquality.pdf

Nutbrown, C. and Clough, P. (2004) 'Inclusion in the Early Years: Conversations with European Educators', *European Journal of Special Needs Education,* 19(3): 311–39.

Nutbrown, C. and Clough, P. (2013) *Inclusion in the Early Years.* London: Sage.

Nutbrown, C., Hannon, P. and Collier, S. (1996) *Early Literacy Education with Parents: A Framework for Practice* (Video). Sheffield: The REAL Project/University of Sheffield, Sheffield University Television.

Nutbrown, C. and Hannon, P. (eds) (1997) *Preparing for Early Literacy Education with Parents: A Professional Development Manual.* Sheffield/Nottingham: NES Arnold/University of Sheffield REAL Project.

Nutbrown, C. and Hannon, P. (2003) 'Children's perspectives on early literacy: issues and methodologies', *Journal of Early Childhood Literacy,* 3(2): 115–45.

Nutbrown, C. Hannon, P. and Morgan, A. (2005) *Early Literacy Work with Families: Policy, Practice and Research.* London: Sage.

Nutbrown, C., and Jones, H. (2006) *Daring Discoveries: Arts-based learning in the early years.* Doncaster: Creative Partnerships/Darts.

Oldfield, L. (2001) *Free to Learn: Introducing Steiner Waldorf Early Childhood Education*. Stroud: Hawthorn Press.

Owen, R. (1920). *The Life of Robert Owen: Written by Himself*. London: G. Bell and Sons.

Parker, C. (2002) 'Working with families on curriculum: developing shared understandings of children's mark making', in C. Nutbrown (ed.), *Research Studies in Early Childhood Education*. Stoke-on-Trent: Trentham.

Parker, D. (2005) *John Newsom: A Hertfordshire Educationist*. Hertfordshire: University of Hertfordshire Press.

Payton, S. (1984) *Developing Awareness of Print: A Child's First Steps Towards Literacy*. Birmingham: Educational Review Occasional Papers No. 2, University of Birmingham.

Penner, T. (1992) 'Socrates and the early dialogues', in R. Kraut (ed.), *The Cambridge Companion to Plato*. Cambridge: Cambridge University Press.

Pereera, S. (2000) 'Living with special educational needs: mothers' perspectives', in P. Clough and C. Nutbrown (2000) *Voices from Arabia: Essays in Educational Research*. Sheffield: University of Sheffield School of Education.

Pestalozzi, J.H. (1801) *How Gertrude Teaches her Children*.

Phillips, S. (2001) 'Special needs or special rights?', in L. Abbott and C. Nutbrown (eds), *Experiencing Reggio Emilia: Implications for Preschool Provision*. Buckingham: Open University Press.

Piaget, J. (1952) 'Jean Piaget (autobiography)', in E. G. Boring (ed.), *A History of Psychology in Autobiography, Vol. 4*. Worcester, MA: Clark University Press, pp. 237–56.

Piaget, J. (1957) *Jan Amos Comenius (1952–1670)*, in *Prospects* (1993), UNESCO International Bureau of Education vol XXIII, 1/2: 173–96. UNESCO International Bureau of Education, 1999.

Piaget, J. (1990) *The Child's Conception of the World*. New York: Littlefield Adams.

Piaget, J. and Inhelder, B. (1969) *The Psychology of the Child* [1966]. New York: Basic Books.

Pramling Samuelsson, I., Carlsson, M.A., Isson, B., Pramling, N. and Wallerstedt, C. (2009) 'The art of teaching children in the arts: music, dance and poetry with children aged 2–8 years old', *International Journal of Early Years Education*, 17(2): 119–36.

QCA (Qualifications and Curriculum Authority) (2000) *Curriculum Guidance for the Foundation Stage*. London: Qualifications and Curriculum Authority.

QCA/DfES (Qualifications and Curriculum Authority/Department for Education and Skills) (2000) *Curriculum Guidance for the Foundation Stage*. London: QCA/DES.

Rahilly, S. and Johnston, E. (2002) 'Opportunity for childcare: the impact of government intiatives in England upon childcare provision', *Social Policy & Administration*, 36(5): 482–95.

Randell, S., Payne-Cook, E. and Marlow, P. (2004) *Ready for School: The Nursery Project: A Joint Initiative between Willowbrook School, Sure Start Exeter and Whipton First School*. National Evaluation of Sure Start.

Reggio Children (1995) *Le Fontane: Da un progetto per la construczione di un Luna Park degli uccellini [The Fountains: From a project for the construction of an amusement park for birds]*. Reggio Emilia: Reggio Children.

Richardson, M. (1935) *Writing and Writing Patterns*. London: University of London Press.

Ritzer, G. (1998) *The McDonaldization Thesis: Explorations and Extensions*. London: Sage.

Roazen, P. (1976) *Erik H. Erikson: The Power and Limits of a Vision*. New York: The Free Press.

Roberts, S. and Howard, S. (2005) 'Watching Teletubbies: television and its very young audience', in J. Marsh (ed.), *Popular Culture, New Media and Digital Literacy in Early Childhood*. London: RoutledgeFalmer.

Rodman, F.R. (2003) *Winnicott: Life and Work*. Cambridge, MA: Perseus Publishing.

Roffey, S. (2001) *Special Needs in the Early Years: Collaboration, Communication and Co-ordination*. London: David Fulton.

Rogers, C. (1969) *Freedom to Learn: A View of What Education Might Become* (1st edn). Columbus, OH: Charles Merill.

Rogers, C. and Freiberg, H.J. (1993) *Freedom to Learn* (3rd edn). New York: Merrill.

Rogers, C.R. (1961) *On Becoming a Person: A Therapist's View of Psychotherapy*. Boston: Houghton Mifflin.

Rogers, C.R. (1980) *A Way of Being*. Boston: Houghton Mifflin.

Roscoe, B. (1990) 'Robin Tanner and the Crafts Study Centre', in B. Roscoe (ed.), *Tributes to Robin Tanner 1904–1988*. Bath: Holburne Museum and Crafts Study Centre.

Ross, D.D. and Brondy, E. (1987) 'Communicating with parents about beginning reading instruction', *Childhood Education,* 63(4): 270–74.

Rusk, R.R. (1954) *The Doctrines of the Great Educators* (2nd edn). London: Macmillan.

Santas, G.X. (1979) *Socrates: Philosophy in Plato's Early Dialogues*. London: Routledge and Kegan Paul.

Santrock, J. (1996) *Child Development*. Dubuque, IA: Brown and Benchmark Publishers.

Schaeffer Macauley, S. (1984) *For the Children's Sake: Foundations of Education for Home and School*. Westchester, IL: Crossway.

Schickedanz, J. (1990) *Adam's Righting Revolutions*. Portsmouth, NH: Heinemann.

Schiller, C. (1951) 'How comes change?', in C. Griffin-Beale (ed.), *Christian Schiller in His Own Words* (1979). London: A. & C. Black.

Schupack, H. and Wilson, B. (1997) *The 'R' Book: Reading, Writing & Spelling: The Multisensory Structured Language Approach*. Baltimore, MD: The International Dyslexia Association's Orton Emeritus Series.

Schweinhart, L.J., Barnes, H.V. and Weikart, D.P. (1993) *Significant Benefits: The HighScope Perry Preschool Study through Age 27*. Monograph of the High Scope Educational Research Foundation, 10. Ypsilanti, MI: High Scope Press.

Selbie, P and Clough, P. (2005) 'Talking early childhood education fictional enquiry with historical figures', *Journal of Early Childhood Research,* 3 (2): 115–26.

Sharp, A. (2003) *Sure Start Ravensdale Breastfeeding Survey,* November. National Evaulation of Sure Start.

Sharp, C. (1995) *School Entry and the Impact of Season of Birth on Attainment. Research Summary,* September. Slough: National Foundation for Educational Research in England and Wales.

Sheffield LEA (1986) *Nursery Education: Guidelines for Curriculum, Organisation and Assessment*. Sheffield: City of Sheffield Education Department.

Silber, K. (1960) *Pestalozzi: The Man and his Work*. London: Routledge and Kegan Paul.

Siraj-Blatchford, I. (1994) *The Early Years: Laying the Foundations for Racial Equality*. Stoke-on-Trent: Trentham Books.

Skinner, B. F. (1938) *The Behavior of Organisms: An Experimental Analysis*. New York: Knopf.

Skinner, B.F. (1953) *Science and Human Behavior*. New York: Macmillan.

Skinner, B.F. (1972) *Beyond Freedom and Dignity*. New York: Knopf.

Skinner, B.F. (1974) *About Behaviorism*. New York: Knopf.

Skinner, B.F. (1976a) *Walden Two*. New York: Macmillan.

Skinner, B.F. (1976b) *Particulars of My Life*. New York: Knopf.

Smith, F. (1976) 'Learning to read by reading', *Language Arts,* 53 (March): 297–9, 322.

Smith, L. (1996) *Critical Readings on Piaget*. London: Routledge.

Spinka, M. (1967) *John Amos Comenius: That Incomparable Moravian* (2nd edn). New York: Russell and Russell.

Steiner, R. (1947) *The Study of Man*. London: Anthroposophic Press.

Steiner, R. (1980) *Rudolf Steiner: An Autobiography*. Blauvelt, NY: Steinerbooks.

Steiner, R. (1995) *The Kingdom of Childhood: Introductory Talks on Waldorf Education*. Seven lectures and answers to questions, given in Torquay 12–20 August 1924. Hudson, NY: Anthroposophic Press.

Steiner, R. (1996) *The Foundations of Human Experience*. Hudson, NY: Anthroposophic Press (originally published as *The Study of Man* 1947).

Sure Start (2003) The New Sure Start Leaflet. Ref: SUULeaflet 01/12/03.

Sutton-Smith, B. (1997) *The Ambiguity of Play*. Cambridge, MA: Harvard University Press.

Sylva, K. (1994) 'The impact of early learning on children's later development', Appendix C in C. Ball, *Start Right: The Importance of Early Learning*. London: Royal Society for the Arts, pp. 84–96.

Sylva, K., Roy, C. and Painter, M. (1980) *Child Watching at Playgroup and Nursery*. London: Grant McIntyre.

Szretzer, R. (1964) 'The origins of full-time compulsory education at five', *British Journal of Educational Studies*, XIII(1): 16–28.

Tanner, L.N. (1997) *Dewey's Laboratory School: Lessons for Today*. New York: Teachers College Press.

Tanner, R. (1977) 'The way we have come', lecture to the Plowden Conference.

Tanner, R. (1989) 'The way we have come' notes from a lecture to a Plowden Conference 1977.

Taylor, J. (2001) *Handwriting: A Teacher's Guides: Multisensory Approaches to Assessing and Improving Handwriting Skills*. London: David Fulton.

Thorne, B. (1992) *Carl Rogers*. London: Sage.

Tickell, Dame C. (2011) *The Early Years: Foundations for life, health and learning*. London: Department of Children, Schools and Families.

Tizard, B., Phelps, J. and Plewis, I. (1975) 'Play in preschool centres: play measures and their relation to age, sex and IQ', *Journal of Child Psychology and Psychiatry*, 17: 251–62.

Tobin, J.J., Wu, D.Y.H. and Davidson, D.H. (1989) *Preschool in Three Cultures: Japan, China and the United States*. London: Yale University Press, Chapter One 'Introduction', pp. 2–11.

Trehub, S. (2003) 'Toward a developmental psychology of music', in G. Avanzini, C. Faienza, D. Minciacchi, L. Lopez and M. Majno (eds), *The Neurosciences and Music: Annals of the New York Academy of Sciences*, 999: 402–13. New York: New York Academy of Sciences.

Trevarthen, C. (1984) 'Emotions in infancy: Regulators of contact and relationships with persons', in *Approaches to Emotion*, ed. K. Scherer and P. Ekman, pp. 129–570. Hillsdale, NJ: Erlbaum.

UK Children's Commissioners (2011) *Midterm Report to the UK State Party on the UN Convention on the Rights of the Child – The Evidence*. Office of the Children's Commissioner, http://www.childrenscommissioner.gov.uk

UNICEF (2005) *Convention on the Rights of the Child: From Abstract Rights to Realities*. Available at: http://www.unicef.org/crc/index_protecting.html

Veerman, P. and Levine, H. (2000) 'Implementing children's rights on a local level: Narrowing the gap between Geneva and the grassroots', *The International Journal of Children's Rights*. New York: Springer.

Visser, J., Cole, T. and Daniels, H. (2003) 'Inclusion for the difficult to include', in M. Nind, K. Sheehy and K. Simmons (eds), *Inclusive Education: Learners and Learning Contexts*. London: David Fulton.

Vygotsky, L.S. (1980) *Mind in Society: The Development of Higher Psychological Processes*. Cambridge, MA: Harvard University Press.

Vygotsky, L.S. (1986) *Thought and Language*. Boston: MIT Press.

Wall, K. (2003) *Special Needs and Early Years: A Practitioners' Guide*. London: Paul Chapman Publishing.

Wallace, E.R. (1983) *Freud and Anthropology: A History and Reappraisal*. New York: International Universities Press.

Walmsley, J. (1969) *Neill & Summerhill: A Pictorial Study*. Baltimore: Penguin.

Wedge, P. and Prosser, H. (1973) *Born to Fail?* London: Arrow Books in association with the National Children's Bureau.

Weinberger, J. (1996) *Literacy Goes to School – the Parents' Role in Young Children's Literacy Learning*. London: Paul Chapman Publishing.

Weinberger, J., Pickstone, C. and Hannon, P. (eds) (2005) *Learning from Sure Start: Working with Young Children and their Families*. Buckingham: Open University Press.

Welchman, K. (2000) *Erik Erikson: His Life, Work, and Significance*. Philadelphia, PA: Open University Press.

Wells, G. (1987) *The Meaning Makers: Children Learning Language and Using Language to Learn*. London: Hodder and Stoughton.

Whalley, M. and the Pen Green Centre team (1997) *Involving Parents in their Children's Learning*. London: Paul Chapman Publishing.

Whalley, M. (2007) *Involving Parents in their Children's Learning* (2nd edn). London: Sage.

Whitehurst, G.J., Epstein, J.N., Angell, A.L., Payne, D.A., Crone, D.A. and Fischel, J.E. (1994) 'Outcomes of an emergent literacy intervention in Head Start', *Journal of Educational Psychology*, 86(4): 542–55.

Winnicott, D. (1947) *Hate in the Transference*. New York: Aron Books.

Winnicott, D. (1953) 'Transitional objects and transitional phenomena', *International Journal of Psychoanalysis*, 34: 89–97.

Winnicott, D.W. (1957) *Mother and Child: A Primer of First Relationships*. New York: Basic Books.

Winnicott, D.W. (1964) *The Child, the Family and the Outside World*. Harmondsworth: Penguin.

Winnicott, D.W. (1965) *The Family and Individual Development*. London: Tavistock Publications.

Winnicott, D.W. (1967) 'The location of cultural experience', *International Journal of Psychoanalysis*, 48(3): 368–72.

Winnicott, D.W. (1971) *Playing and Reality*. London: Tavistock Publications.

Winnicott, D.W. (1984) *Deprivation and Delinquency*. London: Tavistock Publications.

Winnicott, D.W. (1988) *Human Nature*. London: Free Association Books.

Winnicott, D.W. (1993) *Talking to Parents*. Wokingham and Cambridge, MA: Addison-Wesley.

Winnicott, D.W. (1996) *Thinking about Children*. London: Karnac Books.

Wise, L. and Glass, C. (2000) *Working with Hannah: A Special Girl in a Mainstream School*. London: RoutledgeFalmer.

Wokler, R. (1995) *Rousseau*. Oxford: Oxford University Press.

Wollheim, R. (1971) *Freud*. London: Fontana.

Wood, D., McMahon, L. and Cranstoun, Y. (1980) *Working with Under Fives*. London: Grant McIntyre.

Wood, E. (2008) *The Routledge Reader in Early Childhood Education*. London: Routledge.

Wood E. and Attfield, J. (2005) *Play, Learning and the Early Childhood Curriculum* (2nd edn). London: Paul Chapman Publishing.

Wood, L. and Bennett, N. (1997) 'The rhetoric and reality of play: teachers' thinking and classroom practice', *Early Years*, 17(2): 22–7.

Yelland, N. and Grieshaber, S. (1998) 'Blurring the edges', in N. Yelland (ed.), *Gender in Early Childhood*. London: Routledge. pp. 1–11.

Young, S. (2008) 'Collaboration between 3- and 4-year-olds in self-initiated play on instruments'. *International Journal of Educational Research*, 47: 3–10.

Historical archives and other sources consulted

The British and Foreign School Society Archives
http://www.bfss.org.uk/archive/

Lev Vygotsky Archive
http://www.marxists.org/archive/vygotsky/

Institute of Education of the University of London archives
http://www.ioe.ac.uk/services/4389.html

The Rousseau Association
http://www.rousseauassociation.org/

Steiner Education
http://www.steinerwaldorf.org.uk/

B.F. Skinner Foundation
http://www.bfskinner.org/

Early Childhood Care and Development Website
http://www.ecdgroup.com

Author Index

Subject Index

Pioneer Index

2403 018